"When we see the world through other people's eyes, our horizons are expanded and our lives enriched. Karen Garst's compilation promotes just that. Women's experiences of going from involvement in religious organizations to the freedom they find in atheism and other forms of nonbelief were once conspicuously missing from the volumes of literature documenting the lives of nonbelievers. Just as other major movements, such as civil rights, women's liberation, and gay rights, were advanced more so by individuals sharing their experiences than by the large organizations that often get the credit, as *Women Beyond Belief* shows, so too are individual women helping to lead the new cultural shift in America—the shift away from staying silently subjugated to hegemonic religious systems and the social networks that fuel them and toward having the freedom to live authentic lives. Every exposure to stories that document triumphant transitions validates the experiences of other female nonbelievers, enriches the lives of male nonbelievers, encourages nonbelievers to come out of the closet, and normalizes nonbelief as an acceptable life stance in the larger American culture. Garst's volume of diverse stories, told exactly with the words of the women themselves, can now be counted among the burgeoning tomes of literature that are spearheading that shift."

—**Candace R. M. Gorham, LPC**, *The Ebony Exodus Project: Why Some Women Are Walking Out on Religion—and Others Should Too*

"All three Abrahamic religions are nasty, and women have borne the brunt of the nastiness throughout history. It still persists, and it is moving to listen to women of today telling their personal histories of the various ways in which religion has oppressed them, from childhood on. In their interestingly different ways their testimonies seem to add up to the same story, a story as old as the myth of Eve. I closed the book with uplifted admiration for all these women and for their courage in breaking their historic fetters."

—**Richard Dawkins**, author of *The God Delusion* and *The Magic of Reality*

"When women break free from closed religious groups and Iron Age gender scripts, all manner of daring thoughts and adventures become possible. Sometimes funny, sometimes fierce, often sad and exuberant in turn—these essays invite us along on twenty-two journeys into and out of religion—many from the vantage of a woman who at some point in her life tried to live by a biblical script and then discovered something better. As atheists and freethinkers congregate around shared values and experiences, brave intelligent voices like these will help ensure that the unique experience of women shapes the secular spiritual communities of the future."

—**Valerie Tarico**, psychologist and author of *Trusting Doubt: A Former Evangelical Looks at Old Beliefs in a New Light* and *Deas and Other Imaginings*

"This is one of the most important books on women and religion in the last quarter century."

—**Peter Boghossian**, assistant professor of philosophy at Portland State University and author of *A Manual for Creating Atheists*

"Over the past decade, the number of publications documenting the perspectives of male nonbelievers has skyrocketed, often overshadowing appraisals of the lived experiences of women nonbelievers. Karen Garst's *Women Beyond Belief* is an insightful addition to the small but growing body of work on women who are questioning organized religion. These essays underscore why the process is more onerous for women, who must negotiate the sexist discrimination, respectability politics, and stifling norms of gender and sexuality imposed by religious dogma and tradition. Providing rich testimony from a variety of world views and walks of life, *Women Beyond Belief* is a refreshing snapshot of the cultural and social issues that inform women's transition to secularism and nonbelief."

—**Sikivu Hutchinson**, author of *Moral Combat: Black Atheists, Gender Politics and the Values Wars* and *Godless Americana: Race and Religious Rebels*

"Why would anyone embrace a male-dominated religion in today's world, or any religion for that matter? Specifically, why would women embrace the religion of their male oppressors? Given the stories told in this wonderful tell-all book, they shouldn't. It's one of the main reasons I argue against the Christian faith. I bid all readers to follow the reasoning and examples of the authors in this book. Their stories are quite revealing and fascinating. Highly recommended!"

—**John W. Loftus**, author of *Why I Became an Atheist* and editor of *Christianity Is Not Great*

"As a woman and a rationalist, I have found it hard to understand the plight of women who continue to believe in a personal God and a literalist Bible. *Women Beyond Belief* is a book of revelation, stories of social conditioning and personal self-doubt that have kept women 'in their place' historically and in our modern, supposedly educated world. Besides the sometimes wrenching accounts of eventual awakening, Karen Garst provides a very useful account of the Judeo-Christian tradition's subordination of women that should be read by any woman who still labours under the delusion of a beneficial deity."

—**Meredith Doig**, President of the Rationalist Society of Australia Inc.

"Reading this book makes me so grateful that I was brought up in the relatively gentle and easy-to-abandon Church of England and in a country where most people are now 'nones' and have no religion. Even so, these moving stories remind me that it is women who suffer most under the oppression of a misogynistic, unfair, brutal, and cruel god. From these delightful and varied stories we learn how many women are taught to feel inferior, sinful, wicked, and worthless but also how many escaped, some through sudden realisation and others after long suffering. Any woman who is hovering on the verge of giving up her indoctrination should read this book."

—**Susan Blackmore**, author of *The Meme Machine*

"There are few things more valuable than sharing each other's stories. We learn from others; we gain compassion and understanding of not just them, but also of ourselves. This book invites us into the hearts and worlds of women who have made the life-changing journey from believer to nonbeliever. Each story is unique, filled with anguish, brilliance, pain, and joy, not unlike having a child. And, yet, each story is the same. Each woman was in a very real sense reborn as they shed the cocoon of their old religion for the wings to take flight into fresh air. *Women Beyond Belief* is a testimony to the inner call for truth and the strength of these women to find it for themselves. I found them awe-inspiring."

—**Rebecca Hale**, president of the American Humanist Association and cofounder of EvolveFISH.com and the Freethinkers of Colorado Springs

WOMEN BEYOND BELIEF

Discovering Life without Religion

Edited by Karen L. Garst, PhD

PITCHSTONE PUBLISHING
DURHAM, NORTH CAROLINA

Pitchstone Publishing
Durham, North Carolina
www.pitchstonepublishing.com

10 9 8 7 6 5 4 3 2 1

Library of Congress Cataloging-in-Publication Data

Names: Garst, Karen L., author.
Title: Women beyond belief : discovering life without religion / edited by
  Karen L. Garst, PhD.
Description: Durham, North Carolina : Pitchstone Publishing, [2016]
Identifiers: LCCN 2016013973| ISBN 9781634310826 (pbk. : alk. paper) | ISBN
  9781634310840 (pdf) | ISBN 9781634310857 (mobi)
Subjects: LCSH: Free thought. | Religion—Controversial literature. |
  Women—Religious life.
Classification: LCC BL2747.5 .W64 2016 | DDC 211/.8082—dc23
LC record available at https://lccn.loc.gov/2016013973

CONTENTS

ACKNOWLEDGMENTS

I must first acknowledge my family as my biggest supporters. My husband has accompanied me to meetings, conventions, and debates. My son, who is starting a new business, shared numerous tips on marketing and using social media. My sister proofread the entire manuscript.

Kate Dyer-Seeley, Pacific Northwest mystery writer, was the first to encourage me to write this book and provided me an invaluable referral to Ali McCart Shaw of Indigo Editing, who helped my authors and me craft the best writing for our stories.

Dr. Steven Goldman, an old friend, introduced me early on in this project to Dr. Peter Boghossian, assistant professor of philosophy at Portland State University, author of *A Manual for Creating Atheists*, and creator of the mobile application Atheos. Peter provided invaluable advice, introduced me to people who could assist me, and reached out to his friends in the atheist movement for support of my endeavors. Peter, I couldn't have done it without you!

Kurt Volkan at Pitchstone Publishing was a breeze to work with, communicating well and frequently with me as the process of publishing unfolded. It is not just any publisher who dares to take on a first-time author. Thank you Kurt!

Dennis Lewis at Green Light Digital helped me set up a blog and YouTube Channel and increased my reach to people through social media.

Special thanks to the many podcasters, bloggers, and YouTube video producers who hosted me on their shows in anticipation of the book's publication. Through social media I have "met" many like-minded individuals who have provided me with inspiration and support throughout this process. I only hope I have the chance to meet some of them in person. Shanna Babilonia of myiobi.com and Kristi Winters, who runs TheAtheistHub YouTube Channel, deserve special recognition for their help and friendship.

Finally, it is to my authors that I reserve the highest praise. Thank you for coming along on this ride, for delving into issues you thought you had buried once and for all, and for having the courage to speak out about the damage religion has done. This book couldn't have happened without you!

—**Karen L. Garst**

INTRODUCTION

Karen L. Garst

Until 2014, I was content with my own journey to atheism and the conclusions I had reached. While I shared my views with friends and family, I never joined a secular or humanist community. My passivity abruptly changed on June 30, 2014, when the US Supreme Court issued its decision in *Burwell v. Hobby Lobby Stores, Inc.* Five out of nine of the justices decided that Hobby Lobby, a privately held company, did not need to provide certain methods of birth control to its female employees under the Affordable Care Act because of the owners' religious beliefs. Earlier, the Supreme Court had ruled that corporations were entitled to certain constitutional rights. The five justices who supported the decision in this case were all men who had previously indicated they were Roman Catholic. While their professed religion was certainly not part of the written opinion, I found it hard to believe that their religion played no role. The Catholic Church has long opposed any form of birth control. These justices would have been exposed to this teaching from their earliest years. For many, religion is one of those factors in our cultural-social environment that shapes our lives and thus it is difficult to shield our opinions from its influence.

Because this judicial decision directly affected women, I began to reflect on the long battle for equal rights for women in this country—from the fight for suffrage, to the Civil Rights Act of 1964, to the availability of birth control, to the right to a safe and legal abortion. This led me to examine religion, the basis for Hobby Lobby's lawsuit, and how it affects Western civilization's views toward women. I began a quest to turn my reflection into knowledge and understanding. I reread the Bible in its entirety, as well as many other books exploring religion and women's rights. I read the writings of Elizabeth Cady Stanton and others from the nineteenth-century abolition and suffrage movements. I read Joseph Campbell's writings on mythology. I reread many books of the Jesus Seminar, which revived a study of the historical Jesus in the late twentieth century. And I read many, many recent books by atheist writers. I came to the conclusion that religion has subjugated women throughout history and continues to do so today. The appendix to this volume is a summary of what I learned.

In spite of this history, women in most Western civilizations have made great strides in terms of equal rights in the last hundred years. But decisions such as the one the US Supreme Court made in the Hobby Lobby case point to a gap that still remains. As religion fueled the instigation of this litigation and as religious beliefs played a role in the court's decision, it is time to acknowledge that one of the final barriers to full equality for women is religion. Because of the history of Judeo-Christianity, its teaching, and its written Bible, I do not believe that it can be reformed to provide equal rights for women. Full equality for women, however, is not just a concern for women. Men who want to live in a society that allows each individual to fulfill their potential and follow their dreams should also support full equality for women.

One such recent approach to this society is a movement called the New Atheism. Fueled by the tragic events of the terrorist attacks on September 11, 2001, four authors emerged to the forefront of religious influence on societal perspectives and behavior. The four authors—Sam Harris, Richard Dawkins, Daniel Dennett, and the late Christopher Hitchens—were dubbed the Four Horsemen, an allusion to the four horsemen of the apocalypse discussed in the book of Revelation in Christianity's New Testament. They have made great strides using logic, scientific evidence, and rational thought to break down many long-held religious beliefs: the age of the earth, the lack of evidence for many of the stories in the Bible, the refutation of miracles and supernatural events, and so on. Until recently most of the people who took on science as a profession were men; thus most of these fellow outspoken atheists are men as well.

That is not to say that there are not women scientists, philosophers, historians, and archaeologists who have used their expertise to refute religious beliefs. However, the majority of outspoken atheists and atheist authors are still men. Thus, while there are many books by men who are former pastors or religious adherents, there exist much fewer writings describing women's personal experiences with religion and an examination of the paths they took to leave it behind. I hope to change that. This book is a start.

At first, I reached out to female friends who I knew might be atheists. Some did identify as atheists but did not have time to develop an essay. Some indicated that while they were not religious, they couldn't quite label themselves as atheists or agnostics or simply secular. Some said yes, and their essays are included in this book. I then expanded my outreach to chapters of the Center for Inquiry, the American Humanist Association, and other secular organizations. I attended debates and gave presentations on women and religion. I also reached out through social media to add women from a variety of ages, ethnicities, and experiences.

Together, we envisioned that both men and women considering leaving religion behind might be interested in our experiences. When we have models of behavior that we can identify with, we are more likely to consider a change in our own behavior. Women might be attracted to stories of other women, and men might want to consider what the effect of religion has been on the women in their lives. We envisioned the book would also help those people who have already expressed doubts regarding what they were taught and are looking for some answers and knowledge about others who have decided to leave religion behind. We envisioned that it might provide a new perspective that would encourage self-reflection and open-mindedness. We envisioned that as much as it guides new thought, this book also explores and challenges preconceived notions and norms. Ultimately, we envisioned that it might give courage to those struggling with what, in the end, is a personal and sometimes monumental decision. This book has been written for them.

* * *

Some of the women who have written essays for this book would face additional ostracism from their family and friends were they to profess their atheism openly; thus, they have chosen to use pseudonyms instead. In addition, some of the women prefer to capitalize the word god and some do not. This choice is reflected in their essays.

A PERSONAL EXODUS

Ann Wilcox

We are made of stardust;
why not take a few moments to look up at the family album?
—Natalie Angier, *The Canon*

I remember the morning I woke up and could not believe in God anymore. It was February 2005, and losing my faith was the absolute last thing I ever thought would happen to me (except maybe being abducted by space aliens—maybe). I had known there was a God from the time I was a child. Even though I had stopped attending church almost thirty years before that morning, that belief had permeated all of my assumptions about life. It was like the ultimate computer program that ran in the background, assuring me that everything was going to be okay, no matter what happened.

In fact, for several months before my sudden loss of faith, I had been thinking more about God and wondering who he really was. What if I could find out? What if I could connect with him? I decided I would try. But no sooner had I decided this than I got the news in late January of 2005 that my father had passed away unexpectedly. Although we hadn't talked to each other in years, I was still upset, maybe more so because there was a rift between us that I had never been able to mend. I flew out to be with my family.

It's hard to describe what happened next. I returned home, settled in, and began to think again about the question of God—except that he was gone. My faith had evaporated. I could not believe there was a God anymore, much less figure out who he was. I was flummoxed, to put it mildly. I depended on my belief for certainty and comfort, and I wanted it back, *now*. But I couldn't even pray for it to come back. I could not believe.

I felt as though someone had picked me up and flung me into the ether, and I was falling with nothing to hold on to. I had no idea how to think about my life or my future. I kept trying to find solid ground, but everything in my frame of reference included God. I began to feel like a wind-up toy that kept going around in a circle and running smack dab into a brick wall. Months went by, and then several years, and I was becoming angry and bitter. I had to do something, but I didn't know what.

One day I was browsing through my online movie account, and up popped *The God Who Wasn't There. Ha!* I thought. *There's the title of my life! I'd better check this out.* The film is a documentary that questions the existence of Christ, and although I don't remember all of the particulars, I do remember being provoked by its messages. While I doubted some of the beliefs I had grown up with, I had never considered actively disbelieving them.

I went online and began looking at a few atheist sites. I had never been *here* before, and I kept looking over my shoulder to see if you-know-who was watching—even though I couldn't believe in him anymore. Some web authors were thoughtful; some of them were careless, and I argued with them, talking to my computer. I tried to avoid authors that sounded dogmatic or arrogant—I didn't trust them. I read John Loftus, Valerie Tarico, Marlene Winell, Ed Babinski, Robert Green Ingersoll, and more. I read other people's stories of leaving their faith. They were brave and moving, and I felt for the writers.

Ultimately, though, I read the Bible. As I was reading the skeptics, sometimes they would refer to a verse or a story in the Bible, and I would think, *Wait a minute—is that what it actually says? Is that being taken out of context?* And so I picked up the old family Bible that I had brought home from my father's house, with the white cover, gilt-edged pages, and color illustrations I remembered from my childhood. I opened the Book and began reading. And that's when everything I had been taught to believe as a child completely came apart.

* * *

My parents were devout Fundamentalist Christians who were committed to seeing their children were thoroughly instructed in their true faith, which they were certain was the only way to God. They knew that outside of it lay a miserable life and a horrific afterlife. Their children would not suffer that fate if they could do a single thing to prevent it.

Fundamentalist has become a dirty word in our culture, but originally, the founders of Fundamentalist Christianity were simply trying to return to the fundamental doctrines of Christianity—thus the name. It's a form of Evangelical Christianity, sharing the same doctrine but more conservative in its approach. There are many denominations in Christianity that have fundamentalist churches, but in some cases not all of the churches in that denomination are fundamentalist.

My parents took us to church three times a week. In addition, my father was determined to send his children to Christian schools so we could be educated in an all-encompassing environment of faith. My parents did not have a lot of money, but to them it was worth the price. At school, we went to Bible class daily and chapel twice a week.

What did we learn? While most people are probably familiar with the basic doctrines of Fundamentalist Christianity, they probably don't realize how nonnegotiable they are. In my education, if anyone doubted these doctrines, they were slipping close to hellfire, whether they believed in hellfire or not. Here are the basics.

One God. Sort Of. There was only one God, the God of the Bible, the Creator of the universe. He was omnipotent (all-powerful), omniscient (all-knowing), omnipresent (everywhere at once all the time), and eternal. He was perfect, merciful, just, and loving. Christians believe God is manifested in three persons: God the Father, God the Son (Jesus Christ), and the Holy Spirit, who is, well, a Spirit that directs and enlightens believers. If this seems a little perplexing, that's because it is. As a child, I didn't worry about the explanation but accepted it on faith, as one of the Divine Mysteries of God. I did that *a lot*.

Satan Is Real. We were warned that he was cunning, was ruthless, and would do his best to deceive us in every way. He was our unimaginably powerful enemy, and he was like a roaring lion, walking the earth, seeking to devour us. We were assured that God was more powerful than Satan and could protect us from the Evil One, but I was still afraid. People referred to Satan routinely, blaming him for ordinary events. Flat tire on the way to church? That's Satan trying to keep you away from the Word of God. Want to date a non-Christian? That's Satan trying to take your eyes off the Lord. Feeling down? That's Satan oppressing you (yes, really). If Satan could affect my everyday world like that, how could I be sure he wouldn't harm me?

Adam and Eve, Paradise Lost. In Fundamentalist belief, the story of Adam and Eve in the Garden of Eden explains not only the origin of humans but also of sin and death. Here's the nutshell version: God created the first two humans and put them in a garden paradise. God also put a dangerous tree in the garden, made it attractive, and warned Adam and Eve not to eat the fruit. (I know, I don't get it either. Probably a Divine Mystery.) Along came Satan, disguised as a serpent, and tempted Eve to eat the fruit. She did and shared it with Adam, so that both of them disobeyed God. In our faith, sin was defined as disobedience to God, and this was how sin and death had entered the world. This story has been used to blame women for the fall of the entire human race and to justify their second-class status. More than two millennia after this story was written, I still paid dearly for that interpretation.

Sin, the Abridged Version. In Fundamentalist theology, people don't just commit sin—they *are* sin. Because Adam sinned, every person born after him was born with a sinful nature and is inherently corrupt. As if that weren't enough, there were sins of commission (when you did something you shouldn't) and sins of omission (when you didn't do something you should). If there is another religion that vilifies humans more than Fundamentalist Christianity, then I feel sorry for its adherents.

We were also taught that God was so holy, he could not have sin or sinful beings in his presence. (No one ever explained to me how this worked. *Was it like kryptonite?* I wondered.) In addition, God's innate justice demanded that sin and sinners should be punished. So God was permanently ticked off at all humans, unless they were reconciled to him through salvation. The beauty of this system is that by merely being born—and who hasn't been?!—humans are now in desperate need of salvation, which can only happen if they become Christians.

As a child, I felt guilty for small transgressions, even things that were normal childhood behavior, such as wishing I could stay home from church on Sunday night to watch Disney or snitching an extra cookie when mom wasn't looking. I wanted to be pretty, but I worried that I might be committing the sin of vanity, and I felt conflicted about trying to look nice. As I grew older, I struggled to be good so I could stop feeling flawed and wrong, and I developed a debilitating perfectionism.

Heaven. The Good Place. Heaven was the eternal home of Christians, and what made heaven *Heaven* was the presence of God. But it had pretty impressive fringe benefits too. There was no death, no sorrow, no pain, and no tears. Everyone you ever loved and lost who was a Christian would be there, and you would never be separated from them again. I felt a secure comfort knowing that I would spend eternity there.

Hell. The Other Place. Hell was a real lake of fire, a place of weeping, gnashing of teeth, and torment day and night forever, created by God for the punishment of Satan and his demons (oh, did I forget to mention them?). Anyone who wasn't saved would also be cast into this everlasting inferno as a punishment for his or her disbelief. While my family never attended hellfire-and-brimstone churches, hell was a cornerstone of Fundamentalist theology. At church, my sixth-grade Sunday school teacher read disturbing accounts of unrepentant sinners in the last moments of their lives, who experienced visions of hell before slipping into the horrific Beyond (the book was called *Voices from the Edge of Eternity*, in case you want to rush right out and buy it). The terror of these "first-person" accounts persuaded us of the horrors of hell. Who would do this to children?!

Even though I was pretty sure I wasn't headed there, hell seared my imagination with its vivid imagery and kindled a subliminal fear that pervaded my young life. Sometimes I felt viscerally disturbed about some of my faith's teachings, such as people being stoned to death for something minor or people going to hell when they had never even had a chance to be saved. But those doubts never surfaced into my conscious awareness; I was too afraid.

Salvation. Salvation is *the* core doctrine of Evangelical and Fundamentalist Christianity. Because of sin and hell, humans desperately needed forgiveness from their innate sin. In Fundamentalist theology the forgiveness of sins requires the shedding of blood (for an explanation of why this is so, I refer you to Divine Mystery). So God took mercy on us and sent Jesus to Earth, where he was born to Mary, a virgin (*really* Divine Mystery). He taught and performed miracles for three years, rocking the boats of the established Jewish religious order, who arrested him. They nailed him to a wooden cross and left him to die a bloody, brutal death.

He allowed this to happen so that he could complete his mission of saving humankind. Three days later, Jesus rose from the dead and returned to heaven. God the Father's need for judgment and punishment was now satisfied. Anyone who believed the salvation story could be saved, and they would become children of God, with Jesus as their personal friend.

My church called this story the Good News, because God was merciful enough to save us, but I struggled with feeling guilty about being so bad that Jesus had to die a horrible death for me. In spite of this, it was comforting to know that Jesus was my friend, and I talked to him daily, praying for guidance and direction.

The Bible. In my experience, arguably the most passionately defended belief in Fundamentalist Christianity was this: the Bible is the *only* divinely inspired, perfectly revealed and recorded words of God. The Bible was the literal, absolute Truth, and was historically, scientifically, and theologically accurate. It was sacred and unquestionable. In fact, it was so revered that we pledged allegiance to it every day in school, along with the American flag and the Christian flag (yes, there is a Christian flag, and no, I am not making this up). Moderate Christians, and even some Evangelicals, call this level of reverence for the literal Bible "bibliolatry," an idolatry of the Bible. No wonder.

Most people don't know what's in the Bible and don't fully appreciate what a perfect, literal Bible means. When the Bible says that donkeys talked, that people walked on water, that the sun stood still (meaning the earth would had to have abruptly stopped rotating!), that ninety-year-old women had babies, that people rose from the dead—and it does—that's *exactly* what it means.

It also meant that the frightful descriptions of a punitive God were reliable and accurate. When the Bible says that God killed people with plagues and war and poisonous snakes for failing to worship him, that he exterminated whole populations, including infants and children, that he allowed a father to butcher his daughter as a sacrifice to him, that he ordered the stoning of anyone who picked up sticks on the Sabbath—and it does—that's *exactly* what it means.

And when the Bible says that God is just, loving, and merciful, that's *exactly* what it means. Even my unquestioning mind could not wrap itself around a genocidal God that was supposed to be loving, though I contorted it terribly in trying. God didn't feel loving to me; he felt dangerous, and

I felt guilty that I couldn't order my heart to follow the Bible's greatest commandment: to love him.

There was one notable exception to the literal interpretation of the Bible: the Song of Solomon. This book is an eight-chapter love poem, full of lush, evocative imagery, with descriptions of thighs like jewels, breasts like two young roe (deer), lips like scarlet, and lying between a lover's breasts. Curiously, this book was taken as a metaphor for the *completely* nonsexual relationship between Christ and the Church. It also didn't get much airtime in my grade school Bible class . . .

Human Depravity. This is an unfortunate corollary to the doctrine of sin, and for me it was disastrous. This bit of theology holds that because all humans are corrupt, they cannot trust anything in their own hearts or minds (unless, of course, it *agrees* with God's Word). If something in the Bible didn't make sense to my mind or heart, then my thoughts or feelings should be dismissed and replaced with obedience. Even though there were passages in the Bible that talked about the importance of love, when it came right down to it, obedience trumped compassion. We were told that God loved us, but clearly he would punish us if we didn't follow him. Trust and obey, we were told, over and over. We were also told that we must die to our sinful selves. It was a sin to trust my own heart, to trust my own mind, to follow my own will.

The problem is, my mind, my heart, and my will were the fundamental tools I needed for knowing myself, for connecting with other humans, for making wise choices, for having empathy and showing compassion, for setting clear boundaries, for living a whole and satisfying life.

But when my religion demanded that I believe things that were irrational, mythical, or contrary to human decency, it had to undermine or destroy these fundamental tools. What else would they have done? If they hadn't bent my mind, I might have wondered why there are such an amazing number of things in the Bible that make no sense. If they hadn't suppressed my feelings, I might have decided that human compassion is more important than obedience to dogma, and I might have rebelled at being commanded to love a Being who sends billions of people to hell.

But in my world, it was flirting with eternal fire to question any of this, and I had no desire to take on the Almighty. As submission to this dogma eclipsed my thoughts and feelings, I lost the ability to know what *I* really thought and how *I* really felt. It became almost impossible to give and receive love, or to trust. It became possible to accept things that violated my integrity as well as human decency.

Years later, as I questioned everything, I could not escape the feeling that this religion had tried to kill me. At first, that seemed pretty melodramatic, but as I kept tearing apart my belief system, I gradually understood. Teaching children that they cannot trust their own ability to think, feel, and decide their own lives, and threatening them with something as fearful as hell if they do trust themselves, is an attempted murder of the essential self in an ever-so-quiet form, and Fundamentalist Christianity had unapologetically tried to kill that part of me.

I often wonder what my life would have been like if someone could have assured me that I am a beautiful, imperfect human, and I can trust myself. I can't even imagine.

The World Is Eeeevil. Because the human race was so depraved, by definition the entire world was as well (except those people who were saved). The Bible says that to be friends with the World was to be God's enemy. There was no détente, no common ground. We learned that as Christians we were the light of the World, and because the World loved darkness, we were assured that the World would hate us.

Of course I was scared. The worst thing I could think of in my young life was to be hated, especially for doing the right thing. When I had to go someplace public, I felt lost and apprehensive. I was afraid of the other humans on my planet. How many interesting and wonderful people did I miss knowing?

Look! I'm Invisible! We were taught that there was an entirely invisible cosmos of angels and demons, heaven and hell, good and evil, and God and Satan that was more real than the physical world we could see and touch. Since God and Satan were at war, we learned that we, too, were in a great battle against evil. To this day I sometimes feel like I'm being watched, even when there's no one around.

Women and Other Servants. Some people think the (literal) Bible is a patriarchal, misogynist book that denigrates women. Yep, it is. Here are choice instructions from God's Holy Word:

- "Let the woman learn in silence with all subjection. But I suffer not a woman to teach, nor to usurp authority over the man, but to be in silence. For Adam was first formed, then Eve. And Adam was not deceived, but the woman being deceived was in the transgression" (1 Tim. 2:11–14).

- "For a man . . . is the image and glory of God: but the woman is the glory of the man. For the man is not of the woman; but the woman of the man. Neither was the man created for the woman; but the woman for the man" (1 Cor. 11:7–9).

- "Likewise, ye wives, be in subjection to your own husbands. . . . Let it be . . . the ornament of a meek and quiet spirit, which is in the sight of God of great price" (1 Pet. 3:1–4).

There's more, but that's enough for now, don't you think?

After Eve took the fruit and shared it with Adam, God placed Adam in authority over Eve, to "rule over" her (the Bible's words). God created a hierarchy in which women were fourth, after God the Father, Christ, and then men. We learned that if we obeyed this chain of command, God would bless us, and if we didn't, our lives would not go well.

In my world, this hierarchy was alive and well. At home, my father was clearly the God-appointed head of our home who expected his directives to be followed, and my mother seldom opposed him. I remember her talking back to him once, and he grabbed her and ordered her to stop. She never did that again. One time when I was a young teen, he complained, "I've tried everything I know to discipline her." He felt he had the biblical right to do so. At the time I accepted his words and his authority. When I think about it now, I feel nauseous. There were times when his "discipline" toward us children turned abusive, but my mother never defended us. She too had been indoctrinated to believe that obedience mattered more than compassion. Well into her eighties, my mother still believes this dogma; I resent it more than almost any other Christian doctrine.

Very few of the men in our church would have approved of my father's methods. While the Bible prescribes submission for women, it also admonishes men to love their wives. Most men did, and many were wise enough to treat them with respect. But the fact is, men were still the authority over their wives, and that is still a fine and pleasant servitude for women, or worse, as in my mother's case.

In church, women were never allowed to teach men, and the idea of a woman pastor was sacrilege. In Pioneer Girls (a sort of Christian Girl

Scouts), I learned embroidery and how to always be nice, but I was definitely not taught leadership skills. What's sad is that I learned some of my most powerful lessons about my place as a woman from women, not men—in school my home economics teacher told us the story of a woman who had become a Christian but her husband hadn't, and he took her to a poker game in which she was one of the prizes. Instead of having a little come-to-Jesus chat with him, this virtuous woman submitted to her husband's treatment. Sure enough, my teacher related—her husband had won his own wife in the poker game. If you do your Christian duty and submit, my teacher assured us, God will honor you, even if your husband is an asshole (no, of *course* she didn't use that word, and yes, I *am* still pissed about this).

I might expect this code of belief from a two-thousand-year-old book from the ancient Middle East. But should I expect this from a Being that is supposedly omniscient and perfectly good? I have heard Christians argue that their faith actually elevated the position of woman compared with other cultures of ancient times. This is brain-stunning. First of all, better than awful is still awful. Second, if an omniscient God were handing out instructions on how to behave, why wouldn't he just tell people to do the right thing instead of being only slightly better than the surrounding culture? The Bible does this with slavery as well as the treatment of women, admonishing the Christian slaves of biblical times to obey their masters. Centuries before Christ, the Greek philosopher Zeno decried the practice of slavery; apparently he was light-years ahead of the omniscient, loving Bible God. Why didn't God just say, "Slavery is obscene and should be abolished?" And why didn't God just say, "You can't treat women like second-class citizens! They're every bit as smart as you, and they nurture the entire human race into existence. Get a clue."

Unless, of course, twenty-first-century humans are simply wrong. Maybe slavery really is okay. Maybe women should just stay home and be submissive. Do I hear an "Amen"?!

As I grew up, I developed a deep rancor for this dogma, but I knew it was a sin to feel that way. Once again, I contorted my being into the shape of obedience and buried my feelings. When I hit puberty, I felt betrayed by my body; I was a woman, for sure, and I had already learned what that meant.

Whew. This is the condensed version of my faith's doctrines, and almost everywhere I went—home, school, church—I was surrounded by devout believers. It might seem remarkable to an outsider that we could accept all of these things, but I grew up with them. I had a naturally believing nature, and God and Satan, heaven and hell, angels and demons were as normal in my world as telephones, airplanes, and the evening news. From preschool on, I learned songs about God and stories from the Bible, and I memorized verses from it. A few years ago, I found a test paper from my third-grade Bible class, questioning us to make sure we all knew we were sinners and God could not have us in his presence without salvation. Jesus, if I checked the right answer, was my Savior.

By age twelve, I was an earnest believer. If I couldn't sleep at night, I would go outside and stare at the stars and pray. In high school, I joined the Missionary Club and went on mission trips to Mexico. I sang in youth choir and went to revivals, retreats, and seminars. If I felt guilty about something in my life, I would go to the altar and confess (and if I ever hear "Just As I Am" again, I'm going to go find a hymn book and burn it). I stayed away from the World and followed the unofficial ten commandments, which included not smoking, drinking, dancing, or going to movies, etc. I would "witness" to people on the bus (tell them the Good News and try to get them to become saved) and canvas local neighborhoods, knocking on doors and inviting people to church. As an introvert, I hated these activities, but I wanted to please God. I became concerned for my Mormon friend Jamie; what if she went to hell? I began to pray for everyone I knew who wasn't saved.

In my late teens, I began to struggle with anger and rage, which I tried to keep bottled up. After graduating from my Christian high school, I lived at home while I went to the local university. At first I was worried about the secular atmosphere on campus (the World!), but gradually I relaxed. People there weren't afraid to ask questions, and I rediscovered a long-buried curiosity that all of my classes fueled. I was also anonymous. The campus had over twenty thousand students, which meant I didn't have to be anyone special, and I relaxed my perfectionism a nanometer or two. But the contrast between the environment at school and the autocracy at home brought things to a head, and I decided to get a job and move out of my parents' house.

I continued to go to church, where I met Eric and fell in love. He was funny, sensitive, and as curious as I was, and he didn't seem to care much whether I submitted or not. He was a long-haired hippie from the Jesus

People Movement, and my father did *not* approve. He lectured me about Eric's clothing and his hair, and even warned me that he felt Eric had been involved in witchcraft in his past. I told Eric. "If he doesn't stop talking about me that way," he joked, "I'll turn him into a newt!" I was grateful to have someone in my life who didn't take my family as seriously as I did. Despite my father's disapproval, my buried heart had had enough. This was my chance to be loved, and in a full-blown mutiny, I married Eric. I was twenty-two. At first my father refused to walk me down the aisle, but when he saw that we were not going to change our minds, he relented.

Eric and I settled into a cozy apartment together, and I discovered how unprepared I was for marriage. I had never learned how to care for another person, to show compassion, to communicate, to work things out when there was a problem. Even though neither of us agreed with the submissive-woman model of marriage, it was so ingrained in my mind that I couldn't get free of it. I felt as though I was constantly rebelling against it, even though I didn't believe it. In my family as well as my faith, *love* had been distorted to mean "obedience," and I rebelled against that too. I had no idea how to love anyone, including Eric, even though I really wanted to. In addition, Eric brought his own family issues with him. All of this put a strain on our marriage from the beginning. But we also had a lot of good times. We both loved to learn things. We shared a lovable Labrador, a prolific garden, and summer camping in the mountains. I introduced him to holidays, which his family had seldom celebrated. He made me laugh, almost every day. He was nonjudgmental and kind, and he was good for me. For a while, we attended church, but both of us began to have trouble with the dogma and intolerance (even though people were *ever so nice* about it), and we eventually stopped going, much to my family's dismay.

As the years went by, Eric and I struggled more and more with the issues in our marriage, and the obedience-over-feelings doctrine that I had learned as a child began to tear my life apart. Without an awareness of most of my own thoughts and feelings, how could I love? I felt as though vital parts of me were lost, and I began to despair. I had a growing conviction that my life would never have any meaning. In my twenties I wrote in my journal about a longing to find what I called Deepest Me. In spite of counseling and ten years of trying, I was still inept at trust and relationships. In my thirties our marriage fell apart, and so did I. I figured out the solution to my despair: I would take a .44 Magnum out into the desert, stick it in my mouth, and pull the trigger.

I struggled for months with my suicidal thoughts. I saw a counselor, but I didn't feel like he understood my problems or how to solve them. I think I was saved by several things: (1) My friends. I had people in my life who had taken me into their hearts, and I didn't want to upset them like that. (2) My siblings. I had a sibling who was also struggling with depression; would they commit suicide if I did? I didn't want to find out. (3) My curiosity. Inside of me, a tiny voice kept asking: "But don't you want to know what *could* happen in the future?" In the end I went on. I found a new counselor, and gradually, I learned to manage my life.

As the years went by, I grew further away from my childhood beliefs. I was exposed to all kinds of discoveries and ideas, especially from history, physics, geology, biology, and neuroscience. I doubted the Bible's creation story as well as the existence of hell, although conveniently, I still hoped for an idyllic afterlife. It turned out that the World didn't hate me after all, and I made friends. I moved to Oregon and felt lucky to live in such a beautiful place. I still believed in God—I just didn't think much about who he really was—until my forties, shortly before my father died, and my faith evaporated.

* * *

After my father's passing, in the middle of wrestling with my unwilling unbelief, I picked up the Book again. After my long (and happy) absence from church, I no longer felt like I needed to defend it. I started reading it the only way I knew how: literally.

And *what* a read it was. I read all over again about Adam and Eve, the first sin, and the doom of the human race; Noah and the planet-destroying flood; the virgin birth of Jesus, his death, and resurrection; the teachings of the apostles; and finally, Revelation, which reads like one huge acid trip (not that I would know, of course). There was an amazing assortment of magic and miracles and an entire panoply of fabulous creatures—giants, leviathans, dragons, satyrs, witches, demons, and angels. I am *not* making this up. I started calling it the Magical Mystery Tour.

As a young person, I never found any of this weird or peculiar. This time, it leaped off the pages and slapped me in the face. The stories seemed so blatantly mythological, and God seemed so human and petty. I marveled that it had all once been the unquestionable truth to me.

But even more than the miracles and magic, what struck me was how *bad* the Good Book was. I had forgotten how cruel and unjust God could be, casually wiping out tens of thousands of people for their unbelief. Bears tearing children limb from limb, people being stoned for small offenses, endless blood sacrifices, eternal fiery torture for the lost or unbelieving. Human parents were far more caring than the Bible God. Would you kill your own children for lying? For cursing you? Would you punish your grandchildren for something their parents did? Would you put your own children in harm's way? What wouldn't you do to keep them safe? God behaved far worse than almost any human I had ever heard of.

And then there was the treatment of women. As I reread the Good Book's admonitions to women, my decades-old fury came roaring up from where I had buried it. It seemed obscene to me that I had been taught those things, and I felt outraged.

I suddenly needed to fish or cut bait. For most of my life, I had practiced a benign neglect toward my childhood beliefs, but I could no longer tolerate the myth and the injustice of my religion without confronting it. My unbelief so far had happened without my consent; now I needed to look hard at whether I really believed.

And so I did what I often did when I had to figure something out: I started writing. Day after day, I would come home from work, inhale dinner, and sit down to read and think. I wrote page after page after page, until finally, I had to say, "Enough." My childhood faith did not make sense, and I could not make myself believe.

All of my reasons for unbelief fell into three categories: (1) Things didn't make sense to my mind. The Bible defied credibility and read like myth. (2) Things didn't make sense to my heart. The Bible's God grossly violated basic moral integrity, not to mention the sixth commandment, "Thou shalt not kill" (no, *really*). (3) Things that cause harm. My religion had indoctrinated me with fear and tried to extinguish my essential self in the name of obedience.

I finished my declaration of independence, and put my pen down. *There*, I thought. *That's done, for now.* But I couldn't have been more wrong.

* * *

As I tried to let my beliefs go, my head seemed far ahead of the rest of me. I would think, *That makes no sense*, but I would be assailed by intense fear and doubt. I felt all of my old fears and beliefs still skulking inside, like the biblical leviathan, a sea monster that lurked in the deep. I felt wrong, as though I had committed a terrible crime and I was going to be punished. Whenever I got near anything to do with my religion—a Christian coworker, a bumper sticker, a debate or a speaker, something on the Internet or the news, even (or especially) my own family—I went into a tailspin of dread and doubt for days. I kept thinking the fear would diminish, but it went on for months and months.

My fear was so ingrained that as I wrestled with my beliefs, I had shadowy nightmares, and I felt like things were creeping up on me in the middle of the night. As I sat in my chair reading, there were times when I involuntarily glanced upward, as if lightning might crash through my ceiling. When I attacked my beliefs about Satan, it felt as if he was in my room with me. This was a *complete* surprise, not to mention freaky. After thirty years away from my religion, my mind was still being assaulted with irrational fear for disbelieving.

I found an insightful therapist who understood my struggle. One day, she mentioned the work of Robert Jay Lifton, a psychiatrist who wrote about Chinese mind control techniques during the Korean War. He described eight methods to control people's minds without their agreement.

I found them online and read them. "Wow," I said to myself. I had experienced every single one of them, to a greater or lesser degree, in Fundamentalist Christianity.

Now, if you were to suggest to Fundamentalist Christians that their training and discipleship are mind control tactics, it would probably go over like a stripper at a church picnic. They staked out their territory—our lives—for Christ himself. How could that be wrong?

On the other hand, if a belief system can convince people of an entire invisible world and compel them to give up their will, their heart, their mind, and their authority over their own lives, then it has ultimate control over them. I wondered, *If Christians saw other religions using these tactics, would they call it mind control?*

I finally began to understand why I was still tyrannized by things I didn't believe, and I was *pissed*. I determined that I would tear my religion apart and break its hold on me. It felt like David and Goliath. I stared my religion straight in the knees and picked up my favorite weapon: my pen. I started writing again, furiously. My mind had been brainwashed into this, and I would brainwash it out.

For months I read, researched, and wrote. I dissected the ways my religion had controlled my mind and used fear to thoroughly inoculate me against skepticism. I listed all of my intellectual problems—forty pages of magic, miracles, myths, visions, superstitions, contradictions, absurdities, and contrivances. I listed all of my heart problems—twenty-five pages of violence, injustice, punishment, blood sacrifice, and fear. They weren't just lists; I wrote plenty of commentary, with just a *teensy* bit of sarcasm.

Almost every day I asked myself, *Why are you doing this? Can't you just read a book or something?!* But I had to show my mind in relentless black and white why it was sane and my beliefs were not.

I wrote for nine months, a hundred pages of questions and commentary. I switched from pen to computer so I could write faster. Sometimes I felt like I was in a dark place. Sometimes I pounded on my keyboard, swearing (profanity can be excellent therapy). I remember the week that it finally hit me: I had been raised to live my life according to the mythical stories and barbaric social mores of a bunch of ancient Middle Eastern men. Suddenly, the emperor had no clothes. Even though I hadn't finished, I stopped writing. I felt like my mind was finally getting free, and I could stop doing battle.

* * *

But now what? Really letting go meant traveling without a map. How would I re-create my life? And I had lost so much that I had to ask myself, Okay, what *do* you have? *Me*, I thought. *I have me.* This felt like nothing. I decided that I would try to sit still and pay attention to *my* thoughts and *my* feelings, and that no matter what I found, I would try to accept it, as is, with compassion. That seemed almost useless, but it turned out to be radical. It also turned out to be the hardest thing I've ever done in my life. I had learned a persistent self-hate, and it's taken determination and tenacity to keep at it. I've described it as trying to dig my way out of Alcatraz with a spoon.

It's been breathtakingly hard to get my feelings back. Not only did I have to unbury them, which was painful, but I felt like my emotions made me vulnerable, and after everything I had been through, I just wanted to protect myself. In addition, many emotions, such as hate, envy, sexual desire and anger had been sins in my faith. I had split them off from my self and disowned them in my attempt to be holy. It took me several years to figure out that I needed them *all* back in order to be whole. "Emotions are like trees growing," my therapist once said. "They're not good or bad— they're just part of nature and part of you. You wouldn't try to make trees stop growing, would you?" That was my aha moment. I discovered that there were reasons for all of my feelings, even anger and hate. I began trying to care for them, all of them, and to listen to them instead of judging them. And when I did that, I came away more whole than before, and I found more joy.

I'm not afraid of God or Satan anymore, but I do live with the aftermath of belief. I don't believe in an afterlife, and I'm afraid of death. But I would rather stare that fear in the teeth than ever give up my mind and heart again. I've lost people I loved, but they are still in my heart and will be until I die. Sometimes I still get angry over what I lost. I have trouble trusting, and I am fiercely protective of my own voice. I am still trying to reimagine my beliefs about being a woman; that's a mess. Christianity is still a bad trigger, so I stay away from it. I try not to be too sarcastic, but sometimes sacred cows make the best steaks.

These days I call myself an agnostic. I never wanted to be the A-word, but none of the arguments for the existence of God make sense to me. Although I'm not afraid of God anymore, I am afraid of his people. I understand the good that religion does, but I also understand the harm humans can inflict when they're certain they're right and everyone else is wrong. To many Christians, agnostics and atheists are deluded and even dangerous, and that feels offensive to me—especially coming from people who can do so much damage.

I have many coworkers, family, and friends (only one Christian friend, strangely enough) who still believe things that I think are mildly insane. On my good days, I try to remember how important their beliefs are to them. On my bad days, I want to scream and bang my head on a wall. But that would just hurt my head, and I try not to do that anymore.

I am grateful to have family members who are thoughtful, loyal, and honest, even if they still live in Bible Land.

I have realized that my own mind is incredibly malleable, and it's full of ideas put there by others, not just by my religion. I should be alarmed, but instead I feel free, free to question whatever is in my head and discard it if I think it's trash. I would like to study the Bible from a historical perspective; I think I could make peace with it. I have a whole planet to explore, and I get totally fizzed at the vastness and mystery of the universe! I love that we humans will always have the adventure of discovering more.

Often these days, I can accept my own thoughts and feelings with curiosity and compassion. It's astonishing to me that I can experience compassion that doesn't require any judgment or warping of my being. Sometimes I even have bouts of wonder or joy, free from any dogma or deity, which also amazes me. I've discovered that as I am kinder to myself, I am kinder to other people (although I have a long way to go here . . .).

I have friends who love me as I am—I am so grateful for them! If I want peace, I ponder the moon and listen to the tree frogs, or I run off to the beach and watch white foam flying off of green-glass waves. I still stare up at the stars, but there's no prayer, only peace. These days, that's enough.

The dictionary defines *integrity* as "soundness," "honesty," and "the state of being whole, entire, undiminished, and unimpaired." These are perfect words for how I am beginning to feel; it's as though I am beginning to breathe again.

I still have a life to make. But I am getting me back. All of me. Now *that's* what I call a miracle.

* * *

I realize that nothing happens in a vacuum, and my religion was not the only powerful influence in my life. My parents did the best they knew how; we all do. But in a religion where God the Father was a main character, the role of my real father had a lot to do with my perception of God. It had to have something to do with suddenly losing my faith when my father died. In fact, many Christians would argue that it was his poor example of a loving father that made me leave my faith. But I would argue that even my father was nothing like the violent, unjust God of the Bible. My father didn't make me leave my religion; he only made me look at it.

Another thing that matters is that no one anywhere in my life intentionally harmed me (I even include my father in this, since I've come to believe that he suffered from his own emotional injuries). In fact it's just the opposite. Everyone who taught me his or her truth was earnestly trying to save me from damnation and help me live a right life. As I departed the faith, it became crazy-making to reconcile their intentions with the harm I experienced.

Is there good in religion? Absolutely. To say otherwise would be as wrongheaded as saying all humans are completely corrupt. All over the world, people of faith deliver food, medicine, and education to those without it. In my childhood faith, there were people with compassion, integrity, generosity, wisdom, and courage. But these values don't belong to religion. They belong to the human race, and it's up to each of us to connect with what's best in us and share it with other humans.

I wouldn't wish my experience on anyone, but I have come out of it with a strong sense of my right to question anything anyone tells me, and to discover for myself what I value. That's very freeing as I re-create the rest of my life.

FALLING FOR THE DEVIL

Ceal Wright

*The idea that you're the center of your own narrative
and that you can create your life is a great idea.*

—Julianne Moore

"You must consider him a tool of Satan."

My face refused to remain neutral as my ears took in this sentence. Did I hear him right? With an expression of incredulity and confusion, I looked back at the elder who'd just spoken and the two others on the panel with him, and replied, "Uh, I don't see how that's possible. I don't think you understand—I love him. This isn't just a crush—I *love* him—I wouldn't be with just anybody. Jehovah is a God of love and this is love, so I don't see how that is even remotely connected to Satan."

"Satan is using him to draw you away from Jehovah and is disguising himself as this boy," another elder chimed in.

Oh silly young Ceal, you hadn't realized that you'd fallen in love with the devil.

The fluorescent lights became unbearably bright as I felt my body stiffen, preparing for my reply. I stood my ground and continued to refute their offensive correlation of my love with the devil. Trying to reason and explain my logical feelings (as opposing as that sounds) to this tribunal of elders was futile though. In this Church females were not given equal voice and stature; therefore, for me to come into the room prepared for anything but groveling for forgiveness was tantamount to disrespect. I had naïvely presumed they would treat me with the respect and openness that I had been raised to believe I deserved, and in the heat of that moment, I did not recognize the danger I was in by voicing my thoughts. After a solid two hours of back-and-forth, they left the room for an agonizing ninety minutes to deliberate, during which time I sat alone in the back room of the Kingdom Hall feeling confused, abandoned, and pissed.

Believing still that God was real and his Holy Spirit was directing the men outside, I was convinced by my conditioning that my case would be dealt with justly—after all, this was my first offense in my twenty-three years of life. Finally, they filed into the small room and sat back down. They all read a scripture that they had personally chosen for me and then informed me that they were leaning toward disfellowshipping me—the highest punishment available to them—but by the grace of one elder who had known me for years, they decided to grant me a reprieve to think upon their counsel and come back repentant.

And in that instant, my faith shattered.

My faith had been inherited, as most belief systems are, and I took to it wholeheartedly. I can't say that I'm naturally a gullible person, but there was no compelling reason for me to look elsewhere or question what the Church told me, so I didn't.

I had an amazing childhood. My parents loved and protected me. My experiences were rich and my life full of love and laughter. And if I'm being honest, superiority played a role. Jehovah's Witnesses (from here on referred to as Witnesses or JWs) are raised to believe they are special. I assume other religions teach the same but, I would argue, not to the degree of the Witnesses. The constant rhetoric of the "only true God" and the "Truth" (capital *T* intended) combined with the continual derogative reference to anyone outside of the organization as "worldly" continually reinforce this special position Witnesses believe they hold.

Quick lesson on JW lore. Witnesses believe that God's name is Jehovah, his son's name is Jesus, and the two are separate beings. They believe that God will soon bring about Armageddon and destroy all those who are not faithful. Those who survive will live on a paradise earth and will welcome all of those who have died over the years in the coming Resurrection. Witnesses are most famous for their door-to-door ministry, with which they spread the message by knocking at people's front doors to distribute literature, mainly on weekends.

Being a socially motivated person, I fit in seamlessly. The Witness community is truly that—a community. It allowed me to be known and loved by a great number of people in my ward as well as connected to a worldwide network of people who, I felt, all served the same purpose.

That purpose, however, escapes me now with my current distance from the organization. But I do know that for me, the bottom line of my fulfillment in life has always been a matter of love. When I had a hard decision to make or needed a barometer, I would ask myself, "Am I loved? Are others loved? Are our actions being motivated by love? Am I being motivated by love?" Tough choices always came down to "Is this an act of love?" and the answer would dictate my response. I have always been a gregarious and lively person, ready to hug anyone I feel a connection to or strike up a deep conversation with a stranger on the street. I spread love and joy around whenever I felt inspired.

Being in such a tight organization, therefore, never felt stifling to me. I felt like I could love anyone that was in my circle. Growing up in it never felt like a burden to me, as I later learned it did for other Witness children. I embraced my differences from other children and felt very proud to not celebrate holidays or birthdays, as I felt we had the Truth and it was others who were ignorant. I spent a lot of my childhood defending my beliefs and proving myself with scripture. I would defend creation to my science teacher and take up doctrinal issues such as the Trinity with other children. Despite my strong stance, I do remember feeling the sting of missing out on cake. I loved it but would have to abstain when other mothers brought in birthday treats for their kids. I can attribute my slight obsession with it now to my childhood deprivation.

At a deeper level, besides the profound issue with cake, serious deprivation existed for me in two areas: participating in sports and going to college. As a Witness child, I was taught that everyone besides fellow members are bad association. Being on a sports team was out of the question since my teammates would be worldly and could influence me in subtle ways—not to mention the time it would take away from my service to the organization.

I was athletic and tall for my age and was constantly recruited to play on school sports teams. I remember filling out the application for the swim team in middle school and going so far as trying to forge my mother's signature (a very rebellious act for a goody-goody like me) until she caught me in the act. Trying to explain to the coaches why I couldn't be on their teams was very difficult—something I couldn't prove with scripture—and in hindsight, I see that it's a ridiculous amount of pressure to put on a kid.

JW's excel in the art of indoctrination. The organization keeps its followers on a strict schedule of busywork. At that time my typical week consisted of a Sunday meeting: two hours, Tuesday night meeting: two hours, Thursday book study: one hour, Saturday morning door-to-door ministry: three hours, and one additional night spent on a family study. In addition, we were strongly encouraged to study before all meetings and spend extra time socializing with fellow members.

For similar reasons we were strongly discouraged to pursue education beyond high school. Who needs more wisdom than what Jehovah's organization can offer you? There were no hard rules concerning either of these things, but rather social pressure and the fear of losing status in the congregation kept most people in line.

I'll never forget a conversation I had in sixth grade with my teacher, Mrs. Terrell, during career week. I submitted that I wanted to be a real estate agent, and she questioned me on this choice. I told her that I wouldn't be going to college and I needed a job that would allow me to pioneer (spend seventy hours per month preaching). To her credit she attempted to mask her incredulity and disappointment, but she made it very clear that I would be wasting my potential if I didn't even try to pursue a bachelor's degree. I always sought the approval of my teachers and remember feeling uncomfortable with Mrs. Terrell's disappointment. I tried to explain with the only set of parameters that I had at the time that going to college is not conducive to being a full-time servant of Jehovah. Needless to say, my argument fell flat, but she supported me as well as she could.

It's so clear to me now why education isn't conducive to being a Witness—it makes a person think. It opens your mind and forces you to question things that they wanted members to accept as fact. More importantly, it exposes you to a whole new segment of the population that makes you question what bad association really is.

When I was an early teen, something extraordinary happened— my dad's business was failing and he decided to pursue some additional schooling. The circuit overseer—think of the role of a district manager for

Witnesses—gave him so much grief for not trusting that Jehovah was soon going to bring an "end to this system of things" (their persistent belief that God will destroy the world and reward his faithful). If he'd been a believer, the theory was, he wouldn't spend the time going to school but would simply wait for Jehovah to bring an end to this wicked world. My father stood up for his choice and went to school. I'm so grateful he did this, as it opened the mental door in my parents' minds for me to pursue a college education as well.

* * *

Despite my seemingly complete acceptance of the religion, a few specific instances stick out for me that showed cracks in my faith. When the Harry Potter book series came out when I was a teenager, the JW's reacted as most fundamental religions did—with a resounding "This is from the devil!" to all those who wanted to read it. I wanted to read these books—so I did, but I didn't tell anyone. However, like most teenagers, I had an absolute mess in my car and I often left the books in my backseat. My friend found my book one night and said, "I can't drive with Ceal. We're going to get hit by lightning!" She was being admittedly dramatic, but the judgment was still there: "Rebellious Ceal, reading banned books again."

Masturbation is forbidden within Witness rules. Being the rule follower that I was, I refrained and never indulged in such "self-abuse." Perhaps surprisingly, it was my family who opened my mind to this. My grandmother was very worldly with her PhD in psychology and was influential on my psyche during high school and beyond. I am forever grateful to her for being a secure tether to the outside world, as she took me out of my cocoon and into the world on many vacations with her.

One such vacation was to Palm Springs to visit my Great Aunt CJ and her husband, David. They were the epitome of worldly. Aunt CJ had had lots of affairs and extramarital sex, been married five times, and lived a life of adventures and pleasure until she eventually met and married David, the love of her life. Together they became ministers of a modern New Age church. I spent a week with them in Palm Springs and, being innocent Ceal, was very open about all things in my life. They took me to the movie *Sordid Lives*, and during the scene with full-frontal male nudity, my grandma reached over to cover my eyes, knowing that she was going to get in trouble with my dad if he ever found out she had exposed me to such entertainment. The trip was eye-opening for me—and not just because of movies with nudity, but because it once again allowed me to see worldly people in an intimate way that proved they weren't as scary as I had been taught to believe. I felt freedom of expression and acceptance as I had never experienced in my JW community.

During one final dinner after a week of open and scandalous conversation, the subject of masturbation came up. Since I couldn't really participate in the conversation, being as innocent as I was, I interjected that for me "self-pleasure is wrong and not allowed by Jehovah." I continued using the Witness logic that seemed airtight to me at the time: "Why would you bother teasing yourself if you can't have sex before you are married? Might as well not tempt your body with self-pleasure if you can't have the real thing until you are married." A silent beat passed as my grandmother, obviously uncomfortable, with a tight pink face and pursed lips, gave no retort. On the other side of the table, however, in her classic brash style, my Aunt CJ shot me an intense look that said, "Listen here." Then in a grave tone, she replied, "By all means, pleasure yourself, darling. Pleasure yourself." So I did. And subsequently lost all recollection of my previous defense.

In addition to my non-Witness family, I always had friends who were my willing corruptors. During my college years I worked at a coffee shop where I met many incredibly intelligent and educated young people who were supportive of my naturally curious nature. Once a customer who had developed a rapport with me came in and said something about the shocker. In my naïveté I asked, "What's the shocker?" not knowing that it was a foreplay move. He said, "Two in the pink, one in the stink," with a giant grin on his face and flashed the obscene hand gesture. *Whoa.* Not what I expected to hear. The rest of my coworkers thought that was the best exchange that had ever taken place at the shop and encouraged my inquiries as I began polling other regular customers if they, too, knew what this was or if I was truly the only ignorant one. These bonds with my coworkers served an important purpose in allowing my sheltered self to begin seeing non-Witnesses as equals and not just "the others."

It was about this time that I started to chafe under the rules that applied to women in the Church. I began to see how women were secondary to men in the Church and there was no room to question this. I realized the quote from *Animal Farm*, "All animals are equal, but some animals are more equal than others," applied here too.

I became vocal about the contrast between Jesus's respect for women and the Apostle Paul's more harsh approach. "Why are we following Paul's example?" I questioned. The organization held to the Apostle Paul's edict in Corinthians that "women should be silent in the congregation." They allowed women, called sisters, to comment during various studies but never to address the congregation directly from the stage. I have always been an excellent public speaker, and I looked forward to opportunities to get up in front of people to speak, but I was told that I would never be able to speak directly from the stage. I would watch from my seat in the auditorium as men with far less skill stammered through a painful five-minute discourse. Their only qualification was their gender. Whenever I would vocalize my frustration about this, other women's responses infuriated me. It was always, "Who would want to do that anyway, so who cares?" There was never any room to have talents or desires beyond the status quo. The classic JW response for everything difficult is: "Trust in Jehovah and his organization—the Holy Spirit is directing, he will work it out in the End." That never did fully satisfy me, but it is impossible to argue with that kind of logic, so I shoved my dissention down deep, and it would only come out when I let my guard down.

Thankfully, I had an outlet in college. My parents' mental leap when my dad went to school extended to their children. At first, I tried to please both worlds by continuing to pioneer and go to school at the same time, hopefully showing that I was still a dedicated servant. But soon the demands of both worlds were too much, and I quit pioneering to focus on school.

This resulted in a firestorm of gossip in the congregation. People looked down on me, scorned me, used me as an example of why it's not possible to pursue higher education and still remain dedicated. I felt strongly that I needed to finish my schooling, so I mostly ignored everyone, but I'm not going to pretend that it didn't sting. I have always been a people pleaser, and I absorbed the sentiments that I was letting my congregation down and setting a bad example for young ones. Some of the parents now use my name as an example of what not to be like.

During all of this time, I had managed to stay almost free of romantic entanglements.

That all changed in my last year of college. I met Cooper. I had yet to discover he was Satan's tool.

It started innocently enough. I was going to be on vacation for a couple of weeks of the term and my marketing class was doing a group project, so I needed to be in a group with a strong leader. He stood out as the biggest nerd in the class, so I approached him and asked him to be in my group.

I was working full time, going to school, and trying to maintain my status in the congregation by attending the full onslaught of meetings. This led to virtually no time to actually concentrate on schoolwork. Cooper was the exact opposite of me with only one class and no job, so he was always free and willing to meet me at whatever time I had available to work on our group project together. Picture those meeting spots at a bar late in the evening with tucked-away booths and strong beer, and what you have is the opportunity for romance. Satan was obviously orchestrating all of this, but I believed I was in control and not in any danger of falling for this unassuming, quiet boy.

Unbeknownst to me, what was really taking place was my slow awakening to the fact that worldly people were not the ilk that I had grown up being afraid of. Before that point, my corruptors always had a vice that made it easy for me to dismiss their lifestyle. My best worldly friend and main corruptor, Cal, smoked, participated in recreational drugs, drank too much, and slept with too many needy women; therefore I could dismiss him as part of the crowd that was bad. But now, when faced with Cooper, who was a better human than I was in morality, in genuineness, in decency— my resolve began to quietly weaken.

We began to date, in a very subtle just-hanging-out sort of way. I was comfortable with it because that's how most of the Witnesses I knew dated. But I knew how it would look, me hanging out, unchaperoned, with a non-JW male. In a nutshell—I hid him. Once, we were at a Starbucks and I went inside first while he was parking. I walked in and saw some people that I knew from the congregation, so I panicked and texted him that he had to stay outside until I told him it was safe to come in because I could not be seen with him. He complied, but when I walked out and saw his stone face, I knew he was about to lose his patience with me and the whole situation.

I understood how offended he must have felt, but I had to protect myself. How could he possibly understand how important it was for him to remain hidden? That if anyone saw us together and even glimpsed a hint of the chemistry between us that I could be turned in to the elders? How could he understand the consequences that I would face? I don't think anyone who hasn't experienced the type of strong control JW's exert could possibly fathom what could happen. They think, *What's the big deal? Atoning for sins is easy*, imagining the TV version of Catholic confession in a booth and a penance of ten Hail Marys. The unfortunate reality of being a JW is that anyone can turn you in, and in fact, members are continually encouraged to do so. And the consequences are very tangible, with the strictest punishment being cut off completely from your family and friends.

Cooper was ten times more easygoing than I was, but that incident took awhile for him to get over. I knew there was tension there that I couldn't make him understand so I began to hide him in more subtle ways. I went to see movies with him but only if they were R-rated—knowing that no one I knew would be there. We frequented bars that I knew were considered too worldly for a JW crowd. I'd suggest take-out instead of eating at a restaurant. I'd only go out if I knew most people I knew were at meeting that night. By managing our outings, I was able to avoid confronting him about keeping him hidden.

He knew I was a Witness from the beginning, but like most people on the outside, he didn't understand what that actually entailed. He slowly got the gist of it, however, when I repeatedly broke up with him the way one might unsuccessfully try to give up alcohol, smoking, or fried food. I would resolve not to see him anymore, and then after a day or two, I'd make my way back to "Why can't we at least be friends?" and then "Friends make out, don't they?" I asked him to just convert many times, and to his credit, he never even considered that an option.

Needless to say, all of this put quite the strain on our relationship. Add to that our lack of intimacy. I maintained my abstinence for a solid two years before I finally caved to being human. The bliss was short-lived, however, before the JW guilt training kicked in. Looking back on it now, I realize how indoctrinated I was and how powerful a weapon guilt is. I felt the absolute heavy burden of conscience. I started to tear up on Sunday at a meeting, and a fellow member knew something was up. She said, "You better call the elders." I was devastated but felt compelled to do what I thought at the time was the right thing to do. That's how I found myself in the back room of the Kingdom Hall facing three men and answering the question "Who took whose shirt off first?"

Really. They asked that. I can only assume it was to determine who the aggressor was in the indiscretion, but this just showed me that they had never had a passionate moment in their lives. Who can remember such details in the throes of passion? And beyond that, who cares? And why was I being forced to answer such a question alone in a room with three men?

Two days later, having taken time to consider my pending disfellowshipment, I was scheduled to meet with the tribunal again. This time I was prepared. The elder who had shown me grace had called me and let me know that I needed to ask for help. "Really?" I responded, "I thought that coming to you and confessing my sins implies my asking for help." Apparently not, so I revised my strategy and decided to approach them as a repentant sinner who did not understand the wayward path I had trodden, and as such needed wise counsel from the elders to correct said path while simultaneously swearing off Cooper, who was the devil's tool. My contrived humility worked. The elders were impressed with my turnaround and believed I was truly repentant. As a side note, a year later I found out that one of the elders on the committee who was judging me for my indiscretion was at that same time having an affair with his sister-in-law.

Following my relief at being spared the ultimate punishment, it was difficult to reconcile my belief in an omniscient God and the power of his Holy Spirit with what had just transpired in the back room. I couldn't understand how a loving God would punish me for being honest and truthful in the first meeting and allow dishonesty to warrant the just and compassionate result of forgiveness. What this ultimately told me was that his Holy Spirit wasn't actually guiding the process as I had been led to believe.

For a time, I tried to push those rebellious thoughts out of my mind, go on another Cooper diet, and be the good JW I was expected to be. I found new friends who were interesting and seemed to be solid Witnesses. Unfortunately, another path of trouble arose as I learned that being friends with people who are under the same mental constraints of indoctrination can inadvertently place your fate in their hands.

Having been raised with absolute love and devotion, I always approach a situation or person with complete trust and don't always see what bad things people are capable of. I had stayed in touch with an old friend, Dick, and at some point our groups of friends intersected. He was in a bad place spiritually, as they say, and I was torn between my two worlds. When he became interested in one of my JW friends, Kristin, I let them do what people do and they let me freely admit to loving a worldly boy whom I was supposed to be staying away from. In short, I trusted them with my hidden boyfriend.

Predictably, I had starting seeing Cooper again. Because "good girls" aren't on birth control but are very much able to get pregnant, I was in need of Plan B. At the time, Plan B wasn't available without a prescription in my state so we had to drive across the border to get it from Planned Parenthood. Dick and Kristin drove me to the clinic so I could secure the pill.

Then Dick and Kristin's relationship went south. When Kristin broke up with Dick, he wasn't happy about it, so he chose to confess his wayward ways to the elders in order to get back at her. In that confession he tried to deflect from his own sins by including my indiscretions, using our trip to Planned Parenthood along with a bunch of text messages that were subject to interpretation. I'm foggy on all the details—I imagine my psyche is protecting me—but somehow I heard that the elders were investigating me. I had no idea at the time what that meant, but as it turns out, the elders were considering all of this for months before I even knew I was under the microscope again.

Somehow I finally told my mom what was going on, and I will always love her for her defense of me and her anger toward the men involved. She made me call the elder whom I was friends with and demand to know what was going on. She requested a quick meeting with the chairman of the committee and me.

So here I was again, in the back room of the Kingdom Hall facing just two of the three elders I had faced before. I had flashbacks of the first incident, but this time I had my mom with me. The chairman opened by telling me that he had heard things, but he was very ambiguous as to what. As he questioned me, I felt like I was being called guilty of something far more evil than falling in love. He peppered me with roundabout questions that I could not answer because I had no clue what he was trying to lead me to.

My mom finally interrupted the main interrogator and said, "Would you just tell us what evidence you have against my daughter? You are being *mean*. Just *mean*." I'll never forget her anger at that moment and her use of the word *mean* as if she were talking to a preschooler. This prompted them to finally cite the various pieces of evidence they had, and I easily refuted them. I had learned my lesson from the last incident—that admitting guilt was far more difficult than denying everything from the start. Plus, my cousin had taken me out to dinner and said, "*Lie*, Ceal, just lie." I took that to heart and knew I needed to deny, deny, deny—it was Dick's word against mine. They told me they were going to form a committee based on the evidence of "loose conduct" and I had no choice but to participate.

I don't know if I can properly convey how torn apart I was at this juncture. I was confused about my faith, my family, my love, and my identity, and now I had to face another tribunal and play the game to avoid getting disfellowshipped and having my whole lifestyle and community stripped away from me. With JW's, shunning is very strict, to the point that even your immediate family is coerced into not speaking to you. They tell you that only by shunning will transgressors see the error of their ways and come back to the congregation, and therefore you have just saved their everlasting life. If that guilt isn't enough, they further enforce the rule by threatening anyone who talks to disfellowshipped people with their own excommunication, and again, family and friends are encouraged to report them if they transgress.

Cooper was as supportive as he could be, but he had zero concept of what I was facing. This was my second misdemeanor, so it was very likely they would severely discipline me. This time, though, I was even more prepared—I consulted. My uncle, a former elder, was very empathetic and coached me. I felt like I was preparing for a boxing match where my goal was to feign and deflect. Thankfully, I had my mom in my corner and, surprisingly, my father. I had avoided telling my father anything that was going on for fear of his wrath and disappointment. I didn't expect his support. However, my mom had felt that it was imperative I tell him what was going on, so I did, and his support gave me all the strength I needed.

This time I would begin as a repentant sinner. I knew what they were going to accuse me of, and I chose to go beyond just those sins—not only was I guilty of *porneia* (a Greek word that doesn't have a direct translation but is used to encompass all acts of immorality) but also lying, greed, sloth, impertinence, disrespect, not honoring God, and disobeying elders. I had printed out article after article from *Watchtower* magazines and highlighted key points to show them just how much I had sinned and how desperately I was in need of their help. I stuck to my improbable story that dry humping in a hot tub could get you pregnant, which explains why I went to Planned Parenthood for Plan B. The entire four hours I was in the meeting, my parents sat in the parking lot of the Kingdom Hall waiting for me. I emerged victorious in two ways: I wasn't going to be disfellowshipped, and I was no longer under the spell of the organization as I had again seen clearly that God's Holy Spirit was not guiding the process.

The elders felt they needed to publicly reprove me because too many people knew of the situation, so they needed to warn the congregation while at the same time let them know that they had dealt with the sinner. This was intense for me, as it exposed my fall from grace to my entire community. Although the Church doesn't announce what manner of sins one has committed while publicly reproving, most people already knew, as members had been gossiping. On the positive side, I no longer felt a need to live up to others' high expectations and I could take a break from pleasing people. Unfortunately, there is no easy way to leave the church. Once baptized (in my case at thirteen years old), you are forever a member unless you get disfellowshipped or disassociate yourself, which hold equal consequences of banishment. I felt the need to play the game of participation while trying to figure out how to fade away quietly.

Somewhere in this swirl of drama, Cooper and I broke up for the last time. I was in a crazy emotional mode with all that was going on, and I wasn't kind to him in many of our conversations. I felt like I was risking everything to be with him and he didn't appreciate the sacrifice I was making. We had a big blowout, and he gave me the silent treatment for days. I was devastated. It took a phone call from my grandmother, asking him to at least reach out to me and forgive me regardless of the outcome, to get him to agree to meet with me.

We rendezvoused at the same bar where our early homework sessions had occurred and began the awkward, vulnerable conversation of "What do you really want?" At one point, we reached over the table and grasped hands, and that's when I let my final reservations go. It took that touch of forgiveness, connection, and love to make me realize that I needed to start fighting for him instead of my religion. Sadly, he had taken a job that required him to move three hours away. This was our make-it-or-break-it moment. Now we would have to put forth supreme effort to stay connected.

I also knew that I would now have to commit to an even deeper level of subterfuge in my attempt to fade from the church until I was ready to be open about my relationship.

At a certain point, marriage was put on the table. With Witnesses, because the sin of fornication is so terrible, it's more acceptable to marry than date. Because of the delicate situation I was in, I knew that I couldn't just date forever—we had to make it official for me to be accepted by my family. I honestly don't remember this being a conscious decision. I just knew that was the next step. One day on the phone, I mentioned, "Maybe May is a good month to get married," and he replied, "Did you just propose to me?" And that's how we got engaged.

Now began the arduous task of keeping this fact quiet and trying to come up with a way to have the wedding I wanted within the confines of the community I was still connected to. I took my mom out for crepes to talk about it, and I remember the Nutella crepe—which I would normally think was delicious—tasting like sawdust and my hands shaking when I tried to use a fork. I finally laid it out there on the table—literally, I pulled my ring out—and she was surprisingly supportive. Then she adamantly said, "We cannot tell your father this right now." We agreed to wait until the right time to break the news, and in the meantime, she wanted to meet Cooper properly. I cannot describe what a relief it was to tell my mom what was going on. She was able to meet Cooper and get to know him a bit before all hell broke loose when word started leaking out.

The problem with a small community where everyone is connected is that everyone is connected. In a normal world, news of an engagement would be cause to celebrate and it wouldn't be a secret. A friend of mine who we call Mr. Flappy Lips was an inactive JW who was excited about the news but forgot that he was still connected to the strict community. He let it slip one night to someone, who knew someone, who knew everyone. Once we heard about this slip, my mother insisted we needed to be the ones to tell my dad before he found out through the grapevine. It was then that I finally understood what true anxiety felt like.

My mom took the brunt of it by telling my father I was engaged. I subsequently avoided him for three days until he was ready to talk and I had the courage to face him. I have nothing but the utmost respect for my father and have always wanted nothing but to please him. This was the first time I was truly going my own way. To his credit, he seemed to seek understanding and wasn't condescending or mean to me, which led to an honest conversation.

I made my case. I said, "My whole life I have been taught that I worship a God of love. That is his core trait and principle beneath everything he does for us. 'For God loved the world so much. . . .' I am in love, Dad. And he is a better person than me, more honest than me, and embodies this love. How could a God of love say this is wrong?"

Dad put forth a couple shallow arguments, but he knew they were weak. Finally, a breakthrough happened when I pushed a bit more—staying with my theme of love—and he stopped me. With a struggle of pure emotion he said, "Ceal, I can't. I just can't. I can't go against my principles. I want to see my dad again." And with those words I understood, backed off, and forgave. His dad had died tragically when he was young and he'd never worked through the grief properly—he'd been letting the hope of a resurrection in the future bandage the emotional devastation he'd held on to for forty years. Now at this crossroad in the conversation, I recognized that his desire to believe in a resurrection and his love and understanding of his daughter were colliding and weren't compatible. In his mind, admitting that I was right would somehow undermine his belief and he wouldn't get to see his dad again. I saw this battle in him and understood that he desperately needed to find a neutral path. I felt compassion for him and appreciated that he'd revealed his struggle.

There wasn't much more to say after this interchange except for his final request. He didn't ask me to break it off, but instead to get married as quickly as possible. "Why?" I wondered. He said, "I trust your judgment in people, and I can support him as my son-in-law but not as your boyfriend."

I took that as the closest thing to a father's blessing I was going to get and went with it. I struggled with the loss of the grand wedding I wanted, but I took the advice of a friend and let that go to keep the peace. I quickly made arrangements for our elopement and once again, Cooper went along with this crazy plan. With the support of my worldly family and friends and my mother, we had an amazing elopement. Eighteen people celebrated with us, the justice of the peace performed the ceremony, the beautiful Columbia Gorge was our background, and the sun came out in February to bless us.

I appreciated the freedom of the ceremony. Because I wasn't held to any church tradition, I could direct the proceedings as I saw fit, and we wrote our own vows. Cooper stole the show and cried during his, and subsequently all eighteen people were in tears. The small crowd consisted of the friends and family who had supported us and knew our story intimately: my corruptors. I could not have asked for a more genuine and heartfelt occasion. We celebrated with dinner and champagne and spent the night at the lodge. My mom once again took the heat and went home afterward to tell my father it was done.

Not surprisingly, the gossip storm erupted again and people felt justified in venting to me about how much I had hurt them by getting married to a worldly man. I'll never forget going to my cousin's house and seeing her in tears as she told me, "You hurt me and my family and Jehovah," and eventually asked, "Do you think that Cooper will want to study the Truth with my husband?" I sat there during her ranting and stayed as neutral as possible. My goal was to live through the initial fallout until a new scandal took my place and in the meantime go to meeting on Sunday so my father could say, "She's still going to meetings," to anyone he wanted.

I boldly planned a classic wedding for that summer even though we were already technically married. Cooper had found a job in town and we were finally together all the time, and it felt right to celebrate being truly married.

We had 150 people at the beach, I wore a white dress, and we had lots of cake. It was fun and beautiful and fulfilled my desire for a party. By the time we had the beach wedding, things in the community had calmed down enough that my dad, my grandmother, and some of my Witness friends and family actually came. I felt like we had made it through the worst of the drama and now people were finally adjusting so we could move on.

It's been seven years since that occasion, and I have continued to navigate through the murky world of fading away from the faith. Some people who choose to leave disassociate themselves to make a clean break and publically show that they do not support the beliefs any longer, and I respect and understand their choice in that regard. For someone as social and connected as myself, I never saw that as an option. I have empathy for my family and understand the mind control I see them subjected to. Not everyone has the opportunity for something as powerful as love to come into their life and open their mind to new ideals. It was only by the grace of falling in love with my husband that I was able to see the other side.

I am proud that I have been able to continue to walk the fine line between my two worlds, and I recognize that they will always be a part of my life. Being content with who I am today has become of the utmost importance, and because of love of self, I can find peace with my past and recognize it as a contributor to my present state. Anger and resentment are not becoming, and I have worked hard to abolish them from my mind. I still get worked up when I hear of the injustices that go on in the organization, but I try not to let the anger linger.

I instead find joy in my happy marriage, my continuing relationships with my family, and more importantly, with my new daughter whom I can raise free from the entanglement of organized religion. I feel free to live by my personal philosophy of pursuing love and happiness in this present life without the guilt and foreboding of the future.

The moment my faith shattered marked the beginning of a great expansion of mind and freedom of growth toward untapped potential. The supposed tool of Satan did more for me as a human being than years of following God ever did. As I stood in the light of love and not in the fear of an organization, I found a new belief system based on true character and self-direction. For all this and more, I am grateful.

GROWING UP ATHEIST

Ute Mitchell

The World's Need
So many Gods, so many creeds,
So many paths that wind and wind,
When just the art of being kind
Is all this sad world needs.

—Ella Wheeler Wilcox, from *Poems of Power*

My story begins in Germany, in elementary school to be exact. I was raised by atheist parents, and my understanding of religion and church was limited to a visit with a neighbor's daughter who babysat for my family and played the organ at Sunday masses.

My first true encounter with religious righteousness happened in school, when I was barely seven years old, during PE class. I was in first grade, part of a newly formed class with seventeen other children, and one of my new friends, who sat on the bench next to me, asked, "Are you Catholic or Protestant?" These were the two major religions in Germany. My prompt reply was that in fact I was neither, that my parents did not christen me because they wanted to leave this decision up to me. My friend, in utter shock, announced that I was a heathen and that heathens go to hell. I had no concept of what a heathen was, nor did I understand what this "hell" place meant. I don't recall asking my parents about it, but I am sure I did.

Religious education was a mandatory subject in Germany, and the only kids excused from it were Turkish kids who grew up Muslim. I joined the Protestant class, as my parents felt it was the lesser of two evils, and so for the next few years I learned about the Bible, discussed Bible stories, learned prayers, and sang Christian songs.

At home, religion was not an issue until I was around thirteen years old and the question of confirmation came around. This was to be a church event during which I would accept the Protestant faith and be welcomed into the church. I remember discussing this with my parents, who left this decision entirely up to me. They said they were happy to support me in my decision, if I truly believed in god and wanted to start going to church. I had some time to think about this, and I even tried praying secretly in my room. The part of me that was jealous of my religious friends and their strong belief in a supreme being wanted to believe as well. I wanted to feel held and taken care of, and of course, I really wanted to believe in heaven. I prayed night after night, asking for a sign, for anything that would confirm to me that there was indeed a god up there who held his protective hand over me.

My prayers remained unanswered. I grew desperate and started reasoning with myself about why this god, who was so good to my friends and who supposedly talked to them, would entirely ignore me. I continued to pray in the darkness of my room, but I found only emptiness. One night I simply stopped. My desire to reach a god who didn't answer disappeared. I did not want to go through with confirmation, and I shared this decision with my parents.

I did, however, remain a student in religious education, which had by now become optional. Between the ages of fourteen when I graduated at seventeen, I led several meaningful discussions with my teachers, one of whom was desperate to convert me to her faith while the other simply challenged me to figure things out on my own. He was a believer but not one who viewed me as a lost little sheep. He accepted my skepticism, and he tried to answer my questions to the best of his knowledge and ability. I appreciated his openness and honesty, although he never managed to answer the one question I wanted to have answered the most.

By now, I knew of many different religions: Buddhism, Hinduism, Islam, and the various Christian faiths. I asked my teacher how he knew that, of all these religions, his was the true one. Why would I believe in his god when there appeared to be so many others? He smiled and shook his head. "I don't know," he said. "It's a feeling." While I found this answer to be fascinating, it was not good enough. I was taught in every subject to think critically, to find evidence for my claims. This was true for math, science, biology, physics, and chemistry, all of which were taught as separate subjects in Germany. Yet, in my religious education class, I was asked to leave these skills behind. I was asked to simply believe.

As important as these questions were to me in school, outside of school none of it seemed to matter. I watched the people around me, my friends and family, and found that none of them were overly religious, nor did they even discuss their religion with friends. Their faith was a private matter. I was friends with believers and nonbelievers alike, and the truth is, to this day I am not quite certain who did and didn't believe in any gods, except for those who had church weddings. Some of these weddings came as a surprise to me. Some of my most relaxed friends who never attended Sunday Mass insisted on church weddings. And yet, none of it mattered when it came to our friendships. Some of us had been friends for life. Religion was not going to change that.

I met my American husband and moved to the United States at the age of twenty-five. My husband was also an atheist, and while back then it never occurred to me to ask him if he was atheist, in retrospect I understand how important this really was to me. I knew nothing about life in America, and when I moved to Arizona, I had the expectation that life would continue as usual. My goal was to raise a family and make friends. I joined a MOMS Club, organized events, and soon felt at home.

I tried to ignore the constant talk about god in politics. None of this made sense to me. I had never heard German politicians say, "God bless Germany." Yet American presidential elections appeared to always involve pride in the candidate's Christian belief. To me it seemed quite evident that no atheist would ever be elected president of the United States. I discussed this issue with a friend once and she accepted this fact as normal and even desirable. She said she was never going to give her vote to an atheist. Once again, I was flabbergasted. She smiled at me and said it was okay. She told me that eventually I would find god. I just hadn't tried hard enough yet. She casually invited me to her church and insisted that if only I gave it a try, I would certainly find faith there. It was different and more relaxed than other churches, she said. She couldn't wrap her mind around the fact that there were people out there who were not trying to find god. Everyone was, according to her.

Over the next few years I had many such conversations with friends. While they appeared to like me, they also felt inclined to at least try to convert me to their faith. Each of them was convinced that their church was different, that their faith was better, that all I needed to do was try.

It wasn't until we moved to Oregon that these conversations stopped. Only one friend here has asked me to join her church and felt sorry for my poor, lost soul. Interestingly, it was here in Oregon that I became a much more active and aggressive atheist. I believe it was a combination of things. I read surveys that found that atheists, along with Muslims, were the most hated minority in the country. I was dumbfounded by these numbers. I couldn't and still cannot comprehend how people waste their time hating others simply for a different belief system or lack thereof. I thought of my children, who would be exposed to this kind of hatred, and my heart ached for them. I was sad to think of my children as being excluded or hated because they were the children of atheists. My husband and I had joined an atheist group in our town and frequently discussed this subject. My husband's decision to start a secular Sunday school was well received, and so we started meeting up in a coffee shop, where we played games and read stories to our fellow heathens' kids. Eventually our numbers grew and we moved into a rec center room, and then we had to divide the group by age. Only about a year later, our group was integrated into the newly formed chapter of the Center for Inquiry.

I also became active in Dale McGowan's Foundation Beyond Belief. I communicated with atheists around the country and felt some relief that there appeared to be a growing number. Some of the families I talked to went on to create their own Sunday school programs in other states, though I have not kept in touch with them to see how things are going for them now.

After years of activism, I grew tired of talking about the same message over and over. While I enjoyed the conversations with other nonreligious parents, the constant struggle to look better to our Christian neighbors became old and boring. I understood that there needed to be activism, and I still admire the folks at the Center for Inquiry in Portland for all their work. They make sure that we, as atheists, are heard, that we are seen, and that it is understood that we are not going away. But on a personal level,

I only wanted to live in peace. Oregon is a wonderful place for this. My activism these days consists of being a decent human being. I have friends from all walks of life: an atheist Jew, several Christians, some agnostics, Buddhists, and some unidentified faiths, I'm sure. We have been able to discuss our beliefs or lack thereof in a friendly manner, with no hurt feelings, nor anger toward one another. This is really what I want in life. I want to be accepted for who I am and what I do, and I am most certainly happy to return the favor.

The truth is that I understand faith. It provides a peace of mind that I have searched for my whole life. I understand that people want to be comfortable in their belief that there is an afterlife, a heaven, a nirvana. It means we are more meaningful than our small existence of eighty years on Earth. It means we continue to exist on a spiritual level even after we cease to exist as humans on Earth. It does sound wonderful.

My children are atheists as well, no surprise. Obviously there was a good amount of influence from their parents, and I feel it was the right thing to go about raising them this way. We did have plenty of open-minded discussions, and we as parents have answered some difficult questions. We did tell them that we love them regardless of what happens in their future. If either of them turns to religion when they grow up, this will not diminish our love for them. Of course, we hope that they will think critically and that they will never be guilted into such a decision. Looking at them, though, it appears they will handle themselves just fine. They have been raised to question and second-guess everything, even those things told to them by their own parents.

I don't regret the life I have lived so far. My upbringing, my searching, my years of activism, have all brought me to where I am now. I have met many wonderful people, and I have met many who challenged me to rethink who I am and whether I truly am on the right path. I continue to seek my place in the world as an atheist homeschool mom. I may or may not become more outspoken on the subject of atheism once again, as my kids grow older and start their own lives. In the meantime, I love to live life to the fullest. I am deeply grateful for the things I have, for my health, for the wonderful place I call my home. Nature is my church, and Earth is my religion. I cannot think of a better way to live my life.

THE MANY PHASES OF BECOMING A YOUNG ATHEIST IN LATIN AMERICA

Matilde Reyes

Therefore not alone to aid her own enfranchisement—
valueless without religious liberty—but in order to help preserve
the very life of the Republic, it is imperative that women should unite
upon a platform of opposition to the teaching and aim of the ever most
unscrupulous enemy of freedom—the Church.

—Woman's National Liberal Union Resolutions, 1890

I was born in Lima, Peru, a few decades before our gastronomy had become renowned and in a time when Machu Picchu was a remote place that received few tourists—only adventurous people who wanted to explore what centuries before had been a sacred Inca city, a city wrecked by the Spaniards and their craze to colonize and evangelize the New World. The same craze that made Peru, until present day, a fervently Catholic country.

One of my earliest memories is of a picture hanging on the wall at the landing of the stairs of the house where I spent most of my childhood. A handsome white, blond, bearded man with a heart on fire in a white, red, and green gown. A typical sight in a 1980s Peruvian home—the sacred heart of Jesus. Perhaps we felt we needed someone to save us, from a lousy government, from inflation, from terrorism, and from each other.

An interesting phenomenon in a country that is, in its vast majority, Catholic is that religion is ingrained in your life from the very beginning, but it does not normally become extreme or fundamentalist. Regardless of the shared Catholic beliefs, frequent processions, and commonplace religious imagery even in public buildings (despite the proclaimed separation of church and state), other belief systems—esoteric practices, natural healing, and a disapproval of some of the Church's teachings—are not uncommon. My home was no stranger to these practices. My mother's grandmother and my father's grandmother were both very mystical. They were women who had learned to "read" the Spanish tarot and who "through the cards" would tell people about their future (and sometimes their past). Actually, both women helped sustain their homes, or at least brought in an extra income, with the cards. The cards were so accepted, they were practically another member of my family.

Many times my mother would sit on her bed, playing them, smoking cigarette after cigarette, trying to figure out what the future held for her, for my dad, and for all of us. My mother had gained fame in the family—on both sides—with her accuracy in reading the tarot, therefore reinforcing the idea that she did have a special psychic power. Her power not only manifested itself in the cards, but it also came in dreams—communicating with the dead and having premonitions. In one instance she told her father that his businesses would go down, one by one. Well ... of course they would. He was a lousy businessman, and at that point she was pissed off that he had left my dad jobless (if I remember the story correctly—maybe I should consult the cards!).

These beliefs also come with a heavy emotional charge—they are inherited. My sister never seemed interested in exercising this ability but was nonetheless interested in having her future told to her. However, I was different. I had that eagerness and curiosity for reading cards and communicating with others in a spiritual way. Even after I later renounced the knowledge of a god, I still felt I had this psychic gift. I wonder if my mother foresaw the additional tragedies that would strike the family ten years later.

My later childhood was spent outside of Peru. Due to the terrible state of the economy and politics as well as increasing terrorists attacks, we moved to the United States. Reflecting on it twenty-five years later, I believe the experience of living in a different country and coming in contact with children and people from so many different backgrounds shaped the person I am today, including the fact that I am ever morphing myself, adapting to my surroundings, and trying to evolve.

Five years later, after Peru had stabilized, my parents decided to go back. So, a month after my twelfth birthday, we moved again. My parents were hopeful that the recently improved economy would allow them to open their own business. I don't think the cards ever warned them that they wouldn't.

Going back to Peru was strange. Spending Christmas with family and seeing cousins regularly was something that I wasn't used to. A major shock was going back to the school I had originally attended. When my sister and I had first entered school (the same school my parents had attended, where they met and fell in love), it was owned by a wonderful man who was a philosopher and educator, so the school was not religious and had British influence. However, a few years before our return, it was bought by a shady character who claimed to be an independent investor/educator, but everyone knew he was a puppet of none other than the infamous Opus Dei, fundamentalists of the Catholic Church.

The Opus Dei is a powerful group that was close to Pope John Paul II. They are very conservative and use their teachings to ingrain specific and restrictive gender roles. They are the ones fervently preaching about birth control, and they don't hesitate to pry into the lives of parishioners to ensure their doctrines are followed. They separate their believers by numeraries and supernumeraries. Numeraries are single men and women who make celibacy commitments, dedicating their lives to god whilst keeping their own professions. Supernumeraries are married members of the Opus Dei.

A couple years into secondary school, I was one of the girls chosen to be invited for a leadership course at one of the Opus Dei houses, where they helped "form" young girls. That course opened the door for me to be invited to meetings, Masses, religious retreats, and a friendship with one of the woman numeraries at the Opus Dei house I attended. A friendship that, about eighteen months later, I would run from for no reason other than the constant checking in—aka, harassment—to join them for everything and anything. One thing I realized is that the Opus Dei goes through great lengths to recruit followers. They pressure you into friendship but only if they think you have potential, and apparently this woman thought I had potential. While this was tremendously annoying, it was also flattering, especially for me as a lonely teenager.

A few months into my engagement with the Opus Dei house, my family received terrible news. My cousin had been diagnosed with cancer— several aggressive brain tumors. We were the same age, and feeling this uncertainty, emptiness, and emotional pain was difficult to deal with, having just turned fifteen. My Opus Dei numerary friend prayed for my cousin. We talked about many things, and I went to one of the religious retreats.

It was the peak of my belief in god. I started going to Mass—my grandmother couldn't have been prouder. She was a faithful Catholic who, every Saturday (ever since someone in Peru had said that if you went to church Saturday evening, it counted for Sunday Mass), would beat her breast before reciting the Mea Culpa. Of course, after church was over, she would go back to being her hateful, racist self, but she did still recite the Mea Culpa and pray.

My cousin's deteriorating health struck the entire family very hard. Our grief manifested itself in different forms, and that was the year all our lives changed. Having a grandchild with deteriorating health made my grandmother very bitter. Her depressed and sometimes angry demeanor became more common, and we felt like we had to walk on eggshells around her. Meanwhile, I prayed and hoped that this would all be put behind us, that god would help us, would make my cousin better and subsequently my grandmother, and that we would all get past this with the grace of his blessings.

During that year I had been attending classes in preparation for confirmation in November. Around October we had our religious retreat, and that is probably one of the first times I started to doubt the true existence of god. Each of us had the chance to speak with a teacher who functioned as a religious counselor. Connie was very easy to talk to—she was young and had an easygoing demeanor. We talked about how being fifteen and being preoccupied by my cousin's deteriorating health was overwhelming and painful, and about how I was starting to doubt my faith. She told me she understood, that it was normal to feel doubt, and that it was okay. She encouraged me to trust that god had a plan, he knew best, he put us on this earth, and he could take us away to be in his glory. Wow . . . it hurts to write that eighteen years later.

I proceeded with my confirmation, and a few weeks later, my cousin passed away. How could god do this? How could god take a wonderful, fun, free-spirited fifteen-year-old and make her go through a horribly painful journey toward death? How could he have not heard the prayers? Seen the recovery Masses? Received the healing thoughts and the good vibes? Everyone said god had dropped an angel on this earth and was claiming her back—as if it were a blessing. As ridiculous as it sounds now, it was what people spoke about every time her death came up in a conversation. In those few months I went from believer, to doubter, to hater. The summer of 1998 was the last time I believed in the anthropomorphized concept of the Catholic god. The handsome white, blond, bearded man with a heart on fire in a white, red, and green gown could no longer shield me from reality.

A year later I entered university to study psychology. One of the many aspects of humankind that I was intrigued by was the need for religion and in particular the need for a god. Ironically, I entered a university run by Catholic nuns, where I had to take three theology classes. During my early adulthood, I had difficulty identifying with a belief or even a lack thereof. It was very difficult to not believe in anything, but I'd already stopped believing in the Church's god, so I settled for a "superior energy" that wasn't a judging "god" per se, but a driving force in the universe. My deeply ingrained psychic history was difficult to brush off. Card readings, palm readings, cocoa leaf readings, and everything in between were familiar and exciting, and believing there was some sort of energy that triggered things, that linked us to one another, was comforting. Feeling like a person with a heightened sensitivity made me feel special. When you are lonely, you will cling to anything that makes you feel exceptional, and I needed that at that point.

At twenty-five I went through a depressive episode like I had never had before. In the past I'd had episodes of sadness, but never like this. Depression really makes you reflect on all your beliefs, possibly because it is the point in your life where you feel truly alone. The people around you seem to be blurred voices and images—nothing they say or do can comfort you. The mere thought of a god, magical being, or driving force that permits self-loathing is beyond revolting. I was alone in the world, with only my self-destructive and suicidal thoughts. There was no magic, no god, no energy to save me. After that, I progressed to letting go of card readings, books about chakras, and anything that signified a belief in metaphysics.

Whilst working on my psychology degree, I learned how important the sense of belonging is. How seeing ourselves in others, identifying with any aspect of their lives, develops a sense of community, and that community protects and nourishes us. Often religion or belief in a god fills that need and develops connections between otherwise very different people. Little by little, I was losing that. I preferred the feeling of a lonely truth over a community lie. But with the help of modern medicine and strong relationships—mainly friendships—I overcame depression and my feeling of loss over my religion.

One of the many things that reinforces people's belief in a superior power is coincidences. It is difficult to understand that sometimes events are just the result of a sequence of actions. It is easier to think that destiny had something to do with it, perhaps because it makes us feel like we are important enough for a superior force to intervene in our lives. This happened to me too. In the summer of 2008, I received a Skype message from a stranger who was eager to speak with a Peruvian and know more about the country in the hopes of visiting later that year. We connected in a way that more than fulfilled my need for belonging. *How in the world did he find me?!* I wondered. Some might have called it destiny. But the truth is, well, he typed in criteria that led to my name being one of the first names in the list of results. It was just Skype intervention. We got married a little over four years after that first Skype message, in a beautiful, elegant, romantically secular ceremony.

In the last decade, a lot of my close friends and family members have started to identify themselves as nonreligious, agnostic, or atheist. Therefore, I did not spend much time as a closeted atheist—I was pretty open to my family, who in their own ways had begun to evolve in their beliefs as well.

The day-to-day life of an atheist has not been as difficult as one would think in a deeply religious, superstitious country. However, it is still difficult to swallow seeing children being christened and forced to pray, or thinking that my tax money goes to the Catholic Church despite the supposed separation between church and state. Witnessing the great dominion of religion in the world is difficult. However, the growing number of freethinkers and atheists is a relief that makes me think the world is evolving, no matter how slowly.

ANIMALS, RELIGION, AND THE PROCESS OF ATHEISM

Taylor Duty

The only position that leaves me with no cognitive dissonance is atheism.
It is not a creed. Death is certain, replacing both the siren-song
of Paradise and the dread of Hell. Life on this earth, with all its mystery
and beauty and pain, is then to be lived far more intensely: we stumble
and get up, we are sad, confident, insecure, feel loneliness and joy and love.
There is nothing more; but I want nothing more.

—Ayaan Hirsi Ali

I was raised religious in the loosest sense of the word; attending church on major holidays and the occasional sleepy Sunday, but infrequently enough that it never defined my relationship to the world. That was, until I attended a week-long Seventh-day-Adventist based summer camp in Eastern Oregon. There, religion changed from a peripheral comfort to front and center into my focus.

Atheism is a not exactly a realization but rather a process. That process involves refuting cultural, societal, and often, familial norms that we are cultured to internalize. Religion has an inherent comfort, both in the ideological aspects as well as in the conformance to hegemony that makes existing in society more seamless. But in order to truly become atheist, one must first experience religion as a fundamental tenant of his or her being.

Otherwise, agnosticism is the less contentious path. Adolescents scarcely scratch the surface of understanding themselves, let alone the systems they occupy. At this phase of my life, the process toward atheism really began when I "found" religion on my own.

I went to camp just a few weeks short of my eleventh birthday. I had no real awareness that it was so acutely religiously grounded—I only knew that I was going to do water sports and hang out with my friends (overnight!) for five days in a row and that was okay by me. Upon arrival, I was completely overwhelmed by how *cool* everyone seemed, how rad our camp counselors were (the male counselors were so cute!) and, most of all, how inclusive and welcoming the camp seemed. The environment was novel, challenging, fun, and yet totally comfortable. In retrospect, it was designed to be a place where moldable adolescents came to be inculcated to the tenets of the religion.

Teens counseling adolescents, engaging them in activities where they feel a sense of worth and inclusion becomes significant in their moldable young minds. Groupthink—or as it is commonly coined—"mob mentality" is powerful, especially among youth. The inherent search for acceptance and inclusion is structured and ciphered into a moral manipulation technique. Summer camp is a hothouse for this type of groupthink, and my young mind was not exempt. The songs we sang, wrapped in blankets under a clear, star-lit sky; the prayers we proffered while holding hands in the rustic mess-hall; the late night bible readings by flashlight, five or six of us girls crammed onto one bunk, each convinced me to believe.

More than *anything*, I wanted to assimilate to the mythical, delightful world that was summer camp. I wanted to learn more about what made these people and this place so wonderful and welcoming. I wanted to be a part of this community and understand how I could make the other 51 weeks per year of my life more like summer camp-land, every day. The answer I got was Jesus.

Interestingly, my personal journey with vegetarianism and animal advocacy also began at this time. Later, my beliefs about animals and my passion for them would play a large role in my realization that religion is wholly culturally constructed, so in retrospect, it is intriguing that these two beliefs were born from the same spark.

Seventh Day Adventists follow a vegetarian diet—a lifestyle choice they claim jibes with the tenets of their religion in that it advocates respect and love for all living things while simultaneously allowing individuals to keep clean minds and bodies. Raised a meat-and-potato girl by my Montana-bred parents, I was shocked to see "fakin' bacon" alongside veggies and grains on my metal tray the first day of camp. My friends and I each took bites of the soy-based bacon strips, wrinkling our noses and watching each other quizzically as we wondered why such a wonderful place would do something so horrific as serve fake meat to us growing kids. Back in our cabin, we peppered our counselor with questions about the lack of meat in the camp.

She responded simply: "We believe animals are not treated well in factories and that eating these animals leads to impurities in our own lives."

My ears perked when she spoke of animals in factories, and I bristled. "What do you mean animals are not treated well in factories?" I'd been to Montana; I'd seen cows in pastures, grazing lazily on grass while windowless farm buildings loomed in the distance. When she brought up the notion of animals in factories, I realized I'd assumed these cows lived nice, comfortable lives and when their day was up, a farmer herded them ploddingly into the perilous building and they came out the other-side as neatly packaged steak. It wasn't ideal, but they were animals so they couldn't be treated that poorly, could they?

With sad eyes, my counselor responded, "animals used for meat aren't respected . . ." she started, but stopped as she saw my brow furrow. "It's hard to describe . . . are you interested in seeing a video of what a factory farm really looks like?" Cautiously, I conceded my interest.

The impact of the video was reality-shifting; each consecutive frame altered my closely guarded belief that respect for living beings was universal. As a culture, we exploit the tragedies of war, the realisms of poverty, the sadness of death and disease; but yet, the animals that we utilized day in and day out became insignificant commodities that didn't justify an open discourse or a forthright presentation of the reality that they existed within. Mainstream media didn't present the conditions of factory farms, dairy farms, and other animal-processing facilities.

I was interested. I wanted the reassurance that what she was saying couldn't possibly be true. I wanted to see a video that would set my mind at ease and prove that people were not cruel. I wanted evidence that the world viewed animals the same way that I did. She opened her laptop computer and quietly clicked as several other young campers and I sat in anxious silence. Then she flipped the screen in our direction, still paused on the video thumbnail: a close-up image of a cow's eye staring directly into the camera. In that eye, I immediately registered fear, anxiety, and confusion.

My counselor pressed play and stepped back from the screen. I watched surreal images flash across the screen; creatures tortured, maimed, and slaughtered by human beings. Eventually, the intensity was more than I could handle. The echoes of pained animals, the brutal handling of living Instinctively, I recoiled from the images, but I couldn't look away. There are very few memories as visceral or impactful as this one. I can honestly say it changed my perspective on the world forever.

This, however, is not an essay about animal rights or my ascent to veganism. This is an essay about atheism. I mention the animal component because atheism and animal rights are two sides of the same coin that largely comprise my moral structure and worldview.

Flash-forward four years from that initial video and the pieces start to fall together: I am a devoted vegetarian in a house of meat eaters; an animal rights enthusiast in an elitist, upper-middle class town where raw activism is rarely proffered to the public. My mom is married to a man of Indian descent and his cousin is getting married. My parents, believing that travel is as-or-more valuable than traditional education, decide that they will pull my stepsiblings and me out of high school, fly us to China (because it is "on the way") and then India to attend the wedding.

As I boarded the plane, the first of a series that would eventually land me in India, I was comfortable with my identification as a Christian. My religious identity was situated within the cultural and social norms of my country, my race, and my peers. I really had no reason to push the boundaries of that comfort zone. I heeded to the impetus of the Christian word and I felt stability and solace in the community in which I had immersed myself. So much of religion depends on the attraction to that stability and solace; when people have nothing left they can cling to a community that provides an answer—I, too, was not immune to that draw.

Everything changed when our plane touched down in Mumbai. Stepping out into the dusty, dry Indian sun, my dark clothes concealing my arms and legs in their entirety—as was custom in Indian culture—I remember being immediately struck by the extreme poverty of the country. There was no hiding it: people swarmed over every inch of the city, setting up makeshift shanties in expansive networks of neighborhoods that siphoned power from city streetlights and backed up to the gates surrounding higher caste neighborhoods. India, as one of the poorest democracies in the world, looks and operates so differently from other impoverished nations like, say, the communist structure of China. I won't pretend to understand the complexities or the evolution of the socio-political structure, but I will say that the visceral nature of the poverty and the chaos that grips even the largest cities in India were phenomena unlike anything I had experienced until that point or have experienced since.

What changed my entire worldview on religion, however, was not the chaos that overwhelmed me to the point of tears for the first few days of my time in India; it was the peace that I came to see within that chaos. And that peace was, oh so ironically, grounded in religion.

According to India's 2011 census figures, just under 80% of the country's inhabitants identify as Hindu. That's about the same percentage of Americans that identify as Christian. It's a powerful percentage. Functionally, however, the way that percentage looks and operates is much different between the two countries. In America, there exists an overwhelming concern for political correctness born out of a litigious and media-hyped culture. That, combined with the social acceptance of a "backseat" religion where one can identify as Christian but not attend church or necessarily propagate "Christian values" on a day-to-day basis means that Christianity in America is relatively unobtrusive; its influence resides mainly in political and cultural undertones.

Hinduism in India is quite the opposite. It is visceral and visible. It breathes through the relationships between people and other people, between people and animals, between people and the world around them. It characterizes dress, behavior, speech, media, philosophy and—perhaps most notably—the caste system for which India is so well known. From an outsider's perspective, it is almost immediately apparent whether or not someone identifies as Hindu in India. For me, it was easy to make the connection between the dominant, apparent religion and the cultural and social patterns that I would come to identify closely with during my time there.

The cultural and social patterns I am referring to circulate largely around—you guessed it—animals. Indians as a cultural group, especially Hindus, value animals more highly than Americans do. This, in part, is because the Hindu religious structure circulates around reincarnation—

the belief that forms the basis for the Karma philosophy. Certain animals also express specific symbols or notions that make them more revered. For example, the Cow embodies the concept of female/motherhood and that embodiment gives them an elevated status in Indian culture.

At the time I arrived in India, however, I had no academic frame of reference for this routine treatment of animals—I just saw people treating other living things in a way that reflected my own moral ideologies. Coming from a culturally "normal" American household, this kind of outward uniform respect and demonstrated mindfulness surrounding animals was completely alien. I was struck by the compassion so readily displayed by nearly everyone; despite their own dire economic situation, there was so much tenderness shown for all other living creatures. In a place that should be classified as desolate and poverty-stricken, there was so much grace and beauty in the simplest interactions. The more time I spent there, the more I fell in love with the people and the ideas they embodied.

About eights days into our trip, we left Mumbai and traveled to Delhi, venturing through Japour and briefly visiting the Taj Mahal. I was sitting in a town car with my head pressed against the tinted window so as to make out the world outside the bulletproof glass. I remember suddenly being involuntarily struck by a thought that had been festering under the surface since the moment I'd stepped into the unforgiving Indian sunshine: these people—these compassionate, simple, grateful people—live, breathe and die by their religious tenets. Everything they touch and love is grounded by their unyielding faith in Hinduism and in all of the deities and teachings it espouses. There is so much good in the religion, so much that I identified with on a more visceral level than anything I had ever experienced. And yet, my own religion and culture and upbringing told me that the belief in Hinduism was implicitly wrong. The belief in a religion like Christianity obscures the ability to give credence to the notion that another religion may also be right. The belief in a monotheistic deity inherently precludes the presence of other supreme beings. It was that schism, that fundamental opposition that completely undermined my belief in religion as a whole. It was the first crack in the eventual shattering of the glass that was my faith.

I wasn't able to fully conceptualize my fall from grace (as some might say) while still in India. It wasn't until I returned to America, to my little suburban bubble that was the city of Lake Oswego, that I began to feel the extreme sense of loss and discomfort that comes from the fracturing of a belief system. I felt like I was groping around in a dark room for answers that would give me guidance. I was struggling to understand the world in its current form, without the moral compass that had guided me throughout my adolescence.

But at the end of the day, I kept coming back to one simple realization: I fundamentally did not believe that one religion (Christianity) could tell another religion (Hinduism) that it was wrong, that its deities did not exist, that its moral compass was askew, that the beliefs of its people—while noble—did not coincide with the lord-and-savior Jesus Christ and his father-in-heaven God, and therefore could not possibly be valid. To me, Hinduism embraced beliefs and morals and a lifestyle that was so much more relatable and beautiful than anything Christianity, even in the Seventh Day Adventist form, had ever taught me. The thought of discounting all of it to adhere to a religion that I was essentially born into by way of my geographic location was completely backward. I couldn't get over the notion that devout faith to one religion obliterates the ability to believe in another, despite the fact that so many millions of Hindus formulated their realities and structured their (in my opinion much more meritorious) belief systems based on those religious principles.

So, by the tender age of 18, I had come to the realization that religion was—for lack of a more graceful term—a farce. Despite that tentative realization, however, I was still grasping to understand *why*.

All of the pieces surrounding my religious evolution began to fall into a more coherent picture as I entered college. I was hungry for knowledge and impatient for truth. I brashly dismissed "prerequisites," skipping as many as possible to better prioritize my time and energy in a way that was most intellectually stimulating. Fortunately, at a large state school there were endless paths for learning new information and I began dipping my hand into as many pots as I could find in an attempt to develop my academic niche.

Classes that honed in on social, political, economic and cultural patterns interested me the most. I wasn't really interested in the individual mindsets of people (precluding psychology and sociology), but I was fascinated by why states and societies functioned in the way that they did. Understanding a person and why that person believes or behaves the way he or she does in an individual capacity seems trivial when compared to understanding the evolution and development of societies and cultures on a structural scale. As I began to seek out more classes that catered to that structural interest, I unearthed a concept that continues to hone my understanding of religion and reinforce my decision to formally denounce it: constructivism.

Animal rights, India, religion and the broader experiences that comprised the development of my college-self were clarified as I came to one central realization: so much of our world is culturally constructed. Patterns of humanity serve to reinforce evolved social, political and cultural ideals. Text and language and religion all exist for the purposes of social order and cultural prioritization. The more I understand about the way societies function, the more I understand the systems we have developed to hold them together. One of the most important systems in that framework is religion.

"Faith" is a powerful motivational tool. Religion provides an explanation for the unknown and a justification for literally any atrocity, natural disaster, struggle, or hardship. It is incredibly effective in mass manipulation as well as in the rationalization of sacrifice and accordingly becomes a powerful tool when exploited by individuals and institutions. Human beings *want* to have hope and *want* to believe that there is, for example, life after death—we yearn for concepts that provide a deeper meaning and structure to human life. Religion is an easy sell; in this context its prevalence throughout history and across almost every culture is not difficult to understand. The wide range of religions and their varying associated rituals are constructs created by humans in order to perpetuate socio-political objectives.

Education helped me realize these concepts and reconcile my personal beliefs about religion. In an academic framework, I was finally able to explain and organize many of the beliefs I had developed through my experiences, which ultimately solidified my self-identification as an atheist.

I'm 25 years old now and not once since that day in India when I pressed my forehead against that town car window have I sincerely questioned my atheism. Unlike "faith" in religion, which proclaims that the most devout are the ones who can best quell their insecurities and doubts, atheism continues to come naturally and confidently to me. My grasp on the social and cultural institutions that benefit from religion, as well as my study of constructionism, gives me more confidence in—and proof for— my belief system than any religion ever could. I retain my strong morals because they are what I choose to make my life about—not because they are indoctrinated into me by an antiquated system that thrives on its ability to dictate human behavior.

I believe in atheism because I see no way around it. To quote Richard Dawkins, a fellow atheist with a biology-based rationale (something I've never had): "We are all atheists about most of the gods that humanity has ever believed in. Some of us just go one god further." At the end of the day, I can't deny that it would be nice to learn that I am wrong and that there is some higher power that will save my soul. Until then, I refuse to believe in something that necessitates the condemnation of the ardent faith of so much of humanity.

ON BEING HUMAN

Sandy Olson

I am quite spiritual. . . . But I don't believe in God.
—Helen Mirren

I'm not a person who spends a lot of time thinking about God specifically. There are times when those around me who are dealing with tragedies or nearing their own deaths have asked for prayers. I see that they find comfort in the idea of God or heaven. I see the value in that—for them. When my aunt recently passed away—she was an artist, an independent spirit, and a free thinker—I asked her children if she was religious or believed in God. No one really knew. We only knew that in the last days of her life, she asked us to pray for her, so maybe that answers the question about whether she believed in God. I'm still not sure.

I grew up in the Midwest. My parents were both from small towns in Western Minnesota: Methodists and Lutherans. My grandparents Floyd and Edith were farmers, Grandpa Barney was the small-town lawyer, and Grandma Evie was, well, the wife of the small-town lawyer. They were good people. They lived in the land of Garrison Keillor's Lac qui Parle County. There were Sunday school sessions, quilting bees, and gatherings in the church basement following weddings, anniversaries, and funerals. Of course, these were always potlucks consisting of the famous hotdish, things floating in Jell-O, weak coffee, and homemade cookies or doughnuts. Everyone knew everyone. The community came together. Was this a function of the church or just the nature of small-town Midwestern life?

I was born and raised in a small town in Illinois. It is now considered a suburb of Chicago, but it wasn't then. My religious upbringing was in the Methodist church, so I'll start there. It, too, was a place for Sunday school, spaghetti dinners, coffee and doughnuts following Sunday service, summer church camp up in Wisconsin, and lots of singing. I loved the singing! There was the kids' choir, the adult choir (with that one very loud vibrato voice that made me giggle), and the hymnal book with about four to five hymns at every Sunday service. (The songs were interesting to me because very few people actually knew the tunes, but it seemed not to matter. Those songs were always easy to follow.) There was the Christmas evening nativity service, Palm Sunday special service, and Easter sunrise service. My mom loved to sew me new dresses every Easter, and I always had patent leather shoes, white anklets with lace trim, and a new hat. As an aside, I think my mom was proud when she could get me dressed up like that—the rest of the time I was a rough-and-tumble tomboy. When I was very young, I resisted having my hair combed and my clothes never seemed to match.

When I was really young, Sunday school class was at the same time as the church service. I think this was to keep the kids out of the service. We had a workbook and a "bible" that was a kids' bible full of lots of colorful drawings and shortened versions of everything. Sunday school was puzzling to me. Some of the Ten Commandments made sense. Some didn't. But the stories that I believe were supposed to convince me that Jesus was really the son of God just didn't take. I just didn't believe it. I tried asking questions to make sense of some of this, but they were never answered to my satisfaction—even when I was young and more impressionable. It seemed I just needed to suspend logic and believe. But I couldn't seem to do this. (I should note that I wasn't able to believe in Santa too long either because my brothers spilled the beans pretty early on. I pretended to believe after knowing the truth, and I believe I did this with religion as well. After all, I didn't want to hurt anyone's feelings or risk anything if it all were true.)

In addition to some of the Ten Commandments, other very basic lessons stuck with me. I remember singing the song, "Jesus loves the little children, all little children of the world. Red and yellow. Black and white. They are precious in his sight. Jesus loves the little children of the world."

I didn't mind being in church, and I particularly liked the time we spent in the church kitchen after the service with familiar people and lots of kids running around. I also liked the time my family spent together after the service—usually coming home and doing something like yard work. On fall days we'd come home, change out of our church clothes, and rake piles of leaves and then jump in them. The whole family would be in the yard having a great time.

I was close to my neighbors growing up. They had two girls just a few years older than me. I found that hanging out at their house was sometimes a welcome escape from my two older brothers, who found me a pest and a nuisance (and I was, often intentionally so). My neighbors were Catholics. I remember being with them in the car when they would stop by their church on Friday or Saturday nights for confession. I was so intrigued by this. My friend Patty would get out of the car and walk up the steps to the church. When she came back just a few minutes later, her sister Kathy would then take her turn.

I'd ask Patty lots of questions about confession. She described the confessional booth. "The priest can't see you, and you can't see him." But, I wondered, didn't the priest know who she was just by her voice and the stuff she was saying every week? "What did you tell the priest? What did he say to you?" According to Patty she would report that she wasn't nice to her sister: she had argued with Kathy or had called her names. Her punishment was saying ten Hail Marys. I said, "And then what?" Patty said, "That's it. Then you're forgiven and you can start over." Seemed like a nice concept to me, and I remember asking my parents why we didn't have that in our church.

When I got a little older, my neighbors would take me to church service with them. I think they had some Saturday evening services. This was fascinating and I loved it! We were all supposed to wear something on our heads, but I didn't know why. They did a lot of kneeling, standing, and sitting. That was more fun than just standing or sitting all of the time. Their Lord's Prayer was different from ours: they left off the last clause. Communion—what was that all about? Body and blood of Christ. I didn't understand. I loved the ceremony—the incense, the bells, and the great robes. But there was no singing. An organ, but no singing. I couldn't get over that. Then, the most puzzling of all was the fact that the service was in Latin. After the first time, I asked Patty's mom when we left, "What did the priest say in his sermon?" "I don't know," she answered. Being a pretty annoying little kid with no filter, I said something like, "Well, then what's the point?" I don't remember if she answered that question.

In my church I usually didn't much pay attention to the sermon, but I would catch a few words or get the general theme. My family would often try to talk about it later. It was often about love, family, community, or some stuff I didn't understand. My dad and the other men had a little joke that went something like this, "Hey, I saw you were really praying a lot today." That meant that the guy had his head bowed and was fast asleep!

I remember watching civil rights riots on television around this time or hearing news on the radio, which was frequently playing in our kitchen at home. I asked my mom a lot of questions about why "Negroes" weren't allowed to sit at the lunch counters, or allowed to be on the front of the bus, or whatever else I could glean from these little snippets on the TV news or the radio. Why would anyone argue with this? Why would anyone want to stop people from being treated equally? I mean, I learned that song, "Jesus loves the little children, all little children," regardless of race or color. How could anyone dispute that? (Later in life, I have heard rants by racists—some Christians, some not—and have told them about this song I sang when I was a kid. Didn't that song mean that we were all equal and precious? Kind of stops some of them—probably the Christians—dead in their tracks, because I'm pretty sure they sang that song, too, at some point.)

The early conversations I had with my mom while listening to the radio at a young age had a big impact on me and the direction I would take in my life. When I was about eleven years old, I tried to listen to her explanations of violence in the South and of the assassinations of Martin Luther King Jr. and Bobby Kennedy. Fairness, justice, and equality motivate me still.

My feelings about going to church seemed to take a turn about the time I hit puberty. First, I was the altar girl one Sunday at the service, along with a boy my age from the Sunday school class. We were essentially backstage after we lit the candles and were expected to return when it was time to extinguish them. When we were backstage, this boy grabbed me and tried to kiss me and grope me. It wasn't like kids flirting around. It hurt. I was forceful, pushing him back and even hitting him, but he kept on. I told people about it afterward, but no one seemed to pay much attention. I don't think he ever got in trouble or anything. I avoided him from then on and made excuses not to go to Sunday school. This was around the time I had started my Wednesday after-school confirmation classes. I would make excuses to skip so I didn't have to see this guy. (Sadly, this was just one of several sexual assaults I experienced in my youth.)

At church camp one summer (I loved church camp—log cabins, canoeing, swimming, singing, campfires), there were rumors about the minister and the head deacon's wife, Lois, holding hands or kissing. The minister was married to a very lovely woman, Francine. Then, maybe a year or two later, right after I started high school, the minister announced that he and his wife would be leaving the church to move to a warmer climate for health reasons. The community gathered around and planned a big send-off, with lots of gifts and probably even a collection. A few days later, the truth came out. The minister left his wife behind and ran off with Lois. Lois was the mother of about five young children. She had left her husband and her kids. Turns out, too, that they cleaned out the church coffers.

To make matters worse, the congregation discovered that the supposedly well-educated minister who went by the title Dr. or Rev. Bixby was actually a fraud. He never had a higher education degree. As you can imagine, people were devastated. This man had been their spiritual leader. He had lectured about commitment, family, and the Ten Commandments. I was away at boarding school in another state when this happened. I'm not sure, but I don't think my parents ever went back to that church. I don't know if that congregation ever pulled itself together. The church is still there, but I have no idea what goes on inside it or even if they moved on.

High school was a small coed boarding school in Wisconsin. As my family grappled with my older brothers' wild teenage escapades, I was safely, or so they thought, tucked away in a boarding school. It was tough. The school had a kind of Unitarian approach to religion because the kids came from a variety of religious backgrounds, though mostly some flavor of Christianity. One of my best friends was Jewish, but we didn't talk much about that. The pastor for our school was a former bricklayer. I'm not sure he had any serious religious training, but he seemed to be very spiritual. He loved singing. By this point, I also played the guitar, so he frequently asked me and one of my friends to play and sing in small groups or lead songs during chapel services. As a reflection of the times, the songs we sang were mostly songs like "Turn! Turn! Turn! (To Everything There Is a Season)" and other folk songs. Our pastor talked a lot about practical things, being connected with one's work (body and mind), and finding beauty in nature and work. I was, of course, in the church choir, which was a really good choir with an excellent music director. Throughout high school I found spirituality in music. We sang and played all the time. It comforted me and connected me with my friends.

I must say that I avoided chapel at boarding school unless the choir was performing or my friend and I were asked to lead a song. Chapel was a mandatory session once during the week and again on Sundays. My friends and I made a sport of ditching chapel, which involved finding hiding places where we hoped we wouldn't be caught, like under the bed, in a closet, etc. The last time we were caught, about six of us were crammed into a small closet. Upon discovering us there, the headmistress said, "Really? You would rather be piled on top of each other for an hour in a small closet instead of sitting in chapel for an hour?" She had a point. We were embarrassed. After that, we just went to chapel. Though I really can't tell you what was said. But I did like the Christmas candlelight services, complete with candlelight choir processionals.

Finding a sort of spirituality and sense of community in music was comforting in an otherwise difficult and unfamiliar environment. While I was off in boarding school, my family was dealing with tragedies: one brother's near-fatal car crash as he was driving home from college and, a year later, the disappearance of another brother. At one point during all of this, I felt lost and turned to a small group of born-again Christians. I think I lasted for about two months in this group before I just had to admit it wasn't helping me. I found more interest, meaning, and intrigue in music and politics. I loved the intersection where the two of them met—Bob Dylan's "Blowin' in the Wind," "The Times They Are A-Changin'" and Joni Mitchell songs like "Both Sides Now" or "Big Yellow Taxi."

I also found inspiration in nature and in travel: the fall colors in the Midwest, a fresh and quiet snowfall, the deicing of Earth, and the warmth of the sun. Music seemed to work well with these settings too. It was comforting. I remember several times in the spring or fall in boarding school when we'd hike out to a nearby stream and just sit there singing and playing music. It was a kind of high that I never quite got while sitting in a chapel or doing many of the other things that teenagers do.

I traveled to Europe in high school (and again in college) and found inspiration in the majestic cathedrals with those beautiful stained glass windows in France. I thought a lot about how these places felt spiritual, but for me it wasn't because of God.

In high school I started learning about other religions through literature. Although I found *The Iliad* and *The Odyssey* too dense for my teenage brain, they gave me some food for thought that Greek mythology existed and that not everyone had to believe in a single God or perhaps any God at all. Walt Whitman's *Leaves of Grass* impacted me. Our souls return to nature. A blade of grass? I actually found more comfort in this than I did in the idea of heaven.

When I was in high school the world seemed to be in turmoil: the Vietnam War, Woodstock, and at the end, Watergate. And of course feminism—this idea that I could do whatever I put my mind to. These were exciting times, and it seemed there was no mold I had to fit into. I thought about stories from the bible like Adam and Eve and was offended by how sexist they all were.

When I moved on to college—a small liberal arts school in Southern California—I continued with my pursuit of music as spirituality. I met my husband, a nice Jewish boy who had rejected religion all together, had a band, and loved to sing and play. It was also in college that I had in-depth conversations surrounding the meaning of life and whether there was a higher power, and many of these took place during my late-night sociology study groups. Sociologists like Kant and Hume introduced me to the concepts of humanism, the idea that morals and values come from being human (or from community) and don't require a higher power. I thought back to the Ten Commandments and concluded that most of them just made sense to establish a good social order. People could have written them as much as any God. Is there relative morality? Yes. People do write laws, and through the social contract, we expect those laws to be obeyed. The fact that laws vary by country, state, town, and community reflect some of that relative morality, or value. Of course, there are individual exceptions and circumstances to moral codes as well. As some recent literature suggests, perhaps morality has evolved over time. Interesting food for thought.

Over the course of my life, I've had many chances to put my beliefs to the test, but none as enlightening to me as being a parent and a cancer survivor. As parents, my husband, and I had to address how we wanted to raise our son, Mark. My in-laws pushed for a Jewish upbringing, but since I'm not Jewish and my husband wasn't interested, this was out of the question. I had no objection to our son learning about religion. To the contrary, I wanted to encourage it. But I also didn't want him to feel indoctrinated.

We usually spent Sunday mornings singing and playing music together, often around a big homemade breakfast. That was my own personal nod to Sundays, church, and family time. When he was younger, we tried to take as many opportunities as possible to convene with nature: camping trips, hiking, or cross-country trips. We tried to form bonds with other families who shared our quest for community and shared similar values with us. And it worked for many years. Unfortunately, people move on with their lives: kids grow older, and friends grow apart. That sense of community now seems more shifting, and I keep being drawn closer to family. As to any actual discussion of religion with our son, my husband and I bought a book called *What Is God?* for Mark early on. It was a children's book and contained great and nonjudgmental descriptions of different religions.

Observing how Mark grappled with religion made me examine my own experiences. When Mark was about four years old, I was driving with Mark and one his friends from preschool were sitting in the backseat. His friend came from a Jewish family. The friend's grandfather had just died, and I overheard the following:

"My grandpa is in heaven now."

"How did he get there?"

"I think he drove."

"Can you take your own car to heaven?"

"I think so. Or maybe you have to take a taxi or a bus."

"Well, how did get his stuff there with him?"

"I think they can tow it."

I loved listening in on that conversation. I smiled. It reminded me of my early days in Sunday school and just wanting to understand so badly just what heaven was, whether people floated up to the clouds and how the clouds could support them.

When Mark was about seven years old, his best friend, Robert, attended a very conservative Christian summer camp. When Robert came back from camp one summer, he wanted to share all he had learned. Robert told Mark that if Mark ever told a lie or did anything bad, he would burn in hell. Our son, who was tenderhearted and somewhat anxious as a young child, was terrified and haunted by the notion that he would burn in hell. He couldn't sleep and at times even started crying uncontrollably. My husband finally calmed him down by saying, "I'll tell you what. If you go to hell, I'm going with you and I will protect you." This seemed to work.

The last challenge was when Mark decided he wanted to become a Bar Mitzvah. We told him about all of the studying he would need to do. He still seemed interested. Then we went about finding him someone who could assist him in the process. It was next to impossible. We tried to find a temple to which he could belong. We were willing to pay the fees for him, but we would feel like hypocrites if we had to join. I called around and told people we would fully support him in his journey, that we would pay the fees for him to belong to a temple, but that we couldn't join. No one would help. We then looked for a kind of private tutoring. We were just about to give up when Mark admitted that he was really most interested in the big party like the one his Jewish friend had with a band and lots of presents. That was the end of it.

The first news of my cancer diagnosis sent me into a tailspin. It was aggressive. It was bad. I thought I should try to pray. Something like, "Dear God, if you get me through this, I promise I will . . ." But I couldn't finish the sentence. I just didn't know what to say. I thought of dying. I thought of the blackness. But then I thought, *Well, if I'm dead, I won't know there's blackness or emptiness. Maybe whatever I have contributed to the world will in some way be a part of the collective unconscious.* That seemed okay. Then I put my headphones on and listened to beautiful music and meditation tapes. I envisioned myself sitting by the edge of a stream or an ocean or a lake with no ripples. I smelled the air. I felt the ground: the grass, the dirt, and the sand. It was peaceful. On Sunday I went back to singing music in the morning.

I am a spiritual being even though I'm not sure what that means. I don't believe in any form of religious doctrine, or any doctrine I can put a label on. I reject labels when it comes to my beliefs. I can't say I really call myself an atheist because the more research I've done, the more I'm concerned about the unintended baggage the word carries. I don't believe in God or a higher power. But I do believe in deriving a sense of peace, calm, and feeling from music, from nature, and from beauty. I find meaning in my work. I find love in my relationships. I believe morality and ethics come from humans. I believe that for the most part, humans are beautiful.

Perhaps most important to me: somewhere along the line, I understood that if I am in a position in my life to be able to make the world a better place for people who have been less fortunate than I have been, I should. If I have the capacity to try to level the playing field—to work for fairness, peace, or justice—then I should. In part by sheer luck, I can do that. Did I get that early on from my religious upbringing? From early lessons about the civil rights movement? I don't know.

What about the afterlife? What about heaven or hell? My mom passed away two weeks ago and told me that she believed that when you die you leave behind angels who are all the people whose lives you've touched. Whatever happens, I'm not too worried. I accept that there is probably nothing. Or I may end up as a blade of grass, as a part of the collective unconscious, but most likely there will be blackness. If by chance there is a God, I'm sure she wouldn't care whether or not I believed in her as long as I lived my life morally, honorably, and in service of others.

MY WALK AWAY FROM RELIGION

Ruth Marimo

As my ancestors are free from slavery, I am free from the slavery
of religion. . . . If we had put the energy on Earth and on people
that we put on mythology and on Jesus Christ,
we wouldn't have any hunger or homelessness.

—Butterfly McQueen

I was born and raised in Zimbabwe in Southern Africa. Zimbabwe was colonized by Britain in 1888 and did not gain independence until 1980. The British brought with them Christianity, which is now the spiritual fabric of almost all African nations that were once under colonial rule.

Before Europeans showed up in my country, my ancestors used to worship spirits. They believed their dead loved ones were looking over them, and they did rituals to appease the spirits. Some of those rituals are still carried out today. One of them is called *kurova guva*, which literally translates to "beating the grave." This ritual involves celebrating at the gravesite of the deceased to help him or her transition into the realm of the ancestors. However, because of the popularity of Christianity, these cultural rituals are largely frowned upon and seen as evil and even devil worship. Because of this, our culture has mostly abandoned these rituals.

My very name, I am told, came from the Christian Bible. My grandfather, with whom I never had a relationship, named me after the Ruth in the Old Testament. Growing up in Zimbabwe, Christianity was the only thing I knew existed as far as religion goes. Even today, non-Christian religions and secularism are almost unheard of. *Mwari* is the word for God in Shona, the main native language of Zimbabwe. In my country every single thing is deferred to Mwari, from road accidents that kill hundreds of people at a time to the births of healthy babies—it is all God's will. The devotion to God is so strong that it is not uncommon for believers to stop taking medicine and instead rely on prayer and fasting to heal them when they are ill. It is not uncommon for people to pray for rain, or to pray and fast in order to pass academic exams.

This has given rise to self-appointed prophets who prey on the vulnerable and make claims to have healing powers through God. These pastors and prophets are usually so much wealthier than their congregants, owning fleets of cars and living in mansions. In Zimbabwe people gather in the thousands for all-night prayers, spend nights on top of mountains praying, and center almost everything around the notion of God. Human responsibility and accountability is almost entirely erased from everyday experiences. With the possible exception of prayer, humans do not influence earthly events—God orchestrates everything.

I remember being a teenager and being in church and witnessing everyone entirely transfixed in the whole production that was always church. Everyone sang powerful hymns with their eyes closed and their hands raised to the sky—some people even had tears running down their cheeks. Everyone was praying and falling over because of the power of the Holy Spirit. I remember standing there trying to genuinely pray and wishing to feel all the emotions that everyone else seemed to be feeling, but feeling absolutely nothing. While other people expressed an overwhelming sense of knowing when it came to God, I felt nothing, and I stopped trying to feel it. So while I have only been out as a humanist/atheist the last two years, I really let go of religion way back in my teens.

By the time I completed high school in 1998, the Zimbabwean economy was crumbling and political tensions were starting to rise. Everyone who could leave was considering it, and my aunt just happened to know a Zimbabwean doctor who lived in England and needed a young girl from home to help his family as a live-in domestic maid. So I left Zimbabwe two days after writing my final high school exam and headed for England, where I hoped to study while I worked for the doctor and his family. However, upon my arrival, it was evident that the picture was not as rosy as it had been portrayed. The doctor was only willing to pay me a hundred pounds each month, which was equivalent to about 163 American dollars at the time.

So I had to come up with a different plan. I had acquired an American visa before departing Zimbabwe, and my aunt knew a Zimbabwean lady who lived in Omaha, Nebraska. When my plans of a happy life in England fell through, I made my way to America. My life in America has not been uneventful—so much has happened since I arrived here in July of 1999 that I have actually penned a memoir titled *Outsider: Crossing Borders, Breaking Rules, Gaining Pride* documenting my struggles.

It has taken almost seventeen years of living in America, away from my continent of origin, to come to terms with the fact that I had not been given a choice about Christianity as a child. I never even knew that secularism was an option. I had held on to the idea of God even when I arrived in America. I went out of my way to find churches I felt comfortable in. I attended church even though there was no one making me. Perhaps it was out of my ingrained obligation.

In 2008 I went through a bitter and painful separation in which my ex-husband reported my undocumented status to the Department of Homeland Security. I was immediately arrested, and I spent an entire month in jail fighting deportation. While in jail I felt the deepest despair I have ever endured in my life. I was so depressed that I even contemplated suicide, and in all that pain, I found myself praying and looking for God. I would wait until everyone was asleep and get on my knees and pray for hours at a time, really believing this would make some kind of difference to my outcome. I was finally bailed out after a month, and one of the first things I did was look for a church community I could belong to. I found a very open and affirming LGBTQ church and felt at home.

You see, the reason I needed a church home was because I came out as a lesbian right after I was released from jail, and I immediately dealt with rejection from my family as well as the Zimbabwean community where I live in Nebraska. Homosexuality is incredibly rejected in African culture, largely due to the influence of conservative religions. So I went to an LGBTQ church to feel acceptance from the rejection I was receiving from my other religious communities. At my new church everyone was kind and welcoming, and I felt I was growing as a person and as a member of that church community. Nevertheless, the questions I had always wrestled with about Christianity remained.

I had always struggled with the idea of endless worship. What kind of a God requires constant worship? In everything else we do in life, we eventually finish—from going to school or raising our children, for example—but that is not the case with worship. It is never enough. It is never ending. There is not anything in life I want to do forever, and I certainly do not want to worship some deity forever.

As a black woman, I often wonder why brown and black people are so devoted to Christianity when the Bible was used to enslave their ancestors. As an African, I am well aware that Christianity did not exist in Africa until white people showed up on the continent with Bibles. Our ancestors survived hundreds of years without modern religion. Christianity arrived and created a patriarchal and misogynist culture in Zimbabwe influenced by biblical passages that the man shall be the head of the household and similar sexist edicts. In my country now, many religious sects exist that permit child marriages in which young girls are married off to much older men in rural parts of the country, and these heinous acts go unchecked. My cousin's grandfather belonged to an apostolic faith sect and had at least eight wives, the youngest of which was only fourteen years old. Yet no one saw a problem with this—it was simply what they did in their church. It is utterly heartbreaking, the things that religion has enabled and normalized in developing parts of the world. Sadly, many of these societies just happen to be brown and black societies.

To be an African woman who walks away from believing is almost unheard of, and that is precisely why I think it is so necessary to talk about it. I walked away in order to open a world for my children that no one else in my family history had ever experienced before, and I couldn't be more proud. I had introduced my children to church when they were younger, and I have spent the last two years explaining my reasons for walking away from religion, including my wish for them to grow up open-minded and nonjudgmental. I have explained how much I want them to grow up knowing that only they are responsible for their own actions, that they have the power to decide for themselves what they want out of life, that their fate is not up to some god.

Walking away from religion was not easy. My journey began when my ex-girlfriend, who is an atheist, helped me confront everything that bothered me about religion, and slowly I started to find myself withdrawing. I had been a board member at my church for three years, and one of my first actions was to resign from that post, and then I stopped attending church entirely, though I kept the reason to myself. The hardest thing for me was getting out of religious habit. It took a long time for me to not feel the need to pray before bed or before meals and even just to not feel compelled to get up on a Sunday and get ready to go to church. As soon as members of my church started asking about my absence, I started to explain the reasons and everyone tried to convince me otherwise. It felt like it was a lot harder for other religious people to reconcile with my walking away than it had been for me. Some people actually expressed how hurt they were about my choice to no longer be religious, some people stopped talking to me, and some even unfriended me on social media. But just like with my coming-out journey as a lesbian, I soon discovered that many people were like me, and slowly I began to express my secular views more publicly.

My children and I are at a very comfortable place with our secularism now. They have even begun to engage their peers on the topic and have discovered that other kids also come from nonreligious families. We are very lucky to have friends from all walks of life so my children have the privilege of experiencing the diversity of humanity without judgment. We simply treat people the way we want to be treated and focus on what we are passionate about in life. Instead of spending our time in church on Sundays, we camp and go fishing, take trips to the mall, go to the movies, or just spend time together as a family at home doing household chores or projects. We have discovered how freeing it is to have a whole day to do other things besides church.

All our family remains religious, and we respect their religion without being a part of it. I still hang out with friends from church from time to time, and we have come to a place where we simply respect each other's views.

I feel like a tremendous load has been lifted off my shoulders by letting go of religion.

A LIFE:
MY LONG AND WINDING JOURNEY

Karen Brotzman

This religion and the Bible require of woman everything,
and give her nothing. They ask her support and her love,
and repay her with contempt and oppression.

—Helen H. Gardener, from *Men, Women, and Gods, and Other Lectures*

Part 1: In the Beginning . . .

I was born in the back of a police car, which was transporting my mother (who had gone into labor) from the Western State mental hospital to Tacoma General Hospital. It was May 3, 1946. My dad was in the Navy and mom was in Seattle, living with his parents, Floyd and Bertha. My very pregnant mom was in the mental hospital because she had been found walking the streets, confused and manic. When a police officer walked up to her and asked her what was wrong, she responded by hitting him, hence the commitment to the mental hospital.

When I was three weeks old, my maternal grandmother drove to Tacoma from Williston, North Dakota, and brought us home. My mom was still very unstable, so she and my grandmother decided she should file for a divorce.

I was then sent to live with my mother's oldest sister. My aunt Mildred and her husband, Walter, were the most appropriate of my mom's six brothers and sisters. They lived nearby, with a roomy house and sufficient finances to care for me. I lived with them in Watford City, North Dakota until my mom remarried when I was about three years old. I am so grateful for those years, when I experienced a warm family life where I was loved and tenderly cared for. I believe this period provided me with the tools to make sense of the world around me, allowing me to deal with the challenges that the coming years would hold.

Against my aunt's wishes, I was returned to my mother shortly after her marriage to my stepfather, who worked at Tractor Supply Company in Williston. A few years later, we moved to Fargo, North Dakota, with my half sister and toddler brother. My stepfather, Al, was promoted to the manager of the larger store. For a few weeks, while we were looking for a house, we lived at the store, under construction at the time. We thought it was so much fun! We were on an adventure, moving four hundred miles from our family in Williston. Fargo was so big and interesting. The future looked very bright, and Mom and Dad were happy and hopeful about the changes.

We soon moved into a small house on the southwest side of Fargo and joined a church, First Methodist, just a short distance from home. I'd never gone to church before, that I remembered, and this new experience was awe-inspiring. Over time, the church became a sanctuary for me and my younger half brothers and sisters. I was the oldest of five and "special" for a couple reasons: I had a different father, and my biological father was a quarter Sioux Indian.

We started attending church every Sunday morning, and my mom would drop us off midweek for MYF (Methodist Youth Fellowship) and choir practice too. I was crazy about music, begging for a piano and music lessons for years. I received both when I was eleven years old. Three years later, I started violin lessons with a rented school violin, and my anchors were set.

When I was twelve years old, everything changed. Within weeks of my youngest sister's birth, Mom had her second psychotic event. She was hospitalized for many months, and I was thrust into the new role of mom to my four younger siblings. I was in sixth grade, and the baby was a month old. It was overwhelming. I was sad and fearful that I was not up to the task and worried sick about Mom. Al was stunned, and I was scared by his despair. He hired a woman to take care of the new baby and my two-year-old brother while he was at work. My younger sister Darlene, brother Clair, and I attended school during the day and came home after school to help with the chores.

I started stopping by the library on my way home from school each week, and I checked out books to read almost every night after the smaller children were in bed. I read books on many topics. Some of them I needed, like cooking and gardening. Others were vehicles for transporting me to a different world. My mom loved books, and over the years she collected a library of more than a thousand volumes. They became yet another anchor in my life.

Months later, when Mom came home, I'd grown to a new level of maturity. I was handling everything, and we were okay. Our church family was always there for us—they had helped me whenever and however they could. The women, especially, coached, supported, and held me when I was overwhelmed. They constantly told me I could and would get through this, we all would. The comfort and love they surrounded me with meant all the difference. Mom came home, and we rejoiced together.

But it soon became clear we'd all changed. Mom was heavily medicated and deep inside herself. She hated the meds: they made her mouth dry and her head "heavy." As she slowly began to feel better, smiling and talking, she began skipping meds and rationalized that it was good. She felt great! Our pastor and his wife visited often, encouraging and hopeful. Soon it was obvious to all of us that we were on the same slippery slope as before. Mom was going back to the hospital . . .

I remember sitting in her doctor's office with Al and Darlene. We listened while he explained that schizophrenia could be inherited and usually became obvious during the late teens or early twenties. He said if we made it to thirty, we would usually be okay. There was a chance Mom would improve when she hit menopause, or she could tip into complete insanity. She was hospitalized again.

This was terrifying information and sounded heartbreakingly bleak to my dad, sister, and me.

Over the next seventeen years, the cycle was: commit to hospital, discharge, come home, be rational, stop taking meds, experience increased hallucinations, repeat . . . At various times Mom slit her wrists, tried to kill my youngest sister, got lost in the desert in midsummer, defecated on the neighbors' lawns, and became violent or aggressive. But most of the time, she sat at the kitchen table reading a book while chain-smoking and talking to invisible people.

For now, escape became my goal, and God became more important to me.

Part 2: The Blond Bomber and Escape

My sophomore year of high school, my aunt Midge decided to move from North Dakota to Mesa, Arizona, where her husband had started working. This was a huge shock to me—she had always been an anchor for me, an island of calm in my sea of disruption. Shortly after she left, my friends and I started hanging out with a couple of senior guys, one of whom liked bongo drums and poetry readings at a local teahouse. They introduced me to a friend of theirs who had a car. A few months later we became a couple; he was my first boyfriend.

My family called him the Blond Bomber (BB): tall, of Nordic descent, always cracking jokes, and not at all interested in any more college. He'd dropped out of North Dakota State University after a semester and had a good job at the local grocery store. His family had a farm outside Christine, North Dakota, on the bank of the Red River. The elderly aunt who lived there had died, leaving the place abandoned but fully furnished. I lost my virginity there and became pregnant, almost immediately. The repercussions were harsh—I was not allowed to return to school because of my pregnancy.

The Blond Bomber's parents were not happy with the situation and wanted me to go to the Florence Crittenton Home, have the baby, put it up for adoption, and leave their son out of it. Instead, BB and I got married in late August of 1963.

My family had already planned to move to Mesa, Arizona, after the wedding, following Aunt Midge to the land of opportunity. We kissed goodbye at the reception, and Mom was in especially good spirits. It was six months before I saw them again. On our wedding night, BB and I drove from Fargo to Bloomington, Minnesota, where BB had a job, with me sad and depressed. In the hotel room, I began to cry and my new husband lost his temper. He'd pushed me before and twisted my arm a few times, but this was different. He used his fists now, and all the frustration came pouring out. I only then understood the saying, "jumping from the frying pan into the fire." Fire it was, for the next five years.

BB was a Lutheran and asked me to attend church with him. I was surprised to learn this involved study, testing, and re-baptism. Since I'd been confirmed and baptized in the Methodist Church, I assumed that joining another church would be a simple matter. Many years later, I realized that nearly every church has its traditions and rules, designed to stand apart from all the others. I also found that I liked the additional restrictions and tighter expectations of the Lutheran Church. It had less ornamentation, more priest-like robes and traditions, and it felt like God was really in control. It also felt colder. In a sea of Nordic-looking and -sounding members, I stood out as different. Everyone was very polite, but not warm. It seemed to me to be a cultural thing. I remember the first time I tried to take my husband's hand when we were in public. He pulled his hand away and told me to never touch him like that again. After talking about it, he shared that he'd never seen his parents kiss each other at home or be affectionate in public. That was how it was and should be. And, in some perverse way, it felt right. This Lutheran God was strict and less approachable than the Methodist one I'd known before.

My family was struggling in Arizona, so six months later BB and I left Minnesota and moved down to help. Our baby, a daughter, was born in Mesa. BB and I both got jobs, but less than a year later, I was pregnant again and we moved back to Fargo. My in-laws had visited and wanted the grandchildren near them, as they felt my family was not a good influence on our soon-to-be two children.

It was 1965 and BB soon found a job and an apartment, an upstairs flat in a personal home. Several months after we moved in before our second child was born, Al called to ask if my sister Darlene could come stay with us to attend Fargo Central High School. She was having a rough time juggling school, part-time work at the family Tastee-Freez, and caring for the younger children. He wanted to give her a break.

Though we were having a tight time financially, we agreed to have her come for the school year. However, I was worried about having another person see what our marriage was really like. My dream was that BB would stop abusing me and we could have a more normal life. It was not to be. When our son Jon was born, he was severely jaundiced due to an RH blood issue. My O-negative blood type was fighting Jon's A-positive. He had to stay in the hospital for transfusions until he was stable. Our financial situation was very tenuous, and this was a huge additional expense for us.

When I came home without the baby, BB became violent. Darlene tried to intervene by tugging at him while screaming for help. The landlord heard her and banged on the door. A few days later, Jon was at home and Darlene was on a plane back to Mesa.

I felt trapped, with two children under two, a violent husband, little money, and no prospects for change. My closest family members were in Arizona, and that was where I wanted to be. I called Aunt Midge, and she told me she could give me a room and a job at the day-care center she'd opened in Mesa. I would need to find a way to get down there. I began saving all the spare change I could hide ($13.75 to be exact; gas was about $0.30 per gallon then). It took months, but one day after BB left for work, I put the kids in my Volkswagen Bug and started driving south. It took me three days. In Fargo, BB and his mom were frantic. They eventually offered me money if I would send the kids back and just disappear from their lives. I refused. For the first time in a long time, I felt free. I was back near my family and back with the Methodists. First Methodist Church in Mesa, Arizona.

The pastor of my new church quickly became an anchor in my life. He and his wife enveloped me in love, community, and unconditional support. The music—hymns I'd grown up with—called to the child in me. I felt such joy singing the familiar songs, joining the choir, and making new friends. I especially loved the pastor's wife. She had severe arthritis in both hands and, in spite of the pain she was in, had a ready smile and an open, warm heart. In many ways, they became the parents I never had. I was back where I'd started, highly engaged in church activity and part of a community. The contrast with my Lutheran experience was a welcome change, and I vowed never to live in Fargo again.

About six months after leaving Fargo, there was a knock on the door. BB stood there, speaking many promises, with a carful of stuff behind him. Things would change. He promised never to hit me again, nor ever to move back to North Dakota. He just needed another chance—he'd changed since I'd left him—and he begged for a chance to be a better father to his children.

Confused, I asked my pastor for advice, and he asked to talk to BB. Their talks resulted in BB's being baptized into the church and our reconciliation. The next two years were the best of our marriage, happy times with two small children and a strong support structure. We found a small house to rent in Mesa, and BB went back to his old job installing air conditioners.

I left the day-care center and applied for a new job on the assembly line at the Phoenix Motorola plant. Motorola was to change my life in unexpected ways.

A year later we took a two-week vacation to Fargo and reconnected with BB's family. Soon after our return, I realized I was pregnant with our third child. Peder was a healthy baby with a sunny disposition. While still in the hospital, I pondered the idea of going back to school. I'd been working the swing shift, 3:00 to 11:00 p.m., and would go back to that in a few weeks. Before I'd left on maternity leave, my supervisor suggested I might improve my chances for a better job by taking college classes in the mornings. She said Motorola would pay for them 100 percent. I just needed to buy books. I was twenty-two years old, a high school dropout making $1.87 an hour, married with three children under four and little chance for anything better. I decided to try it.

When the baby was ten days old, I started my first class at Mesa Community College: English 101. The babysitter agreed to take the baby along with the older two. I was very excited, and BB was fine with me taking an English class. One class during the day, what could be the issue? The next semester, I decided things were going so well, I could handle two classes. Motorola paid the tuition and noticed I was getting straight A's.

Soon I was recommended for a training program in a new field. After loads of testing, I was transferred to the new Motorola Integrated Circuit Center in Mesa. There I was assigned to a training program for the Integrated Design Pilot Line. Now I was working 7:00 a.m. to 3:30 p.m., weekdays rather than swing shift. This made everything easier on the family. The next semester I switched my two classes to math and electrical engineering evening courses. I could see a path forward: college, promotions, and stability. BB did not see it quite the same way.

Part 3: Trials and Tribulations
BB was unhappy with my decision, and he went to our pastor to share his many concerns. He had some realistic points: we had small children who needed me at home, and school was another activity taking me away from them. We needed the income from my job, so the shift change and increased salary were welcomed. However, taking classes at night exposed me to unexpected dangers (walking to and from classes is what he expressed; meeting men was what he was afraid of, I learned later).

Both our pastor and his wife strongly recommended I curtail my outside activities and focus on my children. My response was that we didn't have much of a future unless one of us was educated. BB had tried a semester of college and dropped out. I wanted to learn and was good at learning. I wanted to finish what I'd started. It was important for our family. I told them that I was not going to leave school, my job, or my family. We could manage and everything would be okay. We were at an impasse, and I felt like my pastor and his wife were disappointed in me. Then BB's escalation began.

He began stalking me on campus. At first he merely followed me from one class to another, keeping a discrete distance and not saying anything. Then he noticed I would often walk with the same person between classes. Since I was the only female in either my math or EE class, my companion was a man. Michael was a complete techie who worked with me at Motorola and had a wife and family. His presence prompted BB to start catcalling while walking behind us. That scared Michael and angered me. Tension at home escalated.

Physical violence had been an undercurrent in my relationship with BB since before we were married. But never before had it been this bad. I started talking about a divorce. Months of frustration and anger exploded late one fall night, when BB forced the children and me into the living room and kept us awake with slaps on the children's feet and a gun in his hand. Never have I felt such terror and rage at another human being, or fear for my children and myself.

The apex of the night came around 3:00 a.m., when BB took a single .38 special bullet, loaded it into his pistol, spun the chamber, and held it to my head. He asked me if I wanted to die; I said no. He asked me if I was ready to stay; I said no. The children were screaming—BB picked up our five-year-old daughter and threw her against a wall about six feet from where he was standing. She slid to the floor and starting vomiting red Kool-Aid all over the carpet. BB stood still and then left the house. I called the police, they came, and the next day I had a restraining order. These two policemen checked up on me often and gave me their contact information. After BB broke into the house and cut up all my clothing late one night, they stopped him for a traffic violation and had a little talk with him about what would happen if he ever came near me again. He heard them and never did.

I filed for a divorce. In Arizona, if you had children, you were required to attend counseling with the Arizona Conciliation Court social workers before a divorce would be granted. This process typically lasted a year before the court hearing, with the goal being to help couples work through their problems and avoid divorce. We met with our counselor individually and at a joint session. When the counselor asked BB if he understood he could never hit me again, BB looked at me, turned toward him, and said, "She's my wife. I can do anything I want to her." The counselor turned to me, shook his head, and said, "Well, that's it then!" The papers were signed.

I felt transported to heaven, free, free! I had so much to be thankful for and decided to find a new church home, where BB was not a member. I'd find a place where God was real and knowable.

A friend told me her father-in-law, Pastor Brown, had recently founded a Pentecostal church in Mesa. She believed Pentecostals were the true believers, though the word *evangelical* was not as used then as it is today. I was invited to midweek prayer meetings and Sunday services quite regularly, and I felt I'd found a spiritual home. After attending for many months and feeling that warmth, excitement, and inclusion, I was asked to begin the process to become a member and join God's family. The real one. In this Church, that meant less studying and more "laying on of hands." The intention was to invite God's acceptance of me and my family, with the expected sign of said acceptance demonstrated by the ability to speak in tongues. I tried and tried again, week after week. A dozen people faithfully showed up twice a week to lay their hands on my head and fervently pray to God to accept me into his family. But, I could not speak in tongues. I was not acceptable. After the last unsuccessful attempt, Pastor Brown pulled me aside and gently told me, "Sister Karen, if you don't speak in tongues, you and your children are going to burn in hell." I was devastated.

The next day, I went to work and talked about my experience with my coworker Michael. I was frantic about the idea that my failure was condemning my children to hell! What was I going to do? He sat me down and explained that my children would not go to hell. They had not yet reached the age of accountability, so they were safe. He explained that his belief taught that each of us held the keys to our own salvation—we were not judged by others' actions or inactions. He was a member of the Church of Jesus Christ of Latter-day Saints, also known as the Mormon Church. Mesa was (and still is) a strong center for the LDS Church, founded by

Mormon missionaries in the late 1800s and full of their descendants. Michael brought me a Book of Mormon the next day, and I started reading. No missionaries, no pressure, just me and a book.

This was it! I'd found the truth. A kind, loving God and a Church reflecting these attributes. I'd checked out books on pre-Columbian civilizations and seen photos of murals in Central America featuring light and brown people together in one place. The Book of Mormon told stories of early migrations by sea of people coming from Israel before the time of Christ and populating the Americas. The book was real. I'd found God.

Months later, after studying with the missionaries, I told my family that I was going to be baptized into the LDS Church. They were all appalled. How could I join a cult? My youngest sister and the oldest brother were strong Baptists. My brother threatened to block off access to the building where the baptism was to be held so I could not enter and be baptized.

My brother and his friends did not show up. The baptism took place with many of my friends and coworkers in attendance. I was very happy and felt peaceful. My baptism occurred during my twenties, and I did not leave the church until I was over fifty. For most of that period, I was happy to contribute in various ways: I was a member of the Relief Society, the organist for Sunday sacrament meetings, and a member of the Arizona Mormon Choir. Music was once again a significant part of my life. I especially loved the Arizona Mormon Choir summer bus tours through the Arizona backcountry. We performed classical music along with favorite pioneer road songs. It was a safe, comforting time in my life. As a single mom, I had an amazing support structure: home teachers who supported my family and did yard work too, and a group of women friends who supported me in a variety of ways. I appreciated all the church programs that taught my children so much and celebrated their accomplishments. Sports, music, plays—it was all at our fingertips. It was a period filled with a lot of music, laughter, and service to others. Truly, it seemed as if heaven were right here on Earth.

Several years after joining the church, I was sexually involved with a man and had my last child, my son Joseph, out of wedlock. Even through this, my church members stood by me, no recriminations, no judgment, just love and support. Looking back, he was the love of my life, and between this man and the people around me, I began to see that most people were good and that I could transcend the pain of my past experiences and be okay. My family, work, and school continued to be my most serious goals. Juggling my job, family, and classes was challenging. I would not have been able to "do it all" without the support of church members, family, and fantastic childcare. It was a wild ride . . .

Fast forward fifteen years.

Part 4: The End of Faith

Education and a variety of high-tech jobs led me around Arizona and California and eventually landed me an applications engineering job at Intel's Chandler, Arizona, site in 1988. I'd moved back to Arizona when Jon and Peder were teenagers, as they wanted a closer relationship with BB. Within six months of joining Intel, I was moved into a supervisory position for a new division tasked with creating small chips using computer automation for faster creation. These designs were targeted at specific tasks that could be reused in various designs, more quickly and cheaper than any other generally available chip. About a year later, the plant merged four divisions into one. My responsibilities grew fourfold, and our new, much larger team struggled with the added complexity for many months. The results were impressive: shortened design cycles, less rework, and satisfied customers.

Then our success was noted at Intel headquarters in Santa Clara, California. Within a short time, I was asked to interview for a position as the manager of Applications Engineering for Intel Design Technology. I got an offer. This was 1991, and I was moving back to the Bay Area. My youngest son, Joe, was a senior at Mountain View High School in Mesa, and he and Peder did not want to move back to California. I agreed to leave them behind in Mesa until Joe graduated from high school. Peder found a two-bedroom condo that was close to both school and our existing home. I sold the house, bought the condo, and moved by myself to a small apartment in San Jose. The whirlwind began.

My new position was very different from anything I'd done previously. The department, Design Technology (DT), was spread all over the world, and I was managing people anywhere Intel had a facility in the United States. It was not a design job—it was managing people who supported other Intel employees who used DT's software tools to do their jobs. This was an entirely new field for me. I really struggled at first and missed my two youngest sons terribly. I was lonely and overwhelmed with learning so many new things.

Between traveling for Intel business or traveling to Arizona to visit Peder and Joe, I rarely thought about contacting a local ward of the LDS Church. I had the intention, but I never acted upon it. Then something even bigger and unexpected happened: my manager, Jim, decided I was ready for more responsibility.

I'd learned a lot about software tool support during the past year, and DT wanted to expand the development group in Hillsboro, Oregon. Jim knew I had no background or education in software development, but he wanted me to move to Oregon and assume responsibility for software development worldwide. To help me with the technical expertise that I lacked, a new position was created for me to co-manage with Elinora, another manager located at the Intel facility in Haifa, Israel. My manager's thinking was: she was very strong technically, I was strong managerially and everything would work out. We would help each other. I was not as convinced, but I agreed to give it my best effort.

When I broke the news to my family, Joe decided to come with me to Oregon. He'd just graduated from high school in Arizona and wanted to live with me again in this new place neither of us had ever visited. He flew to San Jose, and together we drove up I-5 to Portland. Peder followed us two years later, and Jon eventually made his way north as well. Peder, his wife, and I still live in the area—one of my favorite places in the world.

We arrived safely and rented a house, hoping this job would last for more than a year. Joe enrolled at Portland State University, and I began traveling more than ever. We joined our local ward, and this life became the new normal. I was also seriously in over my head with the new job, co-managing approximately 120 people spread across three sites. The ten-hour time difference meant Eli scheduled weekly meetings at 8:00 a.m. in Haifa that were 10:00 p.m. on the West Coast. Once a week I flew to San Jose for two days, to meet with my manager and about forty employees, including three leads. The stress was building fast.

Additionally, my new bishop was less hands-off than I'd experienced. I began to feel pressured by suggestions: I should get involved with the singles organization; it was time to find a husband and be joined to him for all eternity. This required a "temple recommend," which allows the holder to enter an LDS temple and to be sealed to his/her mate in eternal marriage (marriage beyond death). I'd avoided getting a temple recommend for years, for several reasons: (1) I did not want to assume the added responsibility of "higher vows." The Book of Mormon commands believers not to consume "hot drinks," commonly interpreted to mean tea and coffee. I skirted the issue, in my own mind, by drinking only iced tea and did not want to stop. (2) I did not want to wear the neck-to-knee undergarments, which were required for all members after completing the temple endowment ceremony. These garments are embellished with stitching detailing the wounds Joseph Smith suffered while becoming a martyr. They have strategic openings to enable procreation, which is another strong tenet of the faith. (3) I had no intention of ever marrying again. I also did not want to be "sealed" to some unknown person after death, which is the fate upon death for an endowed woman who has never married in the temple.

Regardless, as my professional life started to take off, my position as a woman in a male-dominated church became more and more concerning. Did I really believe my place was as a wife, mother, and servant to my husband? My bishop thought it was time to get remarried. I started questioning my commitment to any of this.

Meanwhile, spending time in Israel every quarter was opening my eyes to question a lot of things, including the validity of the Bible and the Book of Mormon. My first trips were consumed with visiting antiquity sites. My Jewish friends had a completely different take on a lot of biblical events and what they meant. Saint Paul was a big problem. They pointed out that the Bible documents the different times Paul came to Jerusalem and had to be ushered out of town to avoid the angry mobs. Why did this happen? The Bible is oddly silent on this subject. A coworker gave me a copy of the book *Paul the Mythmaker*, written by a Jewish rabbi. It describes Paul as lying to his converts about his background. He claimed to be something he was not. He was not a Pharisee; he may have been a Sadducee. He worked for the Jewish court, something no Pharisee would be doing. Further evidence: in the Bible we first meet Paul at the stoning of Stephen. This seems to inadvertently verify that he worked for the court. So I started reading a lot more—about how the Bible came to be, how it morphed into what it is today—and I questioned it all. Most importantly, what did I really believe was true? Mostly due to time constraints, I cut down my church activity, though I continued to be a member in good standing, all the way up to the year 2000.

In February of 2000, I retired from Intel (for the first time). Every investment I owned was in Intel stock. In August of that year, the dot-com bubble burst and the stock dropped from $75 a share into the teens. Suddenly things changed dramatically for me, at least financially. That fall, a former employee, who had started his own consulting company, contacted me about a temporary design position at the Tempe, Arizona, Motorola plant. I decided to take the job, in spite of the fact that it had been nearly ten years since I'd done any real design. It had been a few years, but it all came back to me. I enjoyed the focus and creative aspects of design. When this job ended, there were many opportunities on the West Coast, so I took contract after contract. I liked being on the road. Home was a travel trailer pulled from place to place. I was a gypsy, living in campgrounds and moving wherever there was work.

In late 2003, I accepted a long-term contract at a company in San Diego County. I checked into the Oceanside RV Park and began my new assignment. The days were full, and my evenings were long, filled with television. To contribute something meaningful, I began volunteering at the Salvation Army dinners in downtown San Diego, sponsored by a church in Escondido. They provided meals, clothing, and incidentals (toothbrushes, shampoo) to a large group every week. They were light on the preaching and heavy on the warmth and support. The Mormons were still keeping in touch with me, but I was no longer a true believer in the founder's vision, the Book of Mormon, or the sanctity of their traditions, like the temple garments. Leaving was a loss of community for me. I've never since been associated with such fundamentally kind people. I missed that sense of belonging and of being *sure* it was the right place to be. I now defined myself as an agnostic and committed to helping my community insofar as I was able. Months later, a different church began sponsoring the homeless meals. The rules were stricter, and adherence was required: a prayer before eating, reading a specific pamphlet before receiving a haircut, and staying for a prayer meeting after the meal. To me, these demands changed the spirit of the donations, which no longer felt like a gift to me—they felt like compensation. This was not my idea of love or acceptance. I realized I'd changed in a very fundamental way. The authentic *me* was no longer sure there was a God.

Part 5: A New Community

In 2008, after a friend's diagnosis of adrenal cancer, I moved back to the Portland area to be closer to them and my family. Eventually, I returned to where I'd started in 1988—Intel. Shortly after being rehired, I joined an Intel employee group and met a man who would help me fundamentally change my way of thinking. The name of the group was Agnostics and Atheists at Intel (AAI). The president of the organization was, and still is, Bernie D. By chance, he was about to start a series of classes on logical fallacies at the Friendly House in Northwest Portland, immediately after the humanist meeting there on Sunday mornings. I wasn't sure what a humanist was, or a logical fallacy either. But I was impressed with Bernie's leadership of the employee group and wanted to support him. I signed up for the class and bought the textbook at the PSU bookstore.

And so it began. I think my head hurt the entire six weeks of the class—it seemed so hard to get my mind around all the information being presented. So many fallacies! And so many I'd unthinkingly bought into, many times. It had little to do with religion, but it did have something I could relate to: algebraic equations. There are very simple ones, for example: if $A=B$, and $B=C$, then $A=C$. Insert words in the place of each letter and evaluate . . . Okay, I could get this. I entered a marvelous period of exponential growth for me, and it's still unfurling every day.

This one class was like an octopus: long arms stretching out in many directions. One arm led me to the meeting just before our class every week, also in the Friendly House, the Humanists of Greater Portland. They had wonderful guest speakers on a wide variety of topics, and I learned something new every time I attended. Another arm led to a pub for lunches after class. There, I got to know more people, one of whom facilitates an Ethical Philosophy meeting twice a month at various Portland libraries. He introduced me to SHEP (Secular Humanists of East Portland, a Meetup group), and before I knew it, I was involved in community again, free to be me. After three years of Meetups, classes, and parties with SHEP and Ethical Philosophy folks, I learned that community is something you build over time. It doesn't have to be an existing organization, and it doesn't need a strong list of requirements, either. Some meetings are hilarious, some participants get mad, and we usually have diverging opinions. In the end, though, most meetings are thought provoking.

I began to think I could integrate all these parts somehow: myself, my family, and my friends, old and new. To dream I could become part of a circle, instead of divided among many spokes with different purposes and separations. It was time to tell my family I no longer believed in a personal

God. It turned out to be much easier than I'd dared to hope.

I already knew my oldest son would not have an issue with my now evolved atheist label. Three of my children believe in God. My daughter was living in a Scandinavian country with a national religion (no separation of church and state in the far north) and her only concern was that I continue to show up in church when needed, for the grandchildren. I was happy to do that. My youngest son and his wife had enrolled their children in a Christian preschool, and I was most concerned about their potential dissension. They took my news in stride, declaring they did believe in a personal God and that my belief was my decision. And they loved me. My middle son and his wife reacted in much the same way. I was then free of religion and ready to move on . . . to new things and new experiences. I've never been happier!

Postscript

Move on I did. I've become something of an activist on left-leaning policy issues, making homemade signs, chanting at county government meetings, and walking with protest groups against Israeli apartheid and Wall Street. I am surrounded by so many different people, so many different views, many with a commitment to rational, science-based decisions in their lives. Insofar as we are able, that is. I'm not convinced that our brains aren't wired to include a tribal membership, and I'm not sure the divide between "us" and "them" is bridgeable in every disagreement. But I know you and I can sit down and have a conversation about something with a good chance of coming to an accommodation between us.

Here's to *life* and more conversation.

GRAYCE

Gil Brennan

*I distrust those people who know so well what God wants them to do,
because I notice it always coincides with their own desires.*

—Susan B. Anthony, at the National American Woman Suffrage
Association Convention, January 1896

Here I am, happy, enjoying life, sniggering in the playground with my grammar school friends, wearing my navy-blue pleated school skirt just one inch above the knee—nothing more, nothing less (per the school rules)—when the shrill, warbling whistle blows to call us to the dreaded class of the week: Religious Education, which we all call R.E.

At least I have my new biro (pen), multicolored all in one! Oh well, here I go: line up, walk in, sit at desk, stare at the blackboard, wait for the nasty, jaw-clenching sound of chalk scraping on the board. Every Thursday at 11:00 a.m., always the same drill, same boring, tight-collared, bespectacled teacher for whom I have no respect. I don't know what R.E. is supposed to be about except it's so boring, hence the multicolored biro—at least I can write one line in green, one in blue, and so on . . . All I think about is that in forty-five minutes, the bell will sound and everyone will pack their books into their satchels whether the bespectacled one says, "Time," or not.

Now there is yet another conundrum: lunch.

I line up once again, walk to my allotted lunch table, and sit, salivating, as it looks like we are getting the chocolate pudding with pink sauce today! I have to get through the meatballs (called faggots in England) and peas first, though. Worst of all, we have to listen to a prefect talk about Grayce—again. I wish I knew who this Grayce was. She is mentioned every lunchtime, but I never see her. We have to listen to some words that end in *Amen*. I think we have to say them, but I don't know what they are, which is weird, as I hear them every day at school. I am confused. Isn't Grayce female? Why then the *Amen*—that's men right? I think she must be popular, judging by how many days she's mentioned, but still, I never see her.

When I was six and one half years of age, I had to have my tonsils and adenoids out. This was the very first time my mother ever mentioned religion. "If they ask you what religion you are, tell them you are Church of England," Mother said. Although I still didn't understand religion and its strange rituals, this wasn't my first exposure to it. I didn't think to question her, but the only two churches I had ever heard about were Catholics and Protestants. Courtesy of Ireland and the unrest, I knew they were bad!

Off we went to the hospital, loaded with a brand-new coloring book, crayons, and oh joy, my very first multicolored biro! I had my ear pricked and got sent home—quite the disappointment, I can tell you. I got to keep the crayons and book, though, so that was a bonus at the time! I didn't quite understand why I was sent home, as the "What religion are you" question had not been asked yet. My blood did not clot fast enough, so two weeks later, we went through the same scenario, same statement from Mother, more coloring books, more crayons.

Finally the day came when the tonsils and adenoids could go. I did have to stay at the hospital, though, and Mother had to leave. I was on my own, still dreading the religion question and not sure what to say. Finally a tall man in a white robe meandered through the ward. I held my breath and pretended to be asleep, of course!

I was so scared of this person, walking around with what looked like an old, tatty book, holding it reverently with both hands. My turn finally came, and the scary man stood at the bottom of the bed by the cold, gray metal rails, just looking at me. Then came the question. "My Mum told me to say Church of England," I replied, feeling incredibly proud of myself: it worked! The tall, scary man moved on, and I started to breathe again.

Moving On

One year later my family had to move from our house in a small village on the outskirts of Nottingham to a town closer to London. We lived on a small lane, up a bumpy, unincorporated county road with many pheasants, wild pigs, and singing doves. On Sunday mornings we could hear the ringing of church bells emanating from the local stone-built, very old church not far away. It was a beautiful sound, especially on early warm summer mornings with the doves cooing at the same time. I didn't discover the significance of the bells until we moved again, this time to a small village called Bishampton, in Worcestershire.

Bishampton had two pubs—the Dolphin and the Red Lion—one church, and lots of boys! By this time my sister, Anne, and I were becoming interested in boys, early teens that we were then. We discovered at thirteen years of age that we could go to the off-licence (the grown-up version of a Starbucks drive-through, except we were not very grown-up and it was a walk-up window!) at the Dolphin to buy hard cider and a packet of cheese-and-onion crisps. We did think we were naughty but very grown-up. It was at one of these purchases that my sister met Andy Capp (yes, this was his true name!). He was a lot older and happened to have something to do with the church, though I wasn't sure what yet.

The church was at the north end of the village and had been there for years and years. It was a significant part of the village, although we never really knew anyone who actually went there except for weddings, christenings, funerals, or Christmas. It was a beautiful old building, and when Anne and I went inside for the first time—just to see what it was like to be in a church—I really did feel something. I think it was awe at what man had been able to accomplish without the tools of today. It had a musty smell, and there were Bibles in front of every place where anyone could sit. I did not know the name of the rows of benches, but they did not look very comfortable. They were highly polished: I could only assume it was from the number of bottoms sitting on them for hundreds of years and shifting position all the time.

Well, Anne and I discovered that going to said church to practice campanology was a great way to meet the local lads. Campanology is bell ringing, and these church bells were high up in the roof. There were four of them, very large, cast iron, each a slightly different size so they all made a different sound when you pulled on the rope to make them ring. I found it sort of fun, but the furry thing on the long rope was sensual. In the bell tower, my sister could also meet Andy without the wrath of Mother!

While spending time with a few other local kids who also went to bell-ringing practice, I discovered that being christened was something that nearly everyone experienced, except for my siblings and me. I questioned my parents about this, only to be told that if I wanted to be christened, I could, but it would involve going to church and Sunday school. Come on—school on a Sunday? I hated school as it was and lived for the weekends.

My parents had never discussed religion with us. All I remember is that by going to this church with Andy and the other kids, I started to question religion. I was at the inquisitive age—mostly about boys, of course. I was an impressionable teenager who by that time didn't have much parental guidance. Going to bell-ringing practice was a great way to get out of the house and have some fun. Anne would disappear with Andy, the director, behind a long, red velvet curtain. I never did find out what they were up to, but I was pretty sure it was illegal. Or maybe it was just kissing or holding hands. Back in the 1960s, that was acceptable in our eyes.

Campanology is a powerful experience in England. I miss the sound of the church bells to this day, even though I still don't know what they stand for. It is a very English tradition and reminds me of hearing the bells on Sundays when I was growing up.

In my family, Sundays meant no going out. To this day I don't understand why we couldn't go out, as my parents were not religious anymore and spent all their time in the garden. We always had a Sunday lunch, always a roast dinner—a tradition that my husband and I still carry on to this day, even in America.

Well, we ended up moving again, as Anne got caught out whilst babysitting. Andy had gone to see her. Mother also decided to go and see how Anne was getting along, as it was her first babysitting job, when she found Andy hiding behind the sofa!

No more bell ringing for us! Busted, as they say. We had to move again.

This time we moved to Great Malvern, still in Worcestershire but in an upscale community with old Victorian houses. We lived in one of these illustrious-looking homes, three stories high. We had the most wonderful views across the Vale of Evesham. You could often see church spires rising above the low-lying fog and hear the bells chiming on Sundays. It was an eerie sound when there was fog. You would also hear the occasional howling of a dog. I would often frighten myself by remembering *The Hound of the Baskervilles* by Arthur Conan Doyle.

I started to question religion again. I wondered, if I closed my eyes really hard and thought about God, would something happen? Like a bolt, a flash of light, a voice? I thought that if I could make this happen, it might help me be able to pray and become a better scholar and stop raiding my parents' drinks cabinets (I was now fifteen years of age). I kept hearing more and more that if you send a prayer, it would happen. What was *it*, though? I selfishly thought it would be something that would help me do better, as I was not the strongest-willed person.

I also kept hearing about Grayce again, and I realized that maybe there was no girl, that it was a religious practice called grace. I would be invited to friends' houses for the weekend. We would sit down for dinner, and the father, who invariably sat at the head of the table, would bow his head and say, "Let's say Grace." I would mumble, lower my head, and fake it one more time.

Getting over the inquisitive teens and going to all-night parties, I thought that I was invincible. Didn't we all? Church bells kept ringing every Sunday; every store was closed except the sweetie shop at the top of Castle Street in Great Malvern. Anne and I used to walk back through a graveyard adjoining Malvern Priory. It was fascinating to read the old headstones dating so far back for centuries. 1698 was a date I clearly remember. On the headstone of a young girl who had died at the age of fourteen were written the words: "called to rest." I paid no heed to those words, to the true meaning of "called to rest"—they were just words then—but I remembered them.

Moving Forward a Few More Years
Here I am, early twenties, becoming a little more responsible and getting ready to settle down with the love of my life, Tony. Then came the big debate for everyone except me. No, I was not getting married in a church—why would I?

A.   I never went to church.

B.   I had never been christened.

C.   I didn't want to wear white. It gets too dirty.

D.   I had never read the Bible.

Fortunately, Tony felt the same way. We had a super wedding. I wore a beautiful red velvet dress with medieval-type sleeves that had a lot of dainty velvet buttons. We married in the Malvern registry office, which was in the old priory building: it was as beautiful as any church.

Life settled down, and we had a lot of fun times with Tony's sister, Jane, and her husband, Roger. We used to have game nights and pub nights. We admired Claire and Paul, our niece and nephew, who often came along. Jane was never one to mention God, until one night. Oh *that* night, I remember it so well—the night that changed our friendship for many, many years.

Jane and Roger came round and wanted to have a serious talk. Jane had found him, *God!* She had, overnight, become a born-again Christian. Our lives and friendship changed dramatically, all because of God!

Jane had many reasons for this awakening: uppermost was apparently being abused by her father (my father-in-law, for goodness sake!). Roger was not part of this at the time but went along with it, as Jane was so happy.

As part of her rebirth, Jane stopped drinking and started eating brown bread and whole grains. She lost a lot of weight, so I thought, *Hmm, maybe I should try this magic trick.* Just as I had done when I was a child, I went back to sitting on the sofa in the quiet, dark living room when all was still, trying really, really hard to send a thought to him up above. Nope, the lightning bolt still never came; I could not figure this out at all.

By this time Tony and I were starting a family. I was pregnant with a child of unknown sex. It was not a practice in England to find out the sex of your unborn child unless there was a medical need. One of the main reasons was that there was a large Indian and Muslim population in England. One of their so-called religious practices was to have a firstborn son. Many people, if they knew that their unborn child was a female, would abort the pregnancy.

We had such a hard time figuring out a name, but we finally decided upon Frances. That would be okay for a boy or a girl, right? Not until she was born and Tony went to register her did we understand that there were two different ways to spell Frances, either with an *e* for a girl or an *i* for a boy. When asked what her middle name was, Tony told them that she did not have one. "Dis*grace*ful," we were told. See? *There is Grayce again,* I thought. Most people I knew hated their middle names, so we had decided, long before Frances's birth, to take the easy option and let our baby choose her own middle name if she ever wanted one.

We were then inundated with old aunts and uncles concerned about Frances's lack of a middle name saying, "Well, what will you do when she is christened?" We told them that Frances would only be christened if and when she wanted to be, as it is a personal choice and a religious one. Isn't that why there are godfathers and godmothers, to let them be chosen by the child? Christening should be a personal commitment, I felt, not one that is forced upon someone at a tender age when they are not old enough to understand the true meaning of the ceremony itself. That went down really well, I can tell you.

Of course, Jane and Roger would come round, and Jane babysat for us on occasion. Even though our relationship was somewhat different than it used to be, we found a way to work through it until yet another fateful day. Frances was only eighteen months old and had to have hernia surgery. The day before she was due to go in, she had another hernia pop out on the right side, so that was two surgeries on the poor little mite.

We took her to the hospital and said goodbye as the nurse carried her through to the operating theater. Tony and I went back to the car to sit, have some coffee, and listen to the news: it was voting day. When we got to the car, it had been broken into and the radio was stolen. What a horrible moment: our daughter was in surgery at eighteen months of age and our privacy had been violated. I cried so hard, I thought I was going to give myself a hernia. We went back to the hospital and found our baby girl waking up quite okay, just sleepy and crankier than usual.

We arrived home and telephoned family to say all was well. But when we called and spoke to Jane, she said in total disbelief, "Well, did she have to have the surgery?" We of course said, "Yes, but she is fine." To our utter astonishment, Jane told us that we must have done something wrong and upset God, as she had been praying very hard for Frances not to have to have the surgery! OMG, as we say these days, talk about speechless. I refused to speak to her for years and years. This rift in our relationship was very sad, and all because of this God thing. I did have the opportunity to talk to Jane about this two years ago. She didn't remember it at all and was very sorry.

Thirty odd years later, Jane is still very religious but has settled down and does not try to change everyone or the world. The funny thing is that Roger now goes to church and is a believer, as is Tony's mother, who at first was very skeptical about Jane's sudden Christianity and reasons—although we suspect that may be somewhat of a teeny, weeny farce to keep the peace, as that is what my mother-in-law does really well.

USA

Fast-forward ten years. For one reason or another, we moved to the United States, mainly due to the fact that my parents immigrated to the United States for my father's job. He needed some family here so that my mother would quit nagging him to go back home to England! We are now in Oregon.

Wow, what a different lifestyle in the United States. We had no jobs, no house, no friends, nothing. After staying with my parents for a few weeks, we moved into an apartment, found part-time jobs, and enrolled Frances in school. We started to rebuild our lives and get used to the American way.

I clearly remember asking some people the way to a store, and they gave us instructions by churches as landmarks! In England we gave folks instructions by pub names: "Turn left by the Red Lion, next right by the Swan, two more roads down turn right by the Dirty Duck." Voilà! Easy. Here, we were told, "Turn left by the Lutheran Church, two more blocks on the right, turn right by the Church of Christ, and then immediately turn left again after the Church of Latter-day Saints." Heaven help me, what on Earth was a block? And why so many churches that didn't even look like churches to me?

In the UK there were numerous beautiful old churches that were true places of worship, built reverently over many years without the technology we have today. Now centuries old and in disrepair through lack of maintenance, some of these churches are being turned into pubs, hotels, and even an indoor skate park. Developers are doing this to preserve the heritage and history that these buildings have.

As our family's life started to settle into somewhat of a routine in the States, either work colleagues or neighbors would ask us to dinner, which was exciting to us. *These will be friends*, we thought. At last we can meet people and have a social life again. How wrong were we? First it seemed that we were only invited as a novelty because we spoke English English. But more than anything, it appeared that they wanted us to go to their churches. Each time we were invited over, our hosts asked us, "What church are you going to?" or "Would you like to come to our church tomorrow?" We were not sure what to think or say. We were so used to people asking us, "What's your local?"—pub, that is.

Well, needless to say, we never did see some of these people again and certainly never went to their churches.

It then seemed that the only time people ever dressed nicely was on a Sunday to go to church. Why? Does God, or whoever is the prophet of choice, give preference if you're well dressed? We also discovered that many so-called churchgoers are total hypocrites. They repent on Sunday and go back to normal on Monday, repeat on Sunday. Oh yes, and greed. I wondered, *Where does that fit in with so-called religion?* So many unanswered questions and inexplicable exceptions. I finally came to the conclusion that I am not going to sit and try to talk to him/her to see if that lightning bolt ever hits me like a ton of bricks anymore, not after seeing all the hypocrisy that I see here in the United States.

Grayce, Again

Frances grew up to be a great student, daughter, and best friend to me. I cannot forget the day she came home from middle school after having the sex education class. I was peeling a potato at the kitchen sink. She entered the kitchen and said so conversationally, "Mum, when I decide to do you-know-what with a boy . . . "

The potato in my hand was shrinking rapidly. "Yes, darling," I answered, breathing deeply.

She continued, "I am going to make him go the doctor's to make sure he doesn't have AIDS, and I will go with him, as boys lie, you know."

First of all, I had to get a new potato. Secondly, what was she told in this sex education class? And thirdly, I was so proud to think that at the young age of eleven, my daughter could talk to me like that with no embarrassment whatsoever.

Then she followed it all up with, "Also, God won't like it if I do that before I am married."

Of course, we ended up having the discussion about God and that sex has nothing to do with him. "Who told you that?" I asked. School, of course.

Was I upset? Oh yes, and so was Tony. We ended up having a long, unpleasant conversation with the school about this. We almost wanted to pack up and go back to England, where at least if a person was religious and went to church, they did not believe in pushing that onto anyone else. Well, except for Jane!

Years later, Frances met a man named Andy, our now son-in-law, who is a really great person. His family, who is Lutheran, is great too. We have to say Grace when we go for dinner, but they understand our beliefs and do not ever try to change us. We all tolerate our different thoughts. Andy does not follow in his parents' beliefs after having to go to Sunday school for many years. His brother and sister still go to the Lutheran Church, but none of them ever admonish us for not believing—so refreshing.

Frances and Andy gave birth to Lily, our precious granddaughter, several years ago. They decided to give her a middle name after Andy's grandmother, who was a lovely lady. Her name was Grayce with a *y*. So you see, Grayce is still in my world but in a completely different way, and I would not be without her.

WELL BEYOND BELIEF

Kay Pullen

Scully: I was raised to believe that God has His reasons,
however mysterious.

Mulder: He may well have His reasons,
but He seems to use a lot of psychotics to carry out His job orders.

—*The X-Files,* "All Souls" (1998)

I am a mother, a lawyer, a vegetarian, and a book-loving, left-leaning, football-obsessed atheist. In roughly that order, although I'm not sure atheist would even make the list if that wasn't the topic of this essay. I guess you could call me a lukewarm atheist in that I don't have any major issues or gripes with religion in general—I just don't believe in any of it. Nevertheless, like most people, religion has had an unavoidable impact on my life for both bad and good. Although I have been an atheist for many years now, I know there are remnants of earlier teachings that are still within me. I have also absorbed, dissected, or rejected ideas from the constant barrage of religious messages that pervade our society. I am fascinated by most people's strong desire to believe and to belong—I think I understand it: I just don't feel it. And I am happy with that.

My path to atheism was pretty much a quiet and steady falling away: no dramatic incidents, no epiphanies. I was raised a Catholic, in what most would consider a very religious family. I went to mass every week and sang in the choir. Overall my experiences were positive. Sure, the homilies (sermons) could be boring and the wooden pews uncomfortable, but the stained glass was lovely and the music was good. I was taught to raise my voice in praise and gladness, to be charitable and forgiving to others, and to admit to and atone for my transgressions. That's one thing I do miss: I'm not sure I've ever again felt as light and free as I used to feel right after confession.

The first religious concept I remember feeling troubled about was that there was just one true religion and anyone who followed a wrong one was basically doomed. That seemed really unfair and also kind of random. Why would god blame you for following what your parents taught you? Why should a mean person who lucked into the one true religion get better treatment than a kind one whose parents picked wrong? I remember asking questions like that in catechism class and never getting satisfactory answers.

The question was finally resolved when I read *The Chronicles of Narnia*, a children's book series by C. S. Lewis (who I much later learned was also a Catholic theologian). The final book in the series deals with the end of the world. In Narnia, the good god was Aslan and the bad god was Tash. When the world ended, all of the good people were pulled toward Aslan and the bad people to Tash. It didn't matter which god they had worshipped in life, just how they had lived their lives. Of course, there was a fair amount of confusion as some people wandered about, unable to reconcile the doomsday reality with their dearly held belief systems. Others adapted pretty quickly and embraced the wonderful new world they had discovered. This all made perfect sense to me, so I adopted it as my version of heaven— complete with talking animals and at least one giant, heroic mouse.

Some of my other earlier confusions were easily satisfied by explanations that many things in the bible, the old testament in particular, were stories—which should be read for the underlying message but not taken literally. That helped a lot with Noah's ark, which I had imagined as an eat-or-be-eaten free-for-all. Maybe it bothered me a little that only men could be priests, but I loved *The Sound of Music* and thought being a nun would be much more fun than being a priest anyway. I don't recall thinking my church was any more sexist than the rest of society—maybe less, given how much hope and faith we devoted to Mary. Our church allowed altar girls as well as boys, and the women seemed to pretty much run the place.

As I grew older, I questioned more of what I was taught. It just didn't make sense in some fundamental ways. Like, what sort of god says you will only be forgiven if you first kill his son? That's twisted. And the original sin was eating from the tree of knowledge . . . so god wants us to be stupid? Why? Then there's the Catholic-specific idea of transubstantiation, which is just gross. For the non-Catholics out there, transubstantiation is the miracle that occurs when, after being blessed by the priest, ordinary bread and wine become the actual body and blood of Jesus Christ. Then you eat and drink it.

I also began to learn more about other religions, and frankly none of those made sense to me either. I didn't have much exposure to world religions, but learned more about the faiths of people I knew. I was particularly interested in and puzzled by the rest of the Protestant groups, most of which seemed exactly the same to me. I was surprised to find out that some people took bible stories literally and others believed in other books. I realized that most Christian faiths had a lot in common, and most religions had at least one thing in common: the core belief that their way was the one and only right way. That brought me right back to the problem Narnia had solved when I was younger—why the religion you practiced was more important than how you lived your life. Looking at it with a slightly more sophisticated thought process, I reached a new conclusion. Either most of these believers were wrong (other than the lucky group that picked right) or all of them were wrong about the existence of a single path. Rejecting the single-path concept, I was left with the conclusion that everyone who believes there is one true religion is wrong. Taking it further, that meant adults could be wrong. Majority opinion could be wrong. Commonly accepted history and tradition could be wrong. Really, anything we accept on faith could be wrong.

This realization altered my worldview but did not rock my foundation in any way. Again, I had never fully embraced church doctrine. I had always been encouraged by my parents to think for myself, to conduct research and form my own opinions, and to be willing to question authority. I did not reject all of the moral values that were taught to me as religious principles, but when I went to college, I left my religion behind at my parents' house, as forgotten as the not-so-favorite clothing and books that didn't make the final packing cut.

I majored in communications and English and continued to read voraciously. I remember an older English professor who was disgusted that so many young people had not read the bible, which he considered the most important work of literature in Western culture. Some students were mad that he called the bible "literature," and others were mad that he was "pushing religion"—I decided to read the bible. In doing so I concluded the professor was right about its literary importance. But if I had any lingering doubts about the veracity of biblical authority, actually reading the thing as an (almost) adult erased them. I found it to be a massive mess of contradictions and silliness mixed with a lot of senseless violence, a few lovely stories, and a language at times dense and sometimes beautiful. I confess I skimmed a lot, but I plowed through most of it. I certainly did not find it inspirational.

I also took a world religion class and did more reading. I was fascinated by the common threads, such as creation myths, eternal reward versus damnation, and again, the importance of the "one true faith," which I now clearly saw as little more than an effective recruitment and retention technique. Most religions also seemed to share an unhealthy obsession with sex, and some had odd rules about food. Almost all had religious leaders who served as their god's representative on Earth, wielding considerable power, often with self-serving motives.

College encourages you to ask questions, sift the answers, and come to your own conclusions. I was already pretty good at that, and with training, a little maturity, and my newfound freedom from religion, I questioned away. I discovered that I was less politically conservative than my parents. I decided that eating animals was morally wrong but most (if not all) sexual acts between consenting adults were fine so long as no one got hurt. My break from religious practice was permanent and without regret aside from the pain I knew it would cause my parents.

Given my parents' deep faith, I can't imagine how hard it was for them to accept that I had rejected it. To their tremendous and abiding credit, they have never blamed nor shamed me for it. I know my mother still prays for me, and I appreciate it in the spirit she means it. Luckily for her, she has a lot of children. Some of my siblings are religious, and some are not. All of them are good, well-educated, and very, very smart people. It really bothers me when other atheists imply or flat-out state that believers are stupid. My family members are all the evidence I need to the contrary. Some of my siblings are off-the-charts brilliant without any correlation to religious practice. The rest, believers and non, are also quite smart, plus they're exceptionally good-looking.

After college I worked as an editor for a few years, then went to law school, and eventually settled in Oregon, across the country from where I grew up. Unlike a lot of other atheists, I never went on a spiritual quest. Once I lost my religion, I never went looking for it. I was done. Same thing with giving up meat—if vegetarianism is a phase, it's been going on for more than thirty years. I can also tell you that not all young liberals grow more conservative as they age. In another ten years, I expect to be a socialist vegan. The vegan issue helps me relate to people who feel guilty for not fully living their principles because, given what I know about the dairy industry, I am a hypocrite for eating cheese but . . . I will try to do better tomorrow.

There's also a parallel in how we relate to each other. I know people judge me for my lack of religious belief, and I know they wonder if I judge them for eating a hamburger. Yeah, I do, but I don't think you're a bad person—you just haven't yet seen the light. But I promise not to bug you about it if you don't bug me about not seeing your light either.

Between my dietary choices and lack of religious belief (plus a few other oddities that are off topic so I'll leave them out), I have more than thirty years of experience living outside the US cultural mainstream. One thing I know for sure is if you're going to do that, you're going to get asked a lot of questions. So, for the record, here are my short answers, by category:

- Vegetarianism/veganism: I get plenty of protein; a fish is an animal; your bacon smells awful to me; my sharper teeth are good for asparagus; I don't think dominion over animals means what you think it means (and are you really quoting the bible at me?); and yes, my child's doctor has approved her plant-based diet.

- Atheism: No, I don't think you need religion to lead a moral life; I don't need the threat of hell or the promise of heaven to know what actions are right and which are wrong; morality is more about socialization, psychology, and the rule of law than religion; and no, I do not feel the need to believe in a higher power.

Sometimes the questions have rude intentions, but most often people are genuinely curious, especially when it comes to religion. I categorize the questions in two ways: questions about comfort and questions about community. The comfort questions are usually about the existence of a higher power, something to explain the inexplicable. People find it hard to accept that I have no need for that kind of belief. I don't need a higher power—I can live with not knowing what, if anything, comes next. I don't need to be comforted from my fear of death by the promise of a reward in heaven any more than I think the ancient gods created droughts and famines to teach ancient peoples a lesson. Science has given us answers to so many questions that used to be answered only by "god's will." I'll take the power of human ingenuity over prayer any day, but if prayer helps you, then I am happy for you.

The questions about community usually come from the people most strongly connected to religion at some point in their lives. They may belong to the church of their upbringing or be spiritual seekers who move from one group to another looking for a perfect fit. I totally understand the impulse to follow your family or community's religion. I have seen people leave a religious group and be shunned and cut off from friends and even family. It would take tremendous courage to withstand so much loss on principle. I am less certain of the spiritual seekers' motivations. I don't know why they are so desperate to believe and to belong. It's something I've pondered for years, and I have concluded that they are just part of the human condition. We all have fundamental needs to believe and to belong—and religion is only part of it.

There's a great work of fiction that artfully plays with the desires to believe and belong in the face of unexplained disasters and unsolved mysteries. It's called *The X-Files*. This groundbreaking television series of the mid-nineties dwelled in space and tension between science and the supernatural. It's all about trying to explain things that seem beyond explanation, and how that intersects with your needs to believe and to belong.

If you aren't familiar with the series, the rest of this will still make sense, but you would probably be better off leaving right now and watching the show instead. If you're already a fan, please forgive the unnecessary background notes. FBI agent Fox "Spooky" Mulder has been relegated to the agency basement to work on the weird, unsolved cases that no one else wants but uniquely appeal to him. That's because Mulder is on a quest to find the truth ("It's out there!") about the aliens who abducted his sister when they were both young children. Mulder is brilliant and gorgeous (like my siblings) but routinely dismissed by colleagues as a wackadoodle for his unconventional beliefs. Mulder doesn't care. As the flying-saucer poster above his desk states, he just wants to believe and couldn't care less about belonging.

Enter Dana Scully, medical doctor and pure scientist, who follows the rules and has no time for aliens and supernatural nonsense. She is also a faithful Catholic, devoted to her extended family, and not at all happy at being sent to the basement away from the serious people. For Scully, it's important to belong. (Of course she is also brilliant and gorgeous—it's television.) Over the course of several seasons, we see these two struggle with their different motivations, gradually moving more toward the middle. The bigger truth may be out there, but they're never going to find it and will have to be satisfied with smaller successes and short-term answers. That's all they have.

I see the power of belief and belonging in nonreligious contexts as well. Once we commit to a belief, most of us are pretty hard to shake. That's why we accept flimsy excuses from a cheating spouse. We don't want it to be true, plus we think love requires blind faith and trust, so we are the last ones to know the truth. Or we believe Barack Obama was born in Kenya because our personal belief system simply can't accept him as the legitimate president of the United States. We even refuse to believe that our celebrity heroes have feet of clay or worse because it's just too painful. We're invested. We are loyal. We simply have a hard time being wrong. As humans, most of us are very good at filtering out or disregarding information that is discordant with our beliefs. And the more we want to belong to the friends and family who share our beliefs, the longer we will hold on to them.

Lucky for me I still find religion very interesting, because it's so pervasive there is no way of avoiding it. It's woven throughout literature, film, television, music, and politics. Everyone around me is always thanking god and offering prayers when things go wrong. Sometimes it seems sincere, and others pro forma—just something you're supposed to say. Even my favorite football players routinely thank god for their success on the field. Really? I'm sure some of them mean they are thanking god for gifting them with athletic skills, but sometimes it sounds like they think god was on their team's side. Really? Your god cares about the outcome of a sporting event? That god, like the vengeful old testament god, doesn't seem worthy of worship.

Other than reflecting on the religious aspects of everything around me, my only toe dips into religious practice as a full-fledged adult resulted from my most important life role: mother. I never agonized about whether my daughter should be raised in a church, as there was no question she would not. I figured I would answer her questions as they arose, to the best of my ability. We celebrated Christmas and Easter with age-appropriate explanations of the pagan and Christian elements of each, along with discussion of the modern commercial aspects that dominate most holidays. Once she came home from preschool asking if we had been saved. I replied that we had never been in danger so did not need to be saved. She was satisfied for the time.

Some months later she asked if we could go to church. I got out the phone book (clearly this was a long time ago) and looked for a nearby Catholic parish. On Sunday we set off, and as we approached the address I had written down, we encountered some pretty heavy traffic. There were volunteers directing cars into the massive parking lot. We parked, got out, walked toward the church, and were greeted by more volunteers who welcomed us and invited me to take my daughter to the children's program. We went inside what looked like a classroom for a very nice private school. My daughter was fascinated by the elaborate floor-to-ceiling hamster habitat. I chatted with the volunteers, who kept talking about how the lord had called them, moved them, etc. They used the word *lord* an awful lot. Then the children's group leader invited everyone to gather around for a bible lesson. Everyone had a bible. As the leader continued to speak, it finally dawned on me—this was not a Catholic church.

For some reason I panicked. I grabbed my child, who protested loudly at leaving the hamsters behind, and started to leave. A friendly volunteer came right along with me, saying she would bring me into the church service and answer any questions I had. Not knowing what else to do, I went along. We entered an enormous building and stood in the lobby, looking through the glass to the main church where the service was underway. It looked like maybe a thousand people were in there. My guide asked if I would like some literature to review, and I said yes. As soon as she was out of sight, I snatched up my child and ran back to the parking lot. There I noticed that there were a lot of new, expensive-model cars in the lot, and most of them had that metallic fish symbol on the rear end. Definitely not a Catholic church. Taking a right out of the parking lot, I drove maybe half a block and saw the church I had been looking for in the first place. They were right next to each other.

I decided to stop in even though we were pretty late. People were standing in the back with crying children. I knew the songs and joined right in, despite the glare of my clearly embarrassed daughter. Right at communion time, people began to trickle out to get a jump on the exit traffic. These were people I could understand. I felt soothed and at home, almost like I belonged—at least following the oddly harrowing experience of the nameless church. In the end it became nothing more than a funny story to tell on myself, but the really great part is that my daughter never asked to go to church again. She did, however, come away with a strong devotion to small rodents and has had one or more as pets for most of her life.

Since that day I have visited a couple of other places of worship. Most notably, I attended a community event at the local mosque a few years after 9/11. I was excited to have a new cultural experience, and this definitely met my expectations. The thing I remember most, however, was being greeted at the entrance by a woman completely covered in a burka. She surprised me be saying, "Thank y'all so much for coming!" in a true Southern twang. Most of my other church visits have been for weddings, all of which have been lovely. Because I live in Portland, a city known for its low church attendance, most of the weddings I've been to here have been in parks or banquet halls. The last one I attended that took place in a church and had a lot of religious content was a same-sex wedding. Another reminder, like the mosque visit, not to make assumptions.

Like a tourist in a foreign country, I enjoy these church visits and learning about the customs and culture. Viewing religions and the faithful from the outside gives me a special perspective. I see so much fear of Islam from people who are blind to the cruelty and crimes of those who share their own faith. I hear mainstream Protestants talk about how odd they find Mormons and Jehovah's Witnesses. From my vantage point, they are all about equal in strangeness, and at the core, all have a lot in common. The people who believe prayer can help people heal are different from the people who choose prayer in lieu of actual medical care, but they are on the same continuum. So when someone tells me they're a Christian, which happens fairly often, I'm tempted to ask, "What does that mean?" because I really don't know. Are they trying to find out whether I belong to their tribe? Are they warning me not to start chanting or cursing or something? They usually sound like they're proud of it, so sometimes I congratulate them in reply. Then we're at least equally confused by what the other means.

Again, I don't have a problem with religion per se, or with religious people on that basis alone. I'm neutral. I know amazing, inspiring people who are religious and many who are not. I know petty, mean-spirited people, both religious and not. I know many people who find strength, comfort, and a sense of belonging in their religious beliefs and practice. I am happy for them. I would never try to talk them out of a belief system that is a positive influence on their lives. I have things I believe in as well.

I believe that the world is a beautiful place and that we all need to do more to take care of it. I believe that rainbows are an inspiring and beautiful gift from the natural world. I believe that animals are here on Earth for their own purposes, not ours. I believe that the Democratic Party cares more about the little guy and the disadvantaged than the Republican Party does. (I also believe both parties have jerks in their ranks along with some wonderful people and a whole lot of types in between.) I believe that Neil deGrasse Tyson and Johnny Depp are the sexiest men alive. I believe that my beloved professional football team should change its racist name. More importantly I believe that people are intrinsically good and that with guidance, love, and support, most of us will grow up to become good people who want positive things for the world.

I suppose I occasionally feel wistful for the certainty I had in my childhood. I'd definitely feel nostalgia for the glorious choir at midnight mass on Christmas Eve and joy for an Easter sunrise service. I sometimes envy the strength I see other people draw from their religious beliefs. I appreciate the serenity of the "let go and let god" folks. (The "Jesus Take the Wheel" types, on the other hand, are a public safety hazard.) I am glad for people when I see that their religious practices make them happy or inspire them to be charitable and forgiving. That's wonderful. It just never will be an answer for me, and I'm more than okay with that.

HOW I STOPPED BELIEVING

Emma Graham

*Fables should be taught as fables, myths as myths, and miracles
as poetic fantasies. To teach superstitions as truths is a most terrible thing.
The child mind accepts and believes them, and only through great pain and
perhaps tragedy can he be in after years relieved of them.*

—Hypatia of Alexandria

Introduction

This is the story about my journey to religious self-awareness. It is not meant to dictate to anyone what he or she should or shouldn't believe. Belief is a strong conviction and one that is difficult to change. This is also not meant to change anyone's religious beliefs or views.

The following stories reflect how, even as a young child, I questioned religion. It wasn't a quick conclusion that a god or maker does not exist.

The Army Life

My father was an enlisted Army staff sergeant, and our family lived at Fort Jay on Governors Island, New York, from 1960 to 1964. It was great growing up on that island—just a short ferryboat ride away from Manhattan. There's even a Facebook page, Governors Island Brats, where we all share fond memories and photos of living on "the island."

The island had one school, an elementary school. After the sixth grade, students took the ferry to New York. It was in the first grade that I was first exposed to a religious education. In the early 1960s, this was part of all military children's curriculum on Governors Island while attending elementary school, and it happened once a week. The island only had a Catholic and a Protestant church (that I was aware of), and the children were separated by whichever one of these religious options our parents selected for us. I always wonder what happened to the children who weren't Christian but might have attended a synagogue or mosque. I assume these children must also have had religious education, but I'm not sure where since the children I went to school and played with were either Protestant or Catholic.

My mother was from Germany and I can still hear her voice, in her very thick German accent, telling me multiple times before I left for school, "Don't forget. You have to go with Jürgen. He is Protestant and that's our church." Jürgen was a boy about my age who lived in the same building and whose mother was also German. My mother and Mrs. Bailey weren't true friends, but Mrs. Bailey was someone that my mother could speak to in German and reminisce. I nodded in agreement to my mother's directions because I knew I was going to follow her instructions implicitly. But then an incident on the playground happened that made me change my mind.

All of the students met in the playground after our last class of the day. This was when we went to our churches for religious education. All of a sudden, I saw a black-and-white composition book flying toward me like a Frisbee. It was too late. *Bam!* The book's binding side hit me square in my right shoulder. Everyone on the schoolyard stopped talking and looked at me. I was mortified. I turned my head in the direction the book had come from, and it was then I saw a very embarrassed and sheepish Jürgen staring at me. Just then, the teachers instructed us to group into our respective churches, and Jürgen waved me over. I was angry and decided to go instead with my best friend, Jeannie, who just happened to be Catholic. Immediately, I knew I hadn't followed my mother's instructions, but I also knew I didn't want to go with Jürgen. So, Jeannie it was. I don't remember how I got to the Catholic Church. Did we ride a bus? Walk?

We all sat on folding chairs as the priest called role. I heard him mumbling names as each student responded with, "Present." I was frightened. *What will happen when he doesn't find my name on that list? Is this when God strikes me with a lightning bolt?* All of a sudden, the priest stopped calling names and looked directly at me. As I sat there petrified, he looked at me and said, "I think you might be in the wrong church. Is that right?" I nodded. He then told me I could stay this time but needed to make sure I went to the church my parents wanted me to go to the next time.

I was so relieved, but then I realized that I was sitting in the "wrong" church. Wasn't I supposed to feel the wrath of God? I was very confused, but I didn't dwell on this for too long. Now I had to fear the wrath of Mom. *I didn't go to the right church, and Mom will be very, very angry with me*, I thought.

I felt like a doomed prisoner as I walked home with Jeannie. I don't remember any of our conversation on that walk because I kept looking up toward the sky, wondering if this was when God was going to smite me with lightning before I made it home.

When Jeannie and I reached the front doors to the building where we lived, number 866, I realized that nothing had happened to me. I was still alive. Then I immediately remembered that I still had Mom's smite to deal with. I dreaded having to tell her that I had disobeyed.

When I walked in the door, I started to try to explain myself, but her first words to me were, "You went to the wrong church, didn't you?" I nodded in disbelief that she could know this already, and Mom just told me that the next time, I had to go with Jürgen. I was dumbfounded. I didn't get smote with lightning, and my mom wasn't angry with me. When I look back on this early memory, I realize that as a child, I took everything I was told by my parents as the truth, but this experience also planted the seed of doubt about religion for me.

After Governors Island

My mother vehemently opposed my father's new assignment in 1963—South Vietnam—because she had lost her first husband in the early days of WWII. So after twenty-one years of military service, Dad retired and our family moved from Governors Island to Hayward, California, in the fall of 1964.

My younger sister, Joyce, and I grew up in Hayward as part of a typical, religious family, which means we attended church on Sundays. My sister and I would rather have spent Sunday mornings watching cartoons and not having to get dressed in our Sunday best. So Mom compromised. We only had to go to church every other Sunday. Mom was exempt from having to go to church, as she "had already gone to church enough as a child in

Germany." I guess it was now our turn. I never remember Dad complaining about going to church, but then my father had a gift of the gab and could talk off anyone's ear, so church was a social time for him.

We attended Grace Lutheran, and our minister was very old and about ready to retire. He was a nice man, but the sermons were dead boring, especially for two young children. I remember many times, during Pastor Lupkeman's sermons, how my sister and I would quietly whisper something funny and then almost break out in fits of hysterics trying to contain the laughter. Sunday school was much easier to take, so I was always glad when Dad let us do that instead of attending a sermon. Sitting in a Grace Lutheran School classroom that also doubled as a Sunday school class, we were taught about how God created Adam and Eve. As I halfheartedly listened, my mind wandered and I tried to make sense of creation and how it worked with evolution. I had learned from science classes how man had evolved from apes. At least that's the simple way it was explained to me as a young child. That's why the concept of God creating a man and a woman just didn't make sense to me.

I relished that every other Sunday when we didn't go to church. Instead, Mom made a full breakfast with eggs, bacon, biscuits, and Spam. Ah, Spam—that canned meat-by-product of gelatinous saltiness. Since my mother was born and raised in Germany and didn't come to the United States until the early 1950s when she was already in her thirties, she knew nothing about American cuisine. My father was military retired, so we shopped at the Oakland Navy commissary and they sold Spam. As far as my mother was concerned, Spam looked like ham, therefore it had to be all right to eat. But it was also on these Sundays, while lying in bed, I would ponder the universe and where we came from. I wondered where the God that church taught us about had come from and what there was at the end of our universe: Was there a wall? Was it a white void? These Sundays weren't the last time that I questioned the existence of a higher being.

Growing up on Hardeman Street was great. We had a very diverse street, and my sister and I had lots of friends to play with. Two of these friends, sisters Lisa and Cindy, lived up a couple doors and were close to us in age, Lisa being the eldest. We played with them regularly, and they were good company. But as childhood friendships go, we all drifted apart. By the time I got into high school, Lisa and I would greet each other but had other friends.

In my sophomore year, we had a social studies segment on religion. Our assignment was to visit a religion or church we were not familiar with. I had explained my assignment to Lisa and asked her if I could accompany her family one time when they went to church. I picked Lisa because her family had become Pentecostals a few years earlier. Instead of shorts and tennis shoes, Lisa and Cindy now wore long, dowdy print dresses.

Lisa's family went to church in the early evening, and on one of these evenings, I went with them. While sitting in a pew, I noticed that there was a lot of activity in the congregation. This was odd to me because a Lutheran church was quiet and reverent. Here there was loud organ music. I sat there motionless with my three-ring notebook on my lap with my pen in hand and didn't know what to write. This was all too weird for me.

I then saw a train of parishioners dancing up the aisle toward the front of the church where the pastor stood. The dancers included Lisa and Cindy, both dancing as if in a trance—heads moving, arms in the air, wearing those god-awful dresses, and dancing toward the pastor. I then saw the pastor put his hand onto Cindy's forehead, and suddenly her head jerked back, her body went stiff, and she started speaking what sounded to me like gibberish. As Cindy fell onto the floor writhing and kicking her legs, I thought I had somehow been transported into an asylum. I was petrified and didn't move. It seemed like I was in there forever and had no way to escape. I had to sit there and wait for the service to end. That was the last time I hung out with Lisa because I no longer understood who she and her family were. It amazed me at how much influence a religion could have on someone and how it literally changes a person.

My Realization

This next story is difficult to write because it was such a sad time in my life, but it also made me realize the hypocrisy and meanness of some people who call themselves Christians. It begins after Pastor Lupkeman retired and Pastor Waldo arrived. Pastor Waldo was a young pastor with a young wife and family. His sermons were passionate, and I no longer sat in church trying to zone out by staring at Jesus's portrait so long that the image would disappear into a white haze. I was inspired by Pastor Waldo and actually didn't mind going to church because his belief in God was evident.

Not everyone liked the new pastor, though. He was young and wanted change, and this didn't sit well with a group of people in the church. I was too young to know what this group did, but I believe they helped organize church functions and my father attended their meetings. Dad loved belonging to groups and committees. It wasn't so much that he wanted to help with a cause or to help organize a function. For him it meant the undivided attention of a group of people to which he could tell his stories of war and of the shoplifters he arrested at his job as head of security for JCPenney in San Francisco. There was one couple, the Bertels, who seemed to be running the show, but it was actually Mrs. Bertel who was in charge.

One day, Pastor Waldo confided in my father. Dad told Mom about this, but since we were children, my sister and I found out about it much later. Pastor Waldo told my father that Mrs. Bertel had cornered him and come on to him. After Pastor Waldo spurned Mrs. Bertel's advances, she was out for his blood. She did everything in her power to force him to leave Grace Lutheran, and I am sure that encounter was held over his head. Out of the blue, it was announced that Pastor Waldo would take on a teaching position at Concordia College in Oakland, and he would be moving his family close to the campus. Many of us were saddened and shocked by his departure, knowing that he wasn't leaving willingly. And that was it.

Until a tragic and horrific murder shocked the Bay Area.

The news report said that while Pastor Waldo was at college, Mrs. Waldo and their two young children were alone in their Oakland apartment. The doorbell rang and Mrs. Waldo answered it, but not before putting the children into one of the back rooms to play. The man wanted money, and he had a knife. I am not sure if she gave him money, but the man murdered Mrs. Waldo. A neighbor came by, but it was too late. The pastor's wife lay dying while her children played in a back room.

By this time our family, along with at least half the congregation, had left Grace Lutheran for Good Shepherd Lutheran on the other side of town. Even though we knew many of the people, it felt strange to go to a different church. We had a lot of memories from Grace Lutheran.

Mrs. Waldo's father was also now part of this new congregation, and it made it ever so sad when the funeral was held here. As we sat down in the pews, waiting for the ceremony, to all of our shock and horror Mrs. Bertel and some of the committee members arrived. What surprised us most was what she wore—a loud, flower-print dress and a very large hat. She looked like she was attending a garden party instead of a funeral. Everyone turned to look at her. If that's what her intent was, she got it. Everyone whispered, and I could feel disgust and anger well up inside of me. I saw the look of disbelief on Mrs. Waldo's father's face. It was just so very wrong. He was a good Christian man and said nothing.

I was sixteen, and it was then that I realized how hypocritical people who called themselves Christians could be. I wanted no more of it. That was my last regular appearance in a church.

Louise

I met Louise around the fourth grade, and we became friends. She wasn't that best-friends-forever kind of friend, but someone I felt comfortable with. Louise had an infectious laugh, and if she found something incredibly funny, she would laugh so hard, tears would start streaming and sometimes her asthma would kick in. Sometimes a good slap on her back would help her, but usually she just pulled out her inhaler and all was good again. Louise was African American and came from a family of four girls and two boys. Her father, retired Air Force, had a permanent tracheotomy and was a driven, shrewd businessman, while her mother was a loving woman who laughed heartily. This is where Louise got her infectious laughter.

As early childhood friendships go, we drifted apart. This occurred mostly because we were in different classrooms. It wasn't until around my sophomore year of high school that Louise and I started hanging out again. We both never felt comfortable in high school. We weren't popular; we weren't the girls smoking in the bathrooms. We just didn't fit in. We eventually befriended two other like-minded girls, and soon the older boys were calling us the Odd Squad, named for the hit TV show *The Mod Squad*!

After I attended my high school graduation, my father moved the family from Hayward to Buena Park, California, because of a job promotion. I moved with my family and attended Cal State Long Beach. Louise and I maintained a friendship by writing and calling each other.

One summer, Louise came for a visit and stayed at our house. My sister and I were in college and living at home. Mom didn't like the idea of a guest staying with us. We never had guests. Maybe it was the way things were done in Germany or maybe she was worried that she would become the maid. However, she relented and agreed to let Louise stay at our house. One fine morning, according to my sister, Louise went out into our backyard. Then Mom went to my sister and whispered, "She's chanting." That was Louise's Buddhist phase. I liked that phase because she was still my friend and she never brought up her religion in conversation. But somewhere along the way, that changed.

* * *

One day Louise told me that her younger sister Joanie, who was in her late teens, had been diagnosed with type I diabetes. It was a shock to everyone. Joanie was also told she would likely be unable to conceive. Well, to everyone's surprise, including Joanie's, and after a "short pregnancy," little Cristel was born.

Sometime later Louise called me in a panic, saying she was unable to reach Joanie at home. Louise phoned later to tell me that she'd found Joanie unconscious on the floor while little Cristel was in her crib. Louise tried to pour some sugar into Joanie's mouth to revive her, thinking she was in a diabetic coma, but it was too late. Joanie died; she wasn't even twenty years old.

I believe this traumatic event, in part, led Louise to abandon Buddhism and become a born-again Christian. But that change came much later. In the meantime, Louise was still very much a fun person and very much a party animal. We had many good times together. She was my partner in crime.

Years later, after my husband, son, and I moved to Oregon, I received a letter from Louise. In it, she gushed about being a Christian and how she was "on her walk with Jesus." I was in shock. I chose to ignore this in my reply letter to her and just wrote about regular and mundane things.

Sometime later, when email became a viable way to communicate, Louise sent a message and once again mentioned how she was still on her "walk with Jesus." I felt like she was trying to draw me into something that I didn't believe in, and I became upset. In my reply, I said that she could contact me again when she was done walking with Jesus. That was when I had a feeling that I was losing her as a friend. Her life was becoming more religious.

I didn't hear from Louis until a couple of years later when, out of the blue, I got a phone call from her. My heart skipped a beat when I heard her voice. I wasn't sure if she was still the religious zealot or if had she gone back to being my very dear friend, but I wanted to find out. After the uncomfortable formalities of greetings, Louise sounded like my friend. I was hopeful, but that was a ruse because the next thing I knew, it was all about Jesus again. I stopped her and told her that I couldn't talk to her anymore.

It's now been many years since I last heard from her. Maybe it's because we have new phone numbers and email addresses, or maybe it's because I don't want her to find me. I don't think I could go through the hurt again. I've lost a friendship, and it's left a hole in my heart. Once again, I saw religion take over someone's life.

My Evolution

Religion is a difficult drug to give up, as I had learned in my own life, and my husband and I decided not to expose our son to religion for this reason. One day, when my son was ten or eleven, he asked me if he could go with a friend to church. I was stunned. He'd never asked to go to church before. I told him that he could go when he turned eighteen. He would be an adult then and could do what he pleased, but up until that time, I asked him not to go. He didn't, and so far, he never has attended a church.

By the time my husband, son, and I moved to Oregon in 2000, I still felt that even though I didn't believe in a god, that I should believe in something. So, if it wasn't Christianity, I wondered what it should be. I thought about Buddhism and Wicca and even aliens. I include aliens because here again is another belief in something, even though this something is not yet proved. I don't discount some of these UFO reports, as I too have experienced something that couldn't be explained, but it's still not proof. It's exchanging one belief for another.

As I pondered my belief system, I happened to catch the actor Jim Carrey on a talk show discussing a book he'd read on dark matter. I hadn't heard about this until then, and it piqued my interest. I researched the subject and found books relating to dark matter and cosmology. This is when I began reading books written by Stephen Hawking, Neil deGrasse Tyson, Lawrence Krauss, and other scientists.

It was then that I finally came to terms with my spirituality and realized that science was what I needed in my life to explain the world and the universe we live in. I knew I had finally found something that made sense to me, and I began to feel the wonderment and awe about life I had felt as a child on those churchless Sunday mornings. I no longer needed a belief in the unexplainable to make me feel this way.

OF FAITH, FEMINISM, AND MASTER NARRATIVES

Sylvia Benner

Of course, you know, the romance of life in the universe is a constant back-beat to everything that I've ever worked on.

—Ann Druyan

If my life were a graphic novel, it would begin like this:

We are in a dark courtyard, enclosed by walls on three sides. It is the early hours after midnight, the scene illuminated by an almost-full moon. The cobblestones are wet from recent rain.

I am uncertain. There is only one way out, but the enemy is guarding it.

Suddenly, a figure leaps, catlike, onto the wall behind me. The figure jumps off the wall and lands next to me. Crossed on his back are two swords. When he pulls back his hood, I realize it is my father. He draws both swords from their scabbards and hands one to me.

"Go do battle, daughter. If you need me, I'm right behind you."

Now, in reality, I am no warrior princess, and I would most certainly acquit myself poorly in a fight. In reality, I concern myself with nothing as grand as an "enemy" but with more mundane things, like mortgage payments, cat litter boxes, and the correct rendering of "medically acceptable" in the German version of informed consent forms. In reality, my father did not leap onto walls—or anything else, for that matter, because he was rather too heavy and sedentary for that sort of thing. And yet, the story conveys a kind of truth that defies a mere statement or description. It conveys how I *experienced* my father much more effectively than if I were to merely describe him or actual events.

In the same way, narratives can convey to us how we experience *ourselves*. In other words, they can provide meaning and identity. They do this not primarily through their claims and story content but by the kinds of characters they allow and call for: the warrior princess, lone traveler, sage, martyr, magician, king or queen, detective, genius, good Samaritan, soldier in the army of the Lord, or any other character from mythology, fiction, religion, or one's own invention. A good narrative tells us why not to be bored with ourselves. Some of us want to be Captain Janeway when we grow up. This may not be an entirely respectable impulse, but it's great fun. What's more, I have a suspicion that much personal improvement happens by way of imagining ourselves as the person we want to be, often informed by characters we find aspirational. There is altogether too much talk about human role models and not enough about fictional ones, which I consider to be far superior because they strip away all the noise created by human foibles and distill a character down to the essence. They throw into high relief what it is about the character that we aspire to be.

It is fashionable to demand that characters in new works be "realistic." I suppose this is a legitimate standard if one uses fictional narratives to navigate one's way through real-world problems. But that is not how I use fiction. When seeking real-world solutions, trying to find them through fictional narratives seems a bit on the inefficient side, and I would instead opt for paid expert advice, reports from people who have been through it, or peer support. Rather, my chosen fictional characters, including those of my own invention, set my aspiration for the person I *wish to be* as I go through adversity or experience success. The character is never truly achievable, but it gives me a general direction to head for. It serves as a kind of psychological lighthouse.

Most narratives remain safely contained in the realm of the fictional. I know of no *Game of Thrones*, *Lord of the Rings*, or *Star Trek* fan, for example, who confuses her favorite fictional world with reality. And while these stories explore themes of heroism, growth, and personal power, and while they propose value systems, they make no claim to truth. They do not purport to inform the individual who he *actually* is. The characters in the stories are interesting, but the stories propose no way for the reader or viewer to participate in the proceedings. The audience remains locked out.

But there is another kind of narrative, which does make room for individuals to be part of the story, and in some cases, to become its characters. These narratives seek to explain the nature and functioning of the world, the way it is all put together, why things happen the way that they do. They are narratives of the universe and human history. They make truth claims about the world and, by extension, about the individual, who now has to decide whether or not to believe the claims. Such narratives can be religions, of course, but they can also be social and scientific theories. By grouping them together, I do not mean to imply that all such stories are worthy of the same degree of belief. In a perfect world, such belief decisions would proceed rationally, based on evidence. But I suspect that in reality, the decision, more often than not, is made based on whether the story offers a compelling character, and this is where reality-based narratives seem to have a competitive disadvantage to religion.

The most successful narratives tell us why—though our lives seem to be dominated by the mundane—in reality, we are a hero character in a story invisible, unknown, even undetectable, to most. They solve the central problem of human existence: the banality of life.

This is what religions are so extremely good at: the religious narrative makes room for each believer to find self-expression by playing a part in a story that is of cosmic importance. Atheists have much to say about why religions are psychologically powerful. It is said that people believe religious claims because they are afraid to die and some religions tell them that death is not permanent; because religion creates hope for a better world; because people are overwhelmed by the responsibility of constructing an ethical approach to life and are happy to accept their religion's comprehensive ethics package; because they are sexually frustrated and look forward to sexual bliss with seventy-two virgins in paradise. All, any, or none of those may be true.

But my interest here is in a rarely discussed feature of religion: unlike narratives that make no claim to be true, religion allows for participation in the story. You get to do more than root for Frodo—you get to *be* Frodo. If you wonder why I go to popular stories rather than the classics, which allegedly deal with the human condition in a timeless way, it is because religious *narratives* are much more like the former than the latter, despite the fact that religious *scripture* is categorized among the classics. The popular may have less depth, but it has more psychological leverage.

Life's endless string of little necessities—going to work, washing dishes, paying bills, getting oil changes, taking tests and writing papers, getting groceries—are not made of the stuff that holds our attention. Life's little indignities and big crises seem all the harder to bear if we cannot dissolve them in a grand context that gives them meaning. Its triumphs and joys seem diminished because there is no larger context that would give them permanent significance.

Enter religion. Being a mid-level HR manager in your fifteenth year of marriage; juggling the kids' school and social schedules with oil changes, laundry, and utility payments; fighting your neighbors about dog poop and your own body about cholesterol isn't such a mundane existence: you are The Teacher and your real job is to transmit God's eternal truth to the next generation. Finding yourself at the beginning of your second year of graduate school with the realization that urban planning will leave much less room for your artistic ambitions than you had hoped is an easier problem if the real action isn't in this world anyway. And when ferrying grumpy riders on boring bus routes in sweaty August feels a bit pointless, you can remember that being a soldier in the army of the Lord is anything but. Your life becomes a kind of cover for your real identity. The world's Clark Kent to your Superman. It all seems rather exciting, as a matter of fact.

It is this part of religion that I did not understand until after I had become an atheist.

* * *

Letting go of religion was quick and easy. I was sixteen when I had my epiphany. Some time earlier I had undertaken the tedious task of actually reading the Bible, and I concluded that its value system and admonitions were ethically questionable, its claims and assumptions scientifically implausible, and its various accounts inconsistent with one another. One night during my seventeenth year, I tried to make sense of the vast contradiction between the Bible's claims about the world on the one hand, and my twentieth-century worldview on the other. That night, for the first time, I considered the possibility that the Bible was precisely what it seemed to be: mythology. There was my sense. The contradictions dissolved when I downgraded the Bible from truth to claim. I went to bed a Christian around ten thirty and was an atheist by eleven thirty.

While my process was not in any way extraordinary, the speed of the development was. Many atheists report struggling with these questions for a very long time before they are finally left without any reason to persist in their belief in a god.

So what was different in my case? Almost certainly, letting go of God is easier in one's youth, when one has less invested. Maybe it was the fact that I did not face any social pressure to keep my religious belief because in my native Germany, atheism just isn't very shocking, and because my family's reaction the next morning, on learning that I was an atheist, was something like "That's nice, dear. Would you pass the butter, please?" But I think at least part of it was the fact that I had not found for myself an aspirational character in the Christian story, nothing of personal relevance that would have encouraged me to maintain an unjustified belief. I had no idea that such a thing was even possible. I did not learn about this possibility until I was twenty-one.

* * *

I was already an atheist when I met Bettina, a young woman I worked with at the package-processing station of the German postal service in Munich, where I was earning money to continue my temporarily interrupted globetrotting adventures. Bettina invited me to a gospel concert, and since I was unfamiliar with the style, I accepted—and a door to knowledge was opened. The "concert" was packaged in a religious service showcasing an American gospel choir that was touring Germany. I got the full load of Pentecostalism: the passionate preaching, the lively music, the speaking in tongues. I was utterly fascinated. Amused, certainly, but mostly curious. This version of religion was very different from the sleep-inducing Catholic and Lutheran services I was familiar with, as well as the practices of other world religions I had encountered in movies, documentaries, and the study of comparative religion in school.

An Irish coworker who had also attended the service with us was miffed at having been misled about the nature of the event, and scoffed at the proceedings. "They're fuckin' lunatics, aren't they?" He raised his hands, as people had during the service while speaking in tongues. "They're all standin' there, going, 'Beam me up, Scotty!'"

As for me, I started going to church with Bettina every Sunday, attending dinners at her house, joining her for Bible study, asking this hypothetical God to reveal himself to me while Bettina and her friend prayed over me—the whole nine yards. I am with Sam Harris, who says: "I don't *want to be wrong* for a moment *longer than* I have to be" (emphasis mine). I was on a quest for truth, and if I had missed a truth about Christianity, I was determined to be set straight.

Nothing ever did happen to change my mind about the existence of God, but two important things happened during those months: First, I developed an interest in exploring unfamiliar religions and denominations by honestly engaging with people trying to convert me to their way of thinking, and I took every opportunity to do so during my travels with friends who were Jehovah's Witnesses, Latter-day Saints, and Seventh-day Adventists. I highly recommend the practice, as I found it very enlightening. Second, and more important, I learned where religion sets its hooks into the human mind.

Until I met Bettina and delved into her world, I had never understood what a powerful organizing force religion could be in someone's life. I had to acknowledge that, had I not already accommodated myself to the idea that the Bible was a book of mythology, I could easily have been drawn into this passionate life—and would afterward have found it extremely difficult to disentangle my identity from the claims. There would have been too much to lose. Experientially, it was like going through the wardrobe into Narnia. It was like being swept up in a tornado and landing in Oz. Or like suddenly finding myself on the bridge of the starship *Enterprise* three and a half centuries in the future. Bettina and her fellow congregants literally lived in a separate story from the rest of us, and it was a story that reached into every moment of her life. Nothing was exempt from her all-encompassing worldview—every action, from one's education to doing the dishes, was the action of an interesting character in a fascinating story. Bettina had literally been transported into an alternate reality in which there were no meaningless things. It made for a passionate life.

I am convinced that my willingness to let go of Christianity so quickly at the age of sixteen was due to the fact that my identity was not entangled with the Christian story. I had no incentive to defend Christianity from an assault by reason.

Many narratives are passionately defended by their adherents precisely because, by providing a context for aspirational characters that people can assume, they do an enormous amount of work in believers' lives. Unless they are very well supported by evidence, narratives that fail to provide a context for aspirational characters tend to be quickly abandoned. This is the fate that befell a particular narrative about women during the post-war years and through the early sixties, which Betty Friedan called the "feminine mystique" in her 1963 book by that name. It is also what ails third-wave feminism, in sharp contrast to the Christian narrative about women, which seems to push all the right buttons.

Commentators tell us that the percentage of women who identify as feminists is in the neighborhood of just 25 percent. Mind you, this is not a fact I deplore. I am among the majority of gender egalitarians who do not label themselves as feminists, mainly because I do not believe the central claims of feminism that women are worse off than men in the United States or that this alleged net disadvantage is due to women being valued less than men. Mind you, I have no problem with that claim with respect to many developing nations. But from what I hear when I listen in on the public conversation, I get the impression that a good portion of those who do not take on the label of feminist actually *do* believe some or most of those claims and yet still don't accept the label.

How come? I have a hunch that it is because the current incarnation of feminism, i.e., third-wave feminism, has no aspirational characters to offer for women (and certainly not for men). It does not propose to women a vision of themselves that is remotely attractive to them. There are no superheroines in the third wave, only downtrodden victims who, at best, can aspire to muscling down the alleged patriarchal oppressors. This is not done by displaying strength, resilience, intelligence, or anything else that a person might aspire to, but by constantly reminding everybody else, and thereby oneself, of one's victimhood and by identifying ever new circumstances that can be interpreted as victimization. There is no hint of personal power, least of all the sexual variety. There is no vision of women as tough and responsible, as mistresses of their fate. There is a vision only of women as children who are utterly determined by their environment, are to be treated only as members of a group but never as individuals, and who have to be perpetually protected against upset, lest they be permanently traumatized, for example, by jokes about dongles assaulting their sensitive ears and fragile egos. It is a rather Victorian view of women. (For a discussion of the parallels, see Rene Denfeld's 1995 book *The New Victorians.*)

I have never found a place for myself in the feminist narrative, as it has no female characters who are confident, self-determined, and powerful, and who, in the mold of the hero, put that power to use in the service of others. I find modern feminism vaguely insulting and highly unpleasant because it makes me small and stands in complete and utter contradiction both to who I am and who I want to be, and, I assert, to what most women aspire to be—even those who find claims of female oppression and systemic misogyny in the West persuasive.

Feminists are baffled that so many women assent to its principles and claims, and yet shun the label of feminist. I think feminism's character problem is a prime suspect. My advice: invent a version of feminism that does not compel women to see themselves as victims. Maybe feminism can go with my earlier warrior princess theme, or something like a Klingon kind of feminism, where females (as they would be called on the Klingon homeworld) join their males in raucous laughter at raunchy jokes and give as well as they get while telling tales of battle and guzzling gallons of blood wine—before engaging in sex that is more like hand-to-hand combat than like a contractual negotiation about who agrees to exactly what. Well, maybe not quite that. But while the Klingon version of womanhood is also far from my ideal, I find it a damn sight more attractive than the version third-wave feminism has to offer.

Paradoxically, the Christian narrative does a much better job of creating aspirational characters for women. One of the most brilliant ways to smuggle the Christian version of womanhood into the minds of young women is the Twilight series by Stephenie Meyer. I don't want to rehash old conversations, but Twilight is an excellent example of where the Christian narrative outcompetes the feminist narrative in terms of identity.

Twilight, for those who do not habitually read young adult fantasy, is a series of four vampire romances popular with teenage girls that tells the story of the relationship between high school senior Bella Swan and vampire Edward Cullen. For the record, I am talking about the books here. I have not seen the film adaptations. The novels have received much justified criticism by feminists: the story glorifies a rather traditional image of women, promotes abstinence before marriage, and lauds the refusal to have an abortion, even to protect the mother's life. Mind you, while I disagree with all this "social conservative" nonsense, I do not think that the only legitimate way to write female characters is the way in which I would write them. When I say the feminist critique is justified, I mean that it correctly identifies the outdated and impractical values conveyed in the novels.

But in one critical point, much of the feminist critique reflects a glaring misunderstanding: there seems to be some measure of consensus among feminist critics that Bella is portrayed as weak, with Edward cast as her protector (or her stalker, in the less charitable interpretations). Nothing could be further from the truth. I will grant that Bella's character starts out as a teenager with all the standard teenage insecurities that come with youth. But throughout the four books, Bella grows in wisdom and power, ultimately acquiring supernatural abilities that turn her into the heroic protector of her entire family. It is true that in the first three books, there is much confusion and danger for Bella, with much rescuing by Edward. But she comes into her own in the fourth book, probably not coincidentally, given the Mormon author, as her role changes to that of wife and mother. The breakthrough in power comes when she finds herself pregnant by Edward during their honeymoon and the rapid development of her human-vampire hybrid fetus is putting her life at risk. Edward, concerned about her survival, argues for an abortion, which Bella steadfastly refuses. When he tries to force an abortion to save his wife's life, she enlists the help of werewolf friends to protect her. Notice the theme: here, abortion is the easy, cowardly, and small-minded solution proposed by a well-meaning man, and her refusal to abort the fetus endangering her life is portrayed as an exercise in choice and female power. She is standing up to her husband to do as she wishes.

Bella's true power is revealed when her family readies for battle with a great enemy. Through intense, sustained training, Bella develops the ability to throw a shield around her family and allies, protecting them from harm. It is the culmination of months of learning and suffering, of growing into wisdom and power. She has grown into a superheroine, more powerful than her husband.

Feminists have certainly acknowledged that the anti-abortion message comes packaged as choice, which is precisely what Meyer claims she is arguing for. But feminist critics seem to read Bella's character as powerless, submitted, and dependent. I have seen hardly any understanding that Bella's character is portrayed as extremely powerful. The book series paints an image not of a woman submitted to a man, but of a woman who outgrows her mate; not of one whose life is expendable and who is put at risk because a life-saving abortion is denied, but of radical self-possession and bodily autonomy, to an extent that Christianity does not generally accord to terminally ill people who want to end their lives to avoid suffering.

Twilight presents the traditional view of womanhood, with abstinence before marriage, refusal to end a pregnancy, and with the role of wife and mother not just as a norm or duty for young women, but as a path to heroism and personal power—and by implication a path to a much more interesting and engaged life than could ever be achieved even in a high-profile career. Every Christian book or blog I have ever read giving advice to Christian women conveys the message that women have a unique, mysterious, almost magical power if only they learn how to use it. Feminism reads the Christian vision as limiting women to specific roles, and thankfully feminist activism has done away with laws that would constrain women to these roles in reality. But Christianity is packaging traditionalism as liberating women from the constraints of modern expectations and empowering them by bringing them back to the true source of their power. Christianity offers a hero's quest while feminism offers the role of a victim. Christianity—personal growth through overcoming obstacles; feminism—an accounting of grievances. Christianity—empowerment as an individual; feminism—identity as a member of a class.

In all honesty, if my only choices were to experience myself through the feminist lens as a character victimized by patriarchal oppression or through the lens of an aspirational character who can grow into personal power, I would choose the latter. Fortunately, I am not so constrained. And fortunately, my belief in a worldview does not depend on whether it offers me the opportunity to participate in the role of a character that is to my liking, as evidenced by the fact that I reject both the Christian *and* the feminist view of the world in general, and of women in particular.

Nevertheless, the ability to project oneself into an aspirational character likely affects the stickiness of a worldview—by which I mean the difficulty that is involved with abandoning it or the ease of adopting it. This might explain the paradox that, as Gallup has found in poll after poll, that "women are significantly more religious than men." (We may be on a path to change in this respect. The Barna Group's 2015 State of Atheism in America poll puts the percentage of women in organized atheism at 43 percent.)

But what of the evidence-based worldview? How easy is it to adopt? How much room does it leave for individuals to find a place for themselves in it? Ideally, once evidence is in play, how good it feels or how comforting or exciting it is should make no difference in terms of our assent to claims, and a good deal of what I regard as cultural progress involves placing ever greater emphasis on evidence-based thinking over compelling narratives. But what if I'm right that narratives provide psychological benefit? Do we have to give up aspirational characters and compelling narratives like the age-old hero's quest if we are to adopt a reality-based worldview?

One may, like Richard Dawkins, be present to "the magic of reality," but there is no getting around the fact that no matter how magnificent the universe, it has no need of us. One is hard-pressed to find a connection between the I and the everything: when we experience ourselves as *part of* the universe, we are utterly insignificant. When we experience ourselves as its observers, we are disconnected from it. Having a worldview that is consistent with reality appears to be in conflict with meaning. It seems to preclude the possibility of aspirational characters and heroism except for the tiny minority of us who get to be heroes of scientific discovery.

Never really having possessed a narrative that assigned me a role in a cosmic play before I became an atheist, all my character creation happened independently of a story. It was never a great burden to be disconnected from ultimate reality, although it did leave an unfulfilled wish. It is only since my involvement with organized atheism, skepticism, and humanism that I have begun to recognize the grand narrative that emerges from evidence, and to merge my aspirations about who I want to be with that narrative.

The reality-based narrative of the world is the narrative of Big History, an approach to the study and teaching of history that examines our origins and development over large time scales from the Big Bang to the present. Using empirical evidence and weaving together knowledge from multiple academic disciplines, it provides a big-picture, science-based view of the history of the universe, the formation of our planet, our species' emergence on it, and the phases of technological, cultural, and moral development that humanity has gone through. (An excellent introduction to the topic is the online class Big History: The Big Bang, Life on Earth, and the Rise of Humanity offered by the Great Courses and taught by Professor David Christian.) Like origin myths, it explains where we came from. Unlike origin myths, this story, to the best of our knowledge, is true and will be refined as we learn more.

But there is more to this story than the past. If we correctly understand the past, we can, with all due caution, guess what the future might hold, and choose our path deliberately. One cannot talk about the future and claim that one's narrative is true. But one can project a possible future and declare aspirations that are based on what we know about the past. Some things I know about the past give me a good deal of hope for the future, not just my own and that of my descendants, but of humanity as a whole.

In 2012, I wrote the following as part of an address for the Portland Center for Inquiry's annual Dark-to-Light celebration:

> Today, we live in the least violent time in human history. Today, we know more about nature than ever before. More humans have the economic means to meet their basic needs, there is more democracy and freedom on the planet, medicine has more power to cure disease and alleviate suffering, and information travels more easily than ever before. Today, torture is universally condemned, and even those who practice it pretend that they do not. Freedom of conscience has become a guiding principle in many societies, and even societies that do not respect this right pay lip service to it. We live in times characterized by greater human wellbeing than ever before.
>
> There is much left to do, to be sure. The benefits I described are extending to ever-increasing numbers of people, but are not yet available to everyone, and to many, only incompletely. There is much left to learn about the universe and our own nature. There is moral progress yet to be made. And yet, however much we still want to improve, whatever is still remiss, to whatever extent human well-being, and the well-being of other sentient organisms, is not realized, it is important to recognize and appreciate how far we've come. Because only then can we ask the question: "What have we been doing right?" and by extension "What do we need to do in order to create the best possible future?"

And here is the answer given by humanism: humanity's achievements so far are the fruits of science and reason. Science gave us the germ theory of disease, antibiotics, anesthetics, surgery, immunizations, computer and information technology, the steam engine and modern transportation, more secure food supplies, as well as greater prosperity, space exploration, knowledge about our universe and our origins on the planet, and much more. Reason gave us moral progress: human rights and individual freedoms, prohibition against torture, an end to the divine right of kings, secular societies, humane justice, a concern for equal opportunity, a commitment to broad-based education and freedom of conscience, among others. . . .

I believe that the great humanist endeavor is to create a society in which science and reason are valued; one in which even people who have no particular interest in science strive to be scientifically literate, because it is akin to being literate, period; a society in which most people strive to think critically and act reasonably, regardless of what particular beliefs they hold. I suspect that humanity's progress will be determined in large part by the extent to which we succeed in this endeavor of shifting society's values. . . .

The faster we switch our interest from resting in heaven to exploring the heavens, the faster we will progress along our path from darkness to light.

According to my narrative, the good fight is the one that promotes science, reason, and freedom of inquiry as the standard model, because this is where I see humanity's progress. I don't know if we will conquer death, eliminate poverty and disease, colonize space, travel faster than light, remove limits to human intelligence, or any number of other things futurists dream about. But I am happy to dream with them—while not confusing the dream with a prediction. Meanwhile, right here and right now, regardless of whether the *Star Trek* vision of the human future will ever materialize, I know that our best outcomes are possible if we continue humanity's transition from superstitious and emotional thinking to reason, to the greatest extent possible given our evolved hardware.

In this good fight, and this good story, there is no need for gods, but there is room for fabulous characters: for sages and teachers, adventurers and superheroes, starship captains, diligent scientists and brilliant thinkers. I think there'll be use for a warrior queen or two.

THE MINORITY ATHEIST

Taressa Straughter

*When we cast off the oppressive mantle of religion, we are free
then to take up the actual work of equality and fairness and justice.
Women can't do this whilst being "protected" from reality
and exposure to the world as religions would dictate.*

—Jamila Bey

"In hell shall you lift your eyes! You're going to wish you would have listened to me." That is exactly what my mom said when I came out as an atheist at age fourteen.

Yes, I know it's really weird to make a decision so early in your life, but I did it anyway. Though I was angry at first because of my mother's reaction, I later felt liberated.

I wouldn't say that I was always an atheist. Of course when you are a kid, you are easily manipulated into believing anything your parents tell you, so for the first few years of my life, I thought god was real. I would pray daily and go to church and sing my little heart out to gospel songs, and it amazes me sometimes how devoted I was as a kid to this invisible being. My family is poor and we never had an easy life—my mother had seven kids and worked day and night so we had food on the table. Till this day, I will never understand how she can still believe in god, even after moving constantly because we couldn't afford to stay in any of our houses or when we were homeless for a couple of months.

My mom is a devoted Pentecostal woman. We went to church Mondays, Wednesdays, Fridays, and twice on Sundays. My mother is what people would call a holy roller or a Jesus freak. As I got older, I started to open my eyes, started to question everything. When I would see commercials about starving babies in Africa or civilians getting killed, raped, or dehumanized by their government officials, I would ask myself, *Where was god? If he is this all-powerful being that is supposed to be benevolent, why is he letting all of this happen to innocent people?* I even asked my mom about this, and all she said was that we are not supposed to question god's actions. I was totally baffled by her response. *Why can't we ask questions? If he is omniscient, he should have no problem answering my questions.*

When I reached my teenage years, I officially embraced being an atheist. My life revolved around science, because to me it answered more questions than the bible ever did. I remember that when I told my mother I was an atheist, she forced me to read the bible. She probably thought that would explain things and make me a believer, but it did the exact opposite. If anything, it made me certain that god didn't exist.

High school was difficult for me—I was so uncomfortable when people would ask me what church I attended or which denomination I was in. When I would tell them I was an atheist, they looked at me as if I'd committed an atrocity. "You don't believe in god? Why?" I was constantly asked in school. When I told them my reason, they judged me. They questioned my morals and said they wouldn't trust me, all because I didn't believe in this transparent being called god. It was crazy, the questions they would ask me. *If anything*, I thought, *I should be asking the questions. Why are they believing in a being that they can't see, feel, or hear?*

Not only was it tough as a teenager being an atheist, but being a black one made my life even tougher. The community I come from is very religious, and my sister and I were the only atheists on our block. They weren't open-minded, so it was uncomfortable for me when they would talk about Jesus or god. Being a black atheist is like being an African elephant almost. I can count how many black atheists I know personally: me and my sister.

As a black atheist, not only do you have white Christians judging you but black Christians as well, and it kind of doesn't make sense to me why a lot of black people are Christian. As Chris Rock put it, "A black Christian is like a black person with no memory." The English slave traders who kept our ancestors in the most inhumane conditions on those disease-ridden ships were Christians. The slave owners who justified beating, raping, and killing slaves by quoting the bible were Christians. The people who created the Jim Crow laws were Christians, and most importantly the founders of the Ku Klux Klan were—you know who—Christians. My ancestors were forced into this religion, and some people even bought in enough to tell their slave masters about the slaves who planned to escape because they were told that they must be obedient slaves in order to get to heaven.

This religion has done more harm to black people than it has done any good. Where was god when people were being lynched? Where was he when Emmett Till was killed? Where was he when segregation was rampant, or when my grandmother and grandfather had to endure racism and could not talk back to white people who degraded them despite identifying as Christians? I just don't understood how people can be so devoted to this religion. Religion in general has not done much good for society, but Christianity of all religions should be the last one a black person pursues. The prayers of black people in those times didn't help combat racism. It took activists who actually did something about it to end it. Prayer has never been the solution; action is the solution.

Sometimes I look at European countries and envy them—their quality of life is so much better. Not only that, but religion has *no* involvement in their politics. If anything, the more religious a European politician sounds, the fewer votes he or she will receive. Americans are too religious. We have a hard time separating church and state. We have these bible-crazed Republicans using god as their debate mechanism, without even using any facts. If you look at European countries, they're more peaceful. Scandinavian countries like Sweden, Denmark, and Norway have the highest percentage of atheists in the world, yet their countries have everything America doesn't: free school, low crime rates, happier lives, and higher college attendance. When I look at these countries, I feel good about myself. There are so many misconceptions about atheists, and yet the countries with the highest percentage of us are the most civilized countries in the world. That shows that you don't need god to have morals. People who do bad things don't lack god—they lack empathy.

I am proud to be an atheist, and I wouldn't change that for the world. In the past couple years, my mother has come to terms with my decision, and I can say that she is more open-minded than she was initially. I'm currently a freshman in college majoring in pre-medicine, I speak three languages, and I'm living my life as a black woman atheist. Atheists still aren't trusted by many Americans, and it hurts to feel ostracized by society, but I hope in the future that America will take some notes from Europeans' progress and be more open-minded.

ESCAPING AND SURVIVING RELIGION

Marsha Abelman

I'm an atheist; I suppose you can call me a sort of libertarian anarchist. I regard religion with fear and suspicion. It's not enough to say that I don't believe in God. I actually regard the system as distressing: I am offended by some of the things said in the Bible and the Koran, and I refute them.

—Emma Thompson, Actress

If only God hadn't answered my first conscious prayer! Ah, I learned too late to be careful what you ask for. I couldn't know at my tender age, as I kneeled and asked God to let my family begin attending church, that religion would so strongly determine the course of my life journey.

I prayed with a fervor and trust that probably only a young child can muster, especially a young child who had been taught to believe in God, Santa, the Tooth Fairy, and yes, even the Easter Bunny. I prayed that my family would go to church, like my grandmother and my cousins did. Soon afterward, my family did begin attending church, and my faith in God was solidified.

Of course God exists! *Of course* he answers prayers! This prayer and answer fueled my religious zeal for a long time.

But it wasn't difficult to be a religious zealot in my time and place.

* * *

I was born in Waco, Texas, part of the post-war baby boom. Waco's official nickname is the "Heart of Texas," and my childhood was literally awash in pride of place. We were Americans in post-war giddiness, a happy time of GI Bill housing; we were Texans living in the biggest and best state; we were Wacoans, proud fans of the Baylor Bears. My earliest memories include going to see the Baylor Bears (both the players at football games and the real bear cub mascots) of Waco's renowned Baptist university, a beloved institution that was older than the state of Texas. In school we drew pictures of bluebonnets, the Texas flag, and the Alamo, and we wore green and gold for our Bears.

We were taught to respect our elders. Any adult anywhere could spank or correct any child. Children were literally to be seen but not heard in my world. We said, "Yes, ma'am," and "Yes, sir," to everyone.

We were taught to love America. There were American flags in every classroom, we said the Pledge of Allegiance every day, and we sang patriotic songs in assemblies. We left the school building one sunny spring morning to walk a few blocks and line the street as President Eisenhower paraded past. He was an impressive figure, making a clasped-hands victory sign while we cheered him as instructed.

We were also taught to love God. We had learned the Pledge of Allegiance in the first grade, but when we returned for second grade, we were told the Pledge of Allegiance had been changed and we needed to relearn it. No longer should we say "one nation indivisible," we were to say "one nation *under God*, indivisible." As a dutiful child who was afraid of disobeying any authority, I worried nervously that I might do it wrong, which etched this notable change in America's history into my mind. In my elementary school, we had prayers before lunch and a classroom Bible reading each morning, and we students were expected to take turns leading those. On Mondays, the teacher asked for a show of hands of all who "went to church and Sunday school yesterday." They sent the count to the principal's office! Before I even knew what peer pressure meant, I felt its heavy weight on my young shoulders.

The problem was, I'd been born to very religious parents who didn't *agree* on religion and who therefore did not attend church. My father was Church of Christ, my mother Southern Baptist, two sects that vehemently disagreed on so many doctrines that they were almost like enemy combatants! I didn't know anything about my parents' thoughts on religion, as religion was never openly discussed. I only knew that I had to make a choice when the Sunday school count was taken: be different or lie. So, fearful and ashamed, I lied. I raised my hand. I added to the number that was scribbled on paper and presumably recorded by the principal.

I really did *want* to go to church, and not just so I could legitimately raise my hand. My paternal grandfather was very religious, preaching the Bible at family gatherings. (From him, I heard that you shouldn't play cards on Sunday and "all women are Jezebels"—things that meant little to me as a child, although they seemed extremely important as we listened to his booming voice punctuated by his fist pounding the table!) However, my maternal grandmother, my source of unconditional love, introduced me to church, a fun place where we sang and did crafts and had cookies. I went to her church during summer visits to her farm in the country. Her small Baptist church was a square wooden building with creaky floors and cardboard fans on each pew. While we tried to shoo away the flies and the heat, a beautiful white Jesus looked up at us from the fans, holding a lamb in one arm and beckoning us with his other arm outstretched. I loved those fans, I loved the musty smell of the old pews, I loved Vacation Bible School, I loved my grandmother's reedy voice singing about Jesus, and I loved the way she put cologne on both of us and gave me a pretty handkerchief to carry. But back at home, we never went to church or talked about Jesus.

Somewhere about this time, my cousins (who lived near my grandmother) all had the same dream about Jesus one night, and the next morning my aunt took them to their Baptist church to be baptized. They were all younger than I was, and I was rather unclear on what their baptism meant. I only knew for sure that they got to go to Sunday school and get Bibles and prizes, and now I was told they were "saved." I felt this was something that I, as the older cousin, should be doing. (After all, I was the one who learned to read first and who read comic books to them. I should know about this!)

That was when I got the idea to pray to God that *my* family would start going to church. And pray I did, with fervor and absolute belief in what I'd been told about God. He would help me, and he would solve my dilemma of not being saved, of not being able to go to Sunday school as my cousins did. I remember sometimes kneeling at my bedroom window, looking up at the sky, and earnestly pleading with God, "*Please* let my family go to church."

I also took home from my grandmother's house a gift she told me to keep quiet about: a copy of *The Little Baptist*, a small children's book about a Baptist child, published before the Civil War (and out of print since 1848). I had learned to read from my grandmother; I loved books; I treasured this gift and hid it in my closet to read later. When I got home from school the next day, it was gone.

And soon thereafter, we began attending church and Sunday school.

Years afterward, I realized that *The Little Baptist* was probably the impetus in our lifestyle change, and I can only imagine what unpleasant words might have been exchanged by the adults in my life about their conflicting denominations. It might have seemed to some that it was out of the blue for our non-church-attending family to suddenly buy some Sunday clothes and go to church, but I was absolutely convinced that God had answered my prayer. Not only that, we began attending the *Church of Christ*, not the *Baptist* Church. I couldn't wait to tell my cousins. Not only were we going to church, but also we were *not going to the Baptist Church*. It was so *obvious* to me that God had chosen one church over another, and I told my cousins that (probably gloatingly, alas!). Only years afterward did I also realize that my overbearing father most likely dictated that choice and that my mother probably had no voice in the decision.

But at last I could raise my hand honestly, with the other kids, when my public school made that terrible incursion into its students' private lives.

I had no idea of the cost to my life "attending church and Sunday school" would have.

* * *

The Church of Christ is a group of loosely affiliated but autonomous congregations that have an unofficial motto, "Speak where the Bible speaks; be silent where the Bible is silent." And if people had questions the elders couldn't answer with a scripture, they would be told "that is not pertinent to your salvation." I carried my Bible on the school bus, reading, underlining, and memorizing. I carried a little book called *Ready Answers to Religious Questions* with indexed reference verses. I was the perfect little Christian soldier, being baptized at the required age (which turned out to be about twelve; my cousins got it wrong again, I thought), and I was always ready to argue religion with my Baptist classmates at school. We exchanged a flurry of theme-paper epistles each day, pages filled with dueling Bible verses we'd looked up the night before, to prove that *our* denomination was the right one. I of course *knew* that God had answered my prayer years ago, sending me to the Church of Christ. I had absolute proof and a desire to convince others.

And thus began the life that had been brought about by a convergence of coincidences: born in a conservative place, at a conservative time in history, and to conservative parents. Other than outright rebellion, there would have been no way for me to escape this childhood and young adulthood. I was the oldest child and tended toward pleasing the adults who rigidly controlled my life (pleasing others was my coping/survival technique). By being punitive and controlling of every aspect of my life, my father very effectively squelched any rebellious thoughts I might have had. He "spanked" (hit) me—for minor infractions like crying, talking back, failure to do chores properly—from the time I was only months old until I graduated from high school. When I was about eight, he punished me for sniffling and rubbing my nose (I had untreated allergies) by painting a circle of mercurochrome on the tip of my nose and making me go to school that way. I went to high school PE classes with bruises on my legs that we would nowadays report to the authorities. He had absolute control.

Although I am a very strong-willed person now, my experiences have taught me how easily children can be subjugated and brainwashed into being submissive. My parents had been taught by their culture and religion that *the man is the boss.* So I was very lucky my authoritarian father *did* allow us to go to church, or I would never have had a friend. Our family had always kept to itself, and as very young children, my brothers and I weren't even allowed to leave our yard or visit other kids' houses. Everyone had to play in our yard. As a teenager, I wasn't allowed to stay after school for any activities or join any school clubs. Without Sunday school and church, and a very active youth group at that church, my social life would have been nonexistent.

My social life was essentially church three times a week.

Youth group was wonderful, led by two trained musicians who were also a married couple. I was allowed to take voice lessons from the wife, and the husband organized our youth group around singing. We actually were excellent singers, because of our church's tradition of a cappella singing and because of this couple's expert instruction. Our chorus sang at weddings and funerals in the region and took fun bus trips around Texas with our earnings, to places like Six Flags or Casa Mañana (a venue for live plays). I never went to a single school event because they were all dances and were considered sinful. After I turned down a couple of invitations by saying, "I'm not allowed to dance," word got around, boys stopped asking me, and I was again the one who was different, who couldn't raise her hand when others did. I wasn't allowed to go swimming if there were to be boys present (*mixed* swimming was considered sinful) or to wear pants (making my climb onto the church hayride most likely immodest). I was not allowed to go to other churches or to any activities with non–Church of Christ school friends. But I had a social life at church. I was happy with that. I knew nothing else.

My parents had no expectations for their children to attend college. They had both graduated high school, and I'm sure that was considered good enough for us. But when my church friends started talking about college, I began to think about it. My father said I should go to Baylor and live at home, but I investigated a Christian college out of town. Only by arranging all my own loans and getting jobs was I allowed to go. I can barely believe I had the initiative to do so, but I did.

Church of Christ colleges at that time were really just authoritarian homes away from home. These colleges shared the nation's obsession with protecting virginity while allowing a double standard that gave a wink and a nod to the cherished adage, "Boys will be boys." Girls' dorms had 10 p.m. curfews, with dorm doors chained overnight. Girls had room checks and got demerits for messy rooms. Girls could not wear pants even to play tennis, girls' dresses had a required length, and girls couldn't date guys from the local Air Force base. Boys had none of those rules; boys could and did go all semester without making their beds; boys stayed out overnight. These restrictive rules sadly felt normal to me, but without the physical punishment. I had more freedom than I'd had at home: I could go on a date that I chose, and I fended off my first grabby boy (the dorm mother's nephew, whom she recommended as a nice boy who was also a preacher's kid). I stayed up late playing card games and talking—against the rules. But I attended daily chapel and devotionals as required. I took Bible courses, and I continued to underline in my Bible.

And I still went to church three times a week.

* * *

Flashing forward through my two unremarkable years at college, I reached a point where I needed more money than college jobs paid, so I returned to Waco to live at home and save money, with the goal of returning to college. However, after church one Sunday, I met my future husband. We were engaged within months. With the Vietnam War raging and the draft board breathing down his neck, he was able to get into USAF Officer Training School and avoid the Army infantry. Following our church wedding in 1967, we honeymooned by driving hundreds of miles to his first assignment. The military was a shock to us and challenged our way of thinking. We felt surrounded by worldly thinking—with people swimming, dancing, and drinking! And *that* was just our church friends!

Only after our release from the turbulent time in the military and our subsequent return to Texas could we settle down enough in our personal lives to begin to assess our religious teachings. We moved to a small town where our church, the white Church of Christ congregation, paid the bills for the black congregation across the tracks. Nice? More like an ulterior motive to maintain segregation. Racism was not usually openly acknowledged, but our jaws dropped when a young father our age said in Sunday school, "I'll kill any n****r who tries to date my daughter." Racism was rampant in the town, in our workplaces, and now we saw it even in church? We'd been raised in Texas, but neither of us had ever bought into the blatant racism that we'd been taught. The ultra-conservative minister's views were extreme to us. It didn't take us long to backslide right out of church. We simply stopped going or answering their phone calls.

The year 1972 was important in my philosophical growth for several reasons. First, my beloved grandmother died that year, and my father informed me that he thought she had gone to hell. She was a woman with a beautiful spirit who helped people at every chance and gave generously, who believed in God, who gave me the only unconditional love I had ever experienced, and who had loved my father like her own son. But he just knew that she hadn't been the "right" religious denomination, and therefore she deserved to burn in hell. (When someone tells me religion does no harm, I just think of this sad story.)

Secondly, I read *The Second Sex* by Simone de Beauvoir in the summer of 1972. This was the first time I'd read that women had been complaining about the misogyny of the world through the ages. I became a feminist that summer. However, I had to stay in the closet for a few more years.

Then a really monumental thing happened. I got pregnant, after we thought we could not have a child. Thinking only of the racism in which we didn't want to raise our child, we moved—to Colorado, attempting to escape the race problems we disliked about Texas. And we went back to church, thinking kids needed it. In fact, church soon became the focus of our lives.

Yes, we went back. Back to church three times a week.

* * *

My husband became a deacon, we both taught Sunday school, we helped build a log lodge for a youth camp, and we learned sign language and began a ministry to the deaf, spending many hours helping deaf members. I eventually became the church secretary. Our little son went to preschool at the church. As when I was a child, our family soon did most things with church people and few things with anyone else. All our friends were at church. They were the people we celebrated birthdays with, went to movies with, traveled with. We took chicken soup to each other after childbirth and surgeries; we comforted each other when we lost our loved ones. We considered them to be our family.

My father had left his lifelong job to become a minister to the deaf after I left home, and his life was completely church-centered now. He told us once, "The Bible is the only book you need." Although my husband and I were also totally immersed in religion by this time, we couldn't ignore the cognitive dissonance we both felt about the Bible. It didn't seem like the "Good Book." We became very disturbed at its stories—so many dreadful stories—as we became Sunday school teachers and as we read it to our child. As a third-grade Sunday school teacher, I was required to teach a story from the Old Testament book of Judges about a man who entertained a traveler passing through his country of Ephraim. Here's the gist of it:

Some "wicked men of the city" came to this old man's house, pounded on the door, and shouted to him, "Bring out the man who came to your house so we can have sex with him." He said, "No, my friends, don't be so vile. Since this man is my guest, don't do this outrageous thing. Look, here is my virgin daughter, and his concubine. I will bring them out to you now, and you can use them and do to them whatever you wish. But as for this man, don't do such an outrageous thing." Long story short, he pushed the visitor's concubine outside, where the men from the city raped her all night. She crawled back to the house and lay there until the man came out. Then he cut her body into twelve pieces and sent the pieces around Israel.

Yes, the story is allegedly symbolism, but what I learned from this horrible story about the abuse of women is that the Bible is completely inappropriate for young children and I shouldn't be teaching this to eight-year-olds! I had studied the Bible all my life, accepting it as the inspired word of God while recognizing that much of it is bizarre; however, realizing that we had introduced this worldview to our own child suddenly made me feel sick.

Another chink in my personal armor of faith was my participation in a book club at church. We read a book of essays on women in early Christianity, each essay written by a different Church of Christ university professor. Each essay concentrated on a particular tradition we had in our church, and each writer concluded that each was just that—a *tradition*, not a decree from God. I asked the preacher, "Well, then why don't we *change* some of these traditions and begin letting women do more and be deaconesses, like in the early church?" He said, "We can't change because we just don't want to offend people."

I couldn't help but think, *I'm people, and I'm offended. Am I chopped liver?* Similar to my childish belief that God answered my prayer, I had a naïve belief that all people valued the truth, even religious people. I had never considered that religion could be practicing deception deliberately!

All my life I'd been told what I could *not* do because I was a girl, what women could *not* do because we were never to usurp authority over a man. As a small girl, before we ever attended church, I had told my parents I wanted to be a preacher when I grew up. They had told me, "Girls can't do that." As a teen in our church, I couldn't start a prayer, lead a song, or do a reading because the Bible said only males could do that. As a woman, I couldn't even teach Sunday school to boys who were over the "age of accountability" (a kind of Protestant equivalent of a bar mitzvah) because that would be taking authority over them and they, even if only twelve or thirteen, were men. I could teach my son at home but could never teach him a lesson in the church building. A seemingly humble duty like passing a collection plate or a communion tray from row to row was forbidden to me because I was a woman. I sat in many services and listened to men give lessons that were poorly written, speak prayers that were products of disorganized minds, and lead songs when they could barely carry a tune.

Foolishly, I soon brought up the subject of my frustrations with traditional women's roles at a family dinner and my father said, "I'm sorry you don't like the place where God put you." Really, what had I expected? He was a diehard in our denomination. And he was a man, who had the privilege of rank in our culture and our religion.

About this time in the religious world, new translations of the Bible were being used in churches. The New International Version is one I remember liking because each book had an explanation at the beginning about the author, the time it was written, and to whom it was written. This was a new way of thinking about the Bible for me. I suddenly saw more clearly that Corinthians (with its anti-woman advice) wasn't dictated from the mind of a deity but was just a letter to some people in Corinth by a man named Paul. I learned that the Bible was generally considered to have been compiled around 367 CE, while other writings were destroyed or cast aside. There were other books called the Apocrypha that some thought to be sacred, yet I'd never even *seen* those. My husband and I talked a lot during this period, really sharing our feelings about the Bible, about the religion we'd been born into, about some disappointing moral hypocrites in our religious lives, about our doubts whether this whole system based on ancient mythology could be truth or was even a system that deserved our support.

I posited: what if I wrote a letter to a friend, offering her marital advice like "Make your husband a glass of tea every evening," and then my letter surfaces years later, some people take it as advice from God, and my words to my friend become a dogma of a religion? Yes, we agreed, it could happen. Apparently this kind of letter-writing-turned-sacred *has* happened. It's called the Bible.

And then our son became a teen, a young man to whom we'd always said, "Ask us anything, and we'll tell you the truth." He now said to us, "You know, this just doesn't make sense." That opened a floodgate for all of us. How *could* we have told him the truth about Santa and about sex but still have perpetuated these myths and made them literally the center of our family's life?

As we talked, I realized that in spite of my conviction that God had answered my first prayer when I was a child, I had been content for the years since then to carry on a one-sided relationship with him. I accepted with blind faith our church's explanation that miracles had ceased, that God didn't speak to people in modern times except to answer our prayers. And even then, his answer could always be no, and we had to accept that.

However, American religion was becoming more charismatic, and even our staid denomination began to get an influx of such members, people who lifted their hands in church, who claimed that God advised them what to buy, where to move, how to rear their kids. They were saying that they were receiving actual communication from God. Once again, my feelings were being ignored, and this time not just by male church leaders but by the Big Man himself. No one had more faith than I had had during my life, and my prayers had been met with silence. As the bumper sticker says, "I gave myself to Jesus, and now he never calls." I can joke now, but it was painful at the time when I realized I'd been talking to myself since that first time I kneeled at my window as a child.

It was also painful to realize that all those years I'd been submissive and silent in church, accepting my place behind every man who ever lived, I was blindly following a tradition created by men. In this case, by literal *males*. God hadn't decreed women were dirty and untouchable because of our biology or that we needed to suffer in childbirth. Men had written those words.

My husband and I came to the same conclusion at the same time. We have always shared many similar viewpoints, and luckily we both agreed on the next step about religion. We left church again, and not by backsliding as before. We left purposefully, openly honest about our unbelief, hoping we could engage our friends in discussions. That never happened, with anyone. The people with whom we'd raised our children, done volunteer work, traveled, camped and hiked, shared our joys and sorrows for twenty years, all turned their backs. It was a shunning, which is not an *official* doctrine of this loosely organized denomination. No one would even go to a movie with us. When we called, our old "friends" were more than willing to preach to us, to say we should come back to church. And my father! My husband let it slip once, early on, that he didn't "really believe all that" anymore. My dad pressured him to answer, "Are you an atheist?" Almost immediately, my dad and his wife packed up and left, going back to Texas a couple of days earlier than planned. Every communication from my dad from that day forward included entreaties to "come back to the Lord." My final interaction with him, back in Texas for my aunt's funeral, was very unpleasant. He died months later, angry and upset, seriously believing that his daughter was going to hell.

Struggling along, feeling alone, we happened upon a group called the Freethinkers of Colorado Springs. Our first awareness that such groups even existed was when we heard their radio show on the local college radio station. A local lawyer, a former Catholic, was talking about atheism, about the hypocrisy of religion, and about abuse he'd endured at the hands of his priest! We read their weekly column, published in the alternative newspaper. Some articles were written by local freethinkers, some by famous freethinkers like Robert Ingersoll or Elizabeth Cady Stanton, and most were new ideas to us. We felt relief and immediate kinship to people who were honest and funny, and who embraced the here and now.

We became members. I joined the board. I wrote some freethought articles for the newspaper, but we had to keep our membership in this group fairly low-key, as I worked in a public school system and my husband owned a business. But the freedom we felt, the freedom from religion, was like a second wind when you're exhausted from running!

Our son's life continued on a freethinker path when he moved to Portland for college. He had broken from religion a bit before we did, and he had really helped us find the courage to leave. We visited him in Portland often and fell in love with the Pacific Northwest. The presence of freethinker groups was a bonus, and we've retired here and are active in local atheist groups.

We found, however, that we expected too much of humans in the Northwest, and the fact that there are so many conservatives still amazes us. It's also disheartening to see dissension among the larger, global atheist community. However, we are happy that progressives across the world are making headway, and we feel that the more open nonbelievers are, the more we will help others come out of their atheist closets, and the larger and more supportive our communities will be.

My experience in religion left me feeling small and insignificant, helpless and unprotected. In religion, there was always a finger pointing at me, accusing me of being bad, of being responsible for Jesus's death (he died for *my* sins, after all), of not having enough faith or being as righteous as I should be. Religion warned me that if I wasn't careful, if I wasn't praying "without ceasing," I might stand before the judgment seat and be found lacking when it was too late to change.

The reward offered for being willing to live a puritanical life was heaven, a place of gold and pearls. But the dangling carrot, the pie in the sky, did not compensate for the losses of pleasure and joy (and dancing!). One had to give up independent thinking in order to please God, and a woman had to give up more than a man; a woman had to accept a submissive role at all times. Without those childhood brainwashings, I might have become a more outspoken person earlier. I think I would have been a great lawyer. I could have been a judge. It was religious tradition that told me I couldn't. Instead, I did the traditionally acceptable female tasks: made many potluck dishes, knocked on doors to pass out religious pamphlets, taught Bible classes, and packed my reluctant child off to church camp. Those would not have been choices either of us would have made if I hadn't been indoctrinated. I hated cooking and my son had an incredibly terrible time at camp! We both would have made different choices had I been reared with a sense of autonomy and the will to fight the traditions of religious patriarchy.

Some of my husband's and my atheist friends who were not raised in religion strive to be conciliatory with religion. They don't imagine a secular world, but rather they imagine coexistence as the only goal. This is worrisome to me, considering the harm that religion has done, and is still doing, to so many people. I understand humans' desire for community and that some people seek a church to be a community that will support them in their lives' ups and downs. What I *cannot* understand is joining, staying in, or supporting any community after you realize the whole system is based on lies and/or harmful beliefs. It would be like staying in the KKK because they use 600 thread count sheets, which are admittedly very nice sheets!

My husband and I have wished we had our youthful, energetic years back so that we could spend them doing things of real value to the world rather than supporting missionaries and promoting false dogmas. Given another chance, we would give our generous financial donations to causes to improve *this* world and make *this* life more pleasant for humans. We regret that we didn't realize earlier that all any of us has for certain is *this life*.

But better late than never!

* * *

This girl who once studied her Bible on the school bus has now had her face on a large Freedom from Religion billboard! I was quite proud for it to say, "Marsha Abelman, atheist." I feel so very lucky to have lived long enough to have escaped—and survived—religion. I know there's no god to answer prayers, and I don't believe in magic lamps with genies, but *if only!* My wish would be that humans would understand the destructive nature of religion and we could have the world John Lennon imagined—a world with "no religion" and "all the people living life in peace."

LEAVING CHRISTIAN BAGGAGE BEHIND

Lilandra Ra

And my punishment for wanting to learn
Is a painful birth from which I may not return
The bible tells me I was made for and from man
And I must do for him everything that I can
I must surrender to his will, yeah I must submit
I can't make the household decisions coz I am unfit
It tells me my place
With ever-lasting grace

—Shelley Segal, "Eve"

The first time I remember hearing about god was after my parents divorced when I had barely started school. I remember the conversation with my dad in his pickup truck with a camper and a CB radio that had plastic lettering identifying his handle, The Flying Dutchman. It went like this:

"Do you know how much you love me?" he said.

"Yes," I stated emphatically, because at that age he was my entire world.

"You should love god more than me."

I don't remember his exact line of reasoning, but I do remember coming away from that conversation with the impression that god must be like some uber-daddy in the sky that I never met. That is not too far off the mark, as Christians often refer to him as a "Heavenly Father."

My dad's family was actually German in origin, not Dutch, and he explained that to me when I later asked about his CB handle. I was too young at the time to ask what the story was behind The Flying Dutchman. So out of curiosity later I looked it up. It turns out that *The Flying Dutchman* was a legendary, cursed ghost ship. The captain defied god that he would sail that night in a bay with rough weather even if he be damned to sail it forever.

I don't know if my dad was referring to his camper as a cursed ship that was doomed to wander without ever making it home or if he just thought that made his truck sound more badass. The truck was home for me and my brother after my dad divorced my mom. He was a former Army career man of twenty-three years. The Army drafted him out of high school for the War in the Pacific, right before he would have graduated.

Later when he did a tour of duty in Vietnam, he met and married my mother, and after that he brought my mother—and me in her belly— from Vietnam. It was the 1970s and there was an economic recession, so times were tough. My parents stayed with my grandmother after my dad was discharged, but jobs were scarce in Pennsylvania, especially for a man without a high school diploma who had spent twenty-three years in the Army. He moved the family south to Texas because of the petroleum industry.

Shortly after the move, my parents divorced; they were certainly two very different people. My brother and I spent some time in The Flying Dutchman moving from campground to campground until my father found a stable job. My mother had to be taken in by the Catholic Church— she spoke broken English and had few marketable skills.

So I grew up in the South, and I don't remember going to church much before my parents divorced, although I'd been christened as a baby. After the divorce, I went to church more than a bit too much. Eventually my father married a native Texan Southern Baptist, who thought my father's Lutheran upbringing was still too Catholic. From then on, whenever I was with my dad, it was church three times a week total, including twice on Sundays. When I was eleven, I decided to answer the altar call to accept Jesus into my heart and be baptized. My Vietnamese Catholic mother was confused by that—I had already been christened.

It wasn't the first time I learned about the differences in the two Christian sects. My mom decided it would be a good idea for us to live with

Vietnamese Catholic nuns. Living with nuns meant even more church, plus praying for an hour morning and night. I was so relieved as a child when I was allowed to do the short rosary path at the end of a long day rather than the longer path of many more Hail Marys in a language I barely understood. Falling asleep during the monotonous droning would get you whipped with this plastic stick. The stick would leave red stripes on your legs. The nuns believed they were sanctioned by god to use violence to make sure you didn't stray from god.

Their god was angry too. They believed so fervently that Catholicism was the righteous path that we were informed matter-of-factly by the nuns that my dad was going to hell for being a Baptist. My dad's church was quick to point out that Catholics were going to hell for idolatry for worshipping Mary. I didn't know what to make of either side of that argument. The question that bothered me was, why would god send that many innocent Catholics or Baptists to hell over worshipping him the wrong way?

As a Christian back then, I learned to put away things that didn't make sense to me, because maybe god knew better. This would be a really long story if I went into detail about everything that didn't make sense to me during the thirty-five years I progressed from a fundamentalist Southern Baptist and Catholic to a doubting Christian, so I'd like to narrow the focus to what I didn't understand in either religion about my identity and place as a woman.

One of the most glaring stories that stood out to me as a young girl was about the Garden of Eden. Any Catholic can tell you about original sin and the guilt associated with it. The fundamentalist analogue to original sin is the fall of man. Imagine what it is like to be groomed as a girl by both sects to believe your gender is literally responsible for suffering and death. What was the most puzzling (even if you believe that story is literally true) was, why would I be still responsible as a woman for something that happened thousands of years ago?

Even though I am biracial, most Americans take me for East Asian, but most East Asians are actually puzzled about my ethnicity. Furthermore, Americans often have negative cultural expectations that Asian women are submissive, but that had little to do with being forced into a submissive mold. The main sources of indoctrination about female submissiveness for me were religious.

The Vietnamese nuns I lived with often lectured against showing any skin or being seductive. They also would enforce unfair gender expectations that women should be skinny and it was okay for a man to be fat. Most of my Vietnamese female relatives were sizes zero to three, but when I finished growing as a teen, I was a size seven. The fat shaming was a constant part of that side of my family. There was this messed-up religious expectation that women were made for men.

The Southern Baptist approach was different, but the message was essentially the same. As far as visibly different ethnicities go in the small church I grew up in, there was me and a Mexican family. Every Mother's Day was the same sermon. Our pastor could have chosen "Honor thy Mother," one of the least misogynistic messages in the Bible. Instead he chose that day to drill into us all: "Wives, submit yourselves to your own husbands as you do to the Lord. For the husband is the head of the wife as Christ is the head of the church, his body, of which he is the Savior. Now as the church submits to Christ, so also wives should submit to their husbands in everything."

In exchange for complete submission from their wives, men were admonished to love their wives as their own body. In retrospect, I see the way the Church and the Bible portrayed a human being as an extension of another is super creepy. It wasn't until I was a young woman that I learned that no man is suitable to be a complete authority over another adult human being. That submitting your wants and needs to the authority of a man is degrading and infantilizing. More importantly, it was a disastrous recipe for abuse.

Religion can often play an undetected role in normalizing abuse. Any system where someone is given authority over another person without having earned it can be manipulated. The pastor himself abused his power in the church to have affairs with some of the church women. He also defended a forty-year-old youth leader who later married one of my younger friends. It isn't a simple matter of unearned authority, either. At the same time that fundamentalist attitudes toward women disempower them, they also deny women the agency to make decisions about their own lives and their children's lives.

Fast-forward to my thirties, and none of the scripts that I was raised with about being a godly woman were helping me to solve real-world adult problems. God couldn't fix them. He didn't really care about me, because he was never there to begin with. Around this time, I started going online to talk to other adults for the support and community I needed. I chose Christian Forums, the largest online message board for Christians. One of the subforums was the Creation/Evolution Debate forum. There I met and debated Aron Ra (before he started producing his well-known YouTube videos about the *Foundational Falsehoods of Creationism*) and other atheists on the topic of evolution.

At the time, I sided with the creationist stance. An important thing to remember is that I was raised in the same part of Texas that gave us Texas school board member Terri Leo. She is one of the infamous board members documented in the PBS documentary *Revisionaries*. The movie was named for the board members' penchant for revising science and sex education textbooks. As reported by the Texas Freedom Network, here is an example of what Leo has said about evolution: "They [scientists] don't want to talk about the science because they lose that argument continually. The science is overwhelmingly against evolution."

As a reporter for Houston Community Newspapers, I knew her well enough to call her on the phone, though we only talked once or twice that way. I am embarrassed to admit that when my brother deconverted in college, I teased him that he believed we came from monkeys. That is evidence of how poorly the state of Texas did on educating me on modern science. It also didn't help that evolution and humanism were roundly ridiculed from the pulpit.

What finally convinced me that evolution makes more sense than creationism was a debate with Aron in which he showed me pictures of a pangolin, among other things. A line that is often used to ridicule evolution says: "No matter how many times it is tried, a dog only gives birth to dogs. Kinds beget their own Kind." A pangolin shows you that morphological characteristics are not that immutable. It looks like a scaly anteater, and it does use a long tongue to lick up insects. However, it is actually more closely related to carnivores like dogs, cats, seals, and bears than to the anteaters and aardvarks. The order Carnivora (bears, dogs, cats, etc,) and the Order Pholidota are both in the Ferae clade. Its physical characteristics are adaptations to an insectivorous lifestyle similar to aardvark and anteaters. If you go back far enough, you can see that all living things are related, not created. In nature there aren't these hard-and-fast lines where a dog is unrelated to any other "kind."

Creationists don't like their children to accept evolution because they are afraid it will make them reject the Garden of Eden story and then their faith altogether. That's how it happened for me, and I feel fortunate because of it. The biblical account of creation contributes to the ignorance of millions of children when it comes to science, myself included.

I couldn't understand why the omnibenevolent deity I was raised to believe in couldn't create a more benevolent system that didn't force humans to rely on killing other organisms to live. The creationists I still talked to had so few explanations because they were limited to the Bible. Of course, their answer was the fall of man, and it was Eve's fault. That explanation hadn't held water for me when I was a child, and it wasn't going to stand up now to a woman who had just learned how ignorant she was raised to be.

By then I had finished a college degree, and for a while I taught in a Christian primary school. The science workbooks promoting Intelligent Design to children just made it more clear to me that Christian beliefs were holding on to ignorant ideas of the past. The workbook actually used a butterfly as an example that one kind doesn't change into another. It proclaimed that butterfly eggs always hatch butterflies. Of course they do; no organism ever outgrows its ancestry. For example, humans still have ancestral traits all the way to Eukarya, as all our cells still have nuclei. So we are still eukaryotes. Evolution isn't metamorphosis. It's gradual change at the population level. There is no such thing as a taxonomic "kind" either. That is a pseudoscience term. Evolution never allows for one "kind," like the dog example, to produce a different "kind." Every organism that ever evolved is just a modified version of whatever its ancestors were.

A butterfly is a species that actually undergoes a startling metamorphosis from a caterpillar to a winged butterfly in its own lifetime. Nature is not fixed and immutable, requiring a deity to tinker with it. Butterflies aren't poofed into place by a god for the purpose of being pollinators with all the biological traits designed to do that. Neither is there this cosmic creator that decided to make butterflies colorful to delight people in the Garden of Eden. Different butterfly colors are various adaptations to attract mates, scare away predators, and camouflage depending on the environment of that particular butterfly species. It angered me that creationists often are successful in inserting their agendas into textbooks, deceiving young minds into being incurious about the way nature works through evolution.

Using the simplistic explanation that god created it that way kills inquiry into finding out why nature actually is the way it is.

As a science teacher, I often get a student incurious about natural things, such as the origin of the solar system. One student actually responded to a film on that subject saying that he didn't need to know where planets came from because god created them. I was raised that way, too, so I don't judge harshly. After having my religion-based science misconceptions remediated, I felt so grateful to understand and know things I had never known before, things I could have died ignorant of.

A few years after first debating with Aron online, I met him in person since we're both Texans. He had just started his own YouTube channel and was working on the series *The Foundational Falsehoods of Creationism*. Aron and I later married, and we still are raising a blended family together. Aron and I travel far and wide because he has become a sought-after speaker at freethinker conferences. We also make a series together called *Living Science* that helps address fundamental misunderstandings of biology that prevent people from seeing why we are still monkeys, amongst other things.

In contrast to the fat-shaming and woman-oppressing religious communities of my youth, the atheist in-person community has been largely accepting of me. I have always been an outsider to both sides of my family's ethnic communities. For the most part, the in-person atheist community is accepting and progressive. Atheist communities in person tend to skew toward liberalism. I have found the most acceptance in liberal communities, where often not being white enough or Asian enough is of less importance.

When I was a freshly minted atheist, I thought atheism—through discarding regressive, religious beliefs—could change many hearts and minds for the better. But it hasn't been so simple. Since then, there has been friction over feminism and other marginalized minorities within the atheist community, which until recently has been majority white and male.

Unfortunately, even some atheist liberals have their blind spots when it comes to socializing with people of color and other marginalized communities. For some reason, Asians are one of the few ethnicities that people still feel okay making deprecating jokes about. Like the one about East Asians eating dogs. Someone even tried to explain to me that it was true, so it was okay to make jokes about it. It isn't so much the truth of the claim; it is the stereotyping of a diverse continent of people. It is being the butt of a joke that attaches disgust with being East Asian in a community of my peers.

Luckily in real-life atheist communities, most people are tolerant and accepting, and in some cases, they even take time to educate themselves on other ethnic communities. There are individuals who understand the importance of welcoming minority atheists into the fold, who have been at the forefront advocating for a more inclusive community. However, the thing that discourages me years later is that we are still having problems understanding each other. As an egregious example, Aron and I have a black friend who speaks at conferences. He has a doctoral degree and is not at all threatening, but actually warm and friendly. At one gathering, someone called security on him.

Furthermore, these fractures are deepened and multiplied online. Having been around awhile, I know that atheists are often fond of debating ideas, both in person and online. And, too, they live in a Christian atmosphere that has for years tried to censor everything deemed unwholesome, from rock music to television. I, for one, grew up being encouraged to listen to Christian music and being lectured on the evils of rock and roll.

So there is this small but vocal backlash in our community that argues against justice for marginalized people because they perceive feedback against making racist jokes, for example, as being told what they can say. The irony is that they defend bigoted speech as free speech, and most categories of it are, except where it crosses the line into abuse and harassment that targets people. Critical voices in response have free speech also. Free speech is a sword that cuts both ways.

The online anti-social justice critics in particular drown out much of the discussion in making the atheist community more welcoming to women and racial minorities. Of the most popular online atheists who are social justice critics and have a following, I don't know of any who are considered an authority in real-life conferences and gatherings.

What concerns me more, moving forward, is that minorities are leaving religion and I would hope that the atheist community would seem to be a welcoming place for them. However, the online hatred discourages them from joining the community. I have seen posts from minorities who now associate atheism with online bigotry. This small slice is so vocal, loud, and disruptive, they make us look bad to new atheists and progressive Christians.

A lot of atheists leave Christianity's regressive social attitudes, particularly its sexist attitudes, behind. But then others remind me that the term *atheist* simply means they don't believe in god, and that doesn't mean that they have to care about social justice. It doesn't prohibit them from caring about it either. For that reason I also consider myself a secular humanist, which encompasses social justice too.

I am encouraged by the efforts of some of our community's organizations, like the American Humanist Association, to be more inclusive and to address social justice head-on. The AHA has even created a position in its organization dedicated to addressing these issues. There are subcommunities popping up everywhere, too, that are more welcoming to everyone regardless of gender, race, class, disability, or sexual orientation.

For me, being an atheist has set me free from ignorance and stifling gender expectations. As a woman, others don't tell me what my place is; I make my own destiny. I wasn't created in the Garden of Eden to be a helper to a man. Learning isn't something to be feared and punished by a control-freak god who values ignorance over knowledge, the supposedly forbidden fruit. It is more difficult to make sense of the world on your own rather than to defer to a book, but it is more honest too.

There is so much more to be learned about ourselves and nature that one book couldn't contain it all. The vastness of the universe and things we don't know about it can be daunting and even scary, but it isn't an evil place where the devil roams about like a roaring lion searching to devour hapless people. It isn't a curse in which humanity is doomed to wander in ignorance like *The Flying Dutchman* because we angered an unforgiving god. The story hasn't been told beginning to end, or Genesis to Revelation. Humanity's story is still being written until some cosmic calamity, or more likely human stupidity, ends it. That is why knowing everything we can to understand the universe and ourselves is important. I don't look in expectation to heaven for a better world than this one. I believe this one is the only one we have, and we have to make it better.

NOW I LAY ME DOWN TO SLEEP

Karen L. Garst

It is not to Bibles, prayer books, catechisms, liturgies, the canon law and church creeds and organizations, that woman owes one step in her progress, for all these alike have been hostile, and still are, to her freedom and development.

—Elizabeth Cady Stanton, "Degraded Status of Woman in the Bible"

Dressed in my new flannel pajamas, I kneel next to my father in front of my bed. We have just moved upstairs from the basement of our house to the newly constructed first floor. I am five years old. The snow is coming down steadily and frosting the panes of the windows. With our hands folded, my father and I recite this prayer: "Now I lay me down to sleep, I pray the Lord my soul to keep. If I should die before I wake, I pray the Lord my soul to take." I remember this now as a comforting ritual that I looked forward to every night when my father was home.

Today, at the age of sixty-five, when my head hits the pillow, this prayer comes to me unbidden. I am nestled comfortably next to my husband in our recently remodeled home on five wooded acres. Instead of snow, a constant rain drums against the windows. But I no longer finish the prayer. Because today I am an atheist and no longer believe in a god or a soul. I also choose not to focus on death but on life and what the next day will bring.

In contrast to some others whose essays you will read in this book, I have mostly positive things to say about my upbringing. I had a great

173

childhood in a safe community, in a comfortable home, and with two loving parents. My mother fostered in me a love of learning that is the essence of who I am today. I strive to learn more about how the world works, how our bodies function, and what other cultures have to teach me. This is what drives me and always will. My father told me that I was the third child he never gave up on having. After my mother passed away, he came to live with me for the last two years of his life.

However, today, as I write this essay about my journey to atheism, I can't help but wonder, *What if?* What if my father hadn't been so religious? What if he hadn't clung so tenaciously to the tenets he had learned from his parents? What if he would have been able to attend college and explore the world of science to which he seemed to be drawn? Would more education have made him look at the world and his religion differently? He was obsessed with an explanation of the origin of Earth's continents and wrote multiple versions of his theory. But when the math did not work out, he tweaked his hypothesis, saying, "God intervened." He sent his exposé far and wide and even created a website about his theories. Needless to say, no scientific publication ever took him seriously.

What if my mother's intelligence and background in literature had led her to explore authors such as Robert Green Ingersoll, a nineteenth-century atheist, or Elizabeth Cady Stanton, a nineteenth-century atheist suffragette? Were their writings even accessible in the library at Northern State Teachers College in Aberdeen, South Dakota, where she received her bachelor's degree? What if she had been exposed to *all* the writings of Martin Luther, the founder of her faith, not just the ones the pastor picked? Would Luther's treatise on "The Jews and Their Lies" have shocked her into questioning her Lutheran faith?

Given the background of their families, the community in which they lived, and the time period, I acknowledge that it would have been hard for my parents to be atheists. But I am still puzzled that my mother never voiced any offense at the dominant role of men and the subjugation of women she encountered in the Church's teachings. She was a strong and independent woman who was highly educated. I am not angry with my parents for raising me in a religious home. But I am disappointed. It took too many years for me to let go of this supernatural deity called god. It took too many years for me to understand that ordinary men wrote the Bible. It took too many years to understand that most religions do not envision or nurture full equality for women. But it is not too late to share my journey and what I have learned with others.

I was born in 1950 in Bismarck, North Dakota. My brother, sister, and I were baptized and confirmed at Trinity Evangelical Lutheran Church. While the town included a few Jewish families that had a small synagogue and a fairly substantial Catholic community with private schools, Lutheranism was the leading denomination and most of my friends were Protestant. German and Norwegian immigrants, just like my grandparents, settled the Dakotas and brought their Lutheranism with them.

While our parents attended church service, we kids attended Sunday school in the annex attached to the church. We even garnered a pin when we had perfect attendance. Mine sits today among other childhood memorabilia in a glass cabinet in my house. The center of the pin says *Lutheran* with the letter *S* on each side of a red cross. A gold wreath surrounds the white center with bars for each year hanging below. Symbols such as these give a community a common reference point. They show belonging and identify the members. You might ask why I have kept this pin if I now reject religion. Why have I kept my Girl Scout sash, my baby ring, my mother's bottle of Chanel No. 5 cologne, my high school ring, and a number of other artifacts? Because they evoke memories of my childhood and family; they make me feel connected to my past.

In Sunday school, volunteer teachers read us stories about the Bible. While I can't remember being upset by these stories, the images they create might seem inappropriate for young children: Adam and Eve, naked but for fig leaves, getting kicked out of Eden; Yahweh destroying every human being on Earth except eight members of Noah's family through a great flood; and the fiery destruction of Sodom and Gomorrah. I can still picture Lot's wife turning into a pillar of salt in a movie of the time. The Christmas story seems a bit better until I remember that in one version, Mary and Joseph had to flee Bethlehem and escape to Egypt to avoid King Herod's massacre of every boy of two years or younger. And of course there is the ever-present symbol of Christ hung on a cross. I don't remember ever questioning the vision of a god who would kill everyone on Earth except for one family or who would send his son to be crucified. It just seemed part of the Sunday experience.

While some of my friends today can't understand how I actually believed these stories, I don't think it's very surprising—the majority of US citizens today believe in them, just as I once did. Children are programmed to believe what their parents tell them. We depend on our parents for everything. As a child, why would I doubt what my parents told me about god? Did I not learn that two and two are four and that green is a different color than red from these very same people? The public school teachers never refuted a single thing I learned at church. In high school, we studied Edith Hamilton's *Mythology*. No English teacher in Bismarck would have compared and contrasted these Greek and Roman myths to the stories in the Bible.

Of course, from time to time I did have some questions about our religion, and I always went to my dad for answers. Dad was clearly the most visibly religious in our family. Every night, he read from his worn black leather Bible. My first question to my father involved a cute Catholic boy who had walked me home one day from first grade. I was definitely infatuated with him. After dinner that evening, I pulled up a chair next to my dad and asked him if a Lutheran could marry a Catholic. Even at the age of seven, I apparently knew which church all my friends attended. I also saw marriage as one of my goals in life. Dad answered my question by saying that marriage was a difficult proposition, and it would be better to marry within the same faith. I didn't marry that first-grade boy. Ironically, I did end up marrying a man raised in the Catholic faith.

When I was ten, I donated my outgrown red winter coat to the church. The church planned to send the donations to orphans in China. This prompted another conversation with my father. In church, I learned that in order to go to heaven, I had to believe that Jesus died for my sins and to accept him as my savior. I was troubled about the orphans in China. What if they had never heard of Jesus? When I asked Dad about this, he seemed to think god had an alternate plan for them. He couldn't accept the notion that they would go to hell, and that comforted me. While hell was not portrayed with fire and brimstone in our church, it was still a frightful place. I was glad that my father thought that the little girl who would wear my red coat wouldn't go to hell.

In ninth grade, when evolution was introduced in a public junior high school science class, I was fascinated and wrote a paper about early hominids. I had no reason to question what the teacher taught us. I had never heard of anyone condemning evolution or prophesying that the world was created in 4004 BCE. I did, however, feel the need to accommodate my new knowledge of evolution with my religion. I did so by imagining that god had probably chosen to award Cro-Magnon the first soul. Or perhaps he waited until *Homo sapiens*.

My pattern of accommodating rather than questioning made sense. My church was almost my entire community: I belonged to Trinity Evangelical Lutheran Church, to Sunday school, and to Luther League, a high school youth group. In fact, I probably wouldn't have had *any* social life without the many outings to the roller-skating rink and the bowling alley with Luther League. I'm not sure my social skills would have suited an atheist or secular label. I don't remember anyone growing up who didn't belong to some church or synagogue. It was hard enough for a skinny, shy girl with homemade clothes to fit in as a conformist. As a nonconformist, nope, I wouldn't have made it.

I loved music, and Trinity Lutheran provided that benefit for me as well. From the first human being that thumped on a rock to create music, humans have been drawn to repetitive chants, songs, or stories said out loud. I have fond memories of singing in both the children's choir and the youth choir. It is perhaps what I miss most now that I don't attend church anymore. In youth choir, we wore long crimson robes with yellow sashes. At the start of the late service, we marched down the center aisle two by two singing "God's Word is our Great Heritage." Even now, when my siblings and I gather together, we have been known to sing it while marching around the living room!

While I never questioned it growing up, I reflected later on the emphasis on men in my religion. At Trinity, all the pastors were men. It was not until 1970 that one of the Lutheran synods ordained a woman. The trinity, a core Church doctrine, also consisted of three men: God the Father; the Holy Spirit (presumably male); and Jesus, the Son of God. While there are some notable women in the Bible, I don't remember them ever being emphasized. The Virgin Mary did not play the same role in Lutheranism as she did in the Catholic Church, so she was rarely talked about. And of course we all knew that Eve was the cause of original sin.

I probably didn't single out the church's male dominance because it was not at all unique in Bismarck. The police officer who came regularly to our grade school was a man. The governor, whose mansion was built across from our house in the 1950s, was a man. The superintendent of Public Instruction was also male. The school principals were all men.

Women were teachers (like my mother), nurses, secretaries, or stay-at-home moms.

As a teacher, my mother always supported and assisted in our education. Yet there was an important gap in my learning that was no doubt influenced by religion. Neither of my parents ever talked to me about sex. After I expressed my total befuddlement regarding *The Story of Menstruation*, a 1946 film sponsored by Kotex that was shown to girls in fifth grade, my mother explained the workings of menstruation. She did this by drawing the female anatomy. No later discussion included how that body worked with the male one. I even remember not getting an answer when I was younger and asked at the zoo, "Mommy, Mommy, why are the llamas riding piggyback?"

When I was in ninth grade, my friend's mother gave her a book about sex. At her house one day, she showed it to me and asked me if I knew what the word *masturbation* meant. Of course I didn't. So we looked it up in the dictionary: the obtuse definition did not enlighten us at all. I had to surreptitiously read one of my older sister's books, *79 Park Avenue* by Harold Robbins, to figure out what sex was all about. In this novel, a storeowner rapes a young girl. I don't think anyone would think this was a healthy way for a child to learn about sex or relationships. Given the early Christian Church's condemnation of sexual desire, it was something my mother's parents probably had never discussed with her either. She told me once that both my father and she were virgins when they married. This lack of sex education did not help me later in my relations with men. Even though I came of age in the early 1970s—the era of free love—I always felt guilty about having sex before marriage. Of course, that didn't stop me.

After high school, my first step in learning more about the origins of my Lutheran faith occurred in my Religion 101 class at Concordia College in Moorhead, Minnesota. My professor introduced us to four different authors of the first five books of the Bible. The first two were named after the different words each author used for god: J for Yahweh and E for Elohim. The other two were D for the Deuteronomist, and P for Priestly, indicating the priests of the temple who edited and rewrote the works of the earlier authors most likely during the exile in Babylon. Texts from these different authors are interwoven throughout as if each editor added bits but left the previous stories intact. Starting with oral traditions, these books were written and edited over a period of several hundred years. The professor also pointed out the two incompatible versions of the creation story in the first two chapters of Genesis: in one, Eve and Adam were created at the same time, and in the other, Eve is created after Adam from his rib. It started to occur to me that this could simply have been a book of stories written by ordinary men not inspired by a supernatural deity. The pastors at Trinity Evangelical Lutheran Church must have learned about this scholarly work in seminary. But they, like most pastors today, didn't venture into discussions that might cause any congregant to question the validity of the writings of the Bible. Just like feeding formula to a baby, the Lutheran Church served congregants simple stories without contradictions and labeled them as divine truth.

In classes at Concordia, I never felt demeaned because I was a woman. Academically, I had always felt an equal to any man. There were, however, some social prohibitions that applied only to women: women were not allowed to smoke on campus (men could) and women had curfews if they lived in a dorm (men did not). Women had to live in someone's home, and men could live in apartments . . . with dishwashers. In addition, Concordia did not permit dances on campus, a prohibition that applied to men and women equally. We just went next door to Moorhead State (today called Minnesota State University Moorhead) to dances on the weekend. I never learned what dancing had to do with religion, especially Lutheranism, and why it was prohibited.

In a Catholicism religion class in my junior year, my professor was Father Emeric Lawrence, OSB. I remember him putting his name on the blackboard and advising us not to get the order of the three letters following his name wrong! My father was a bit taken aback that I was taking a course in Catholicism, but I really enjoyed the professor and what I learned. Each student had access to a Catholic newspaper. Father Lawrence asked us to keep a journal with our reactions to one article each week. The professor then made comments on our entries. It is one of the few items I have kept from that time. My first entry states the following:

> I believe in the Triune God and that Christ died for my sins, but the church has never really reached me. I go and especially adore the liturgy and hymns. Maybe it's the size of my home church that gives me this feeling of impersonality. Although I know that such things are necessary, the financial complex has always left me cold.

Half the service consists of money business. Last year, the parish built a brand new church, which my parents and many others believed was totally unnecessary.

While I was still a believer, I was starting to question the Church and its practices.

Another incident in college brought back the marginalization of women and their roles in society that I had witnessed growing up. I applied for a scholarship to attend Dartmouth College for graduate work. One of the interviewers, the only woman, asked why I should be given the scholarship. "All you will do is get married and have children," she added. I didn't receive the scholarship. I was angry that she had so easily dismissed me, but it did not stop me. I went on and applied to other schools and chose the University of Wisconsin–Madison, where I obtained a master's and a doctorate. I have had a successful career in several widely divergent domains. But who knows what I might have become if I had had more models of professional women? *Father Knows Best* was more than just a television show I watched. It was the message I encountered at home, at school, and at church.

While living in Madison, I rarely attended church. For me, church attendance had always been about family and friends. I found it difficult to go alone to a strange church where I knew no one. My fellow teaching assistants were a diverse lot: many of my friends in this group were Jewish or of some Christian denomination other than Lutheran. One of my Jewish friends told me that he was a secular Jew and explained what that meant. He was probably the first person I had ever met who said he didn't believe in god. During my years in Madison, I didn't pay much attention to religion. I became active in a labor union, taught French, and worked on my degrees. Religion didn't seem to matter very much to me.

In 1980, when I moved to Portland, Oregon, my lack of church attendance continued. Most of the friends I met and formed a community with were active in unions or politics. I also had friends who regularly went to local theater productions. This seemed to fulfill in me the need for community and group affiliation. After purchasing my first house, I did finally join a Lutheran church in Northeast Portland in the mid-1980s. Augustana Lutheran Church, with its aging white congregation, stood in contrast to the many African American families who lived in the area.

Even though my husband and I were married in Augustana and baptized our son there, we were never gung ho congregants.

We moved to the suburbs of Portland in the late 1980s. While talking with a friend, I expressed my disappointment with the new Lutheran church we'd joined. In this church a woman could not be a pastor or serve on the church council. At this time in my life, this was a deal breaker. My friend recommended a New Thought congregation at the nearby Living Enrichment Center. This very liberal church had a membership of several thousand. We could choose lots of activities in addition to Sunday services. Mary Manin Morrissey, the pastor, delivered messages that were very light on religion. Attending a service once with our family, my Catholic mother-in-law summed it up pretty well when she commented, "That was a good speech, but I wouldn't call it a sermon." It was more like listening to Stephen Covey's *The 7 Habits of Highly Effective People*. I liked it that way: little or no doctrine, a diversity of people, and a mild version of Sunday school for our son, who was born in 1990.

Unfortunately, the minister and her husband, the CEO, started to solicit large loans from the congregants. I got involved and spoke to the church council, which was pretty uninvolved with the church's finances. I then confronted the minister herself. I told her that while she was one of the best speakers I had ever heard, she was a con. She was taking money from people when she knew it was very unlikely the church could ever repay them. I informed her that if she would not come clean with the congregation, I would expose what was happening in the media. She didn't and I did. I worked with Jeff Manning, an investigative reporter at the Portland daily *The Oregonian*, and gave him all the information I had. While the state had already begun to investigate the church for securities fraud, the well-researched article by Manning helped turn the tide. Mary's husband took the fall and was sentenced to three years in federal prison. Mary Morrissey paid back little of the money loaned by congregants and is now preaching in California. This was my last effort to be part of a religious community. When LEC closed, my husband and I didn't bother looking for another church. We were done with organized religion.

During the time I attended LEC, however, I came across the Jesus Seminar. In April 8, 1996, *Time* featured this group of scholars with the cover page stating in bold letters "The Search for Jesus." I began to read the books written by members of the seminar and even attended a conference held in Oregon featuring John Dominic Crossan and Marcus Borg, two of its members. I became fascinated with this in-depth look at the New Testament.

Learning about the history behind the New Testament, however, was very different from learning about the history of the Old Testament, as I had done in my first college religion class at Concordia. I had assumed that the disciples wrote the gospels shortly after Jesus's crucifixion, but I learned that Paul wrote his letters around the 50s CE—in other words, about twenty years after the time when Jesus was allegedly crucified. Mark, the earliest gospel written, dates from the time of the destruction of the temple in Jerusalem by the Romans in 70 CE. The gospels of Matthew and Luke date ten years and twenty years later. The gospel of John dates from the end of the first century. I could no longer see these writings as historically accurate portrayals of the life of Jesus.

I also learned from the Jesus Seminar writers that the gospels differ greatly in what they say about Jesus. The letters of Paul state that Jesus was born of a woman, not mentioning she was a virgin. In Mark, Mary had already given birth to four other sons and two daughters before Jesus was born, and there is no reference at all to Bethlehem. Matthew and Luke contain the first legend of the virgin birth.

I also read books that explored the similarities between Christianity and other religions. The prevalence of many gods in other religions who purportedly died and rose from the dead in three days and the multiplicity of deities born of virgins had a strong impact on me. No longer were the stories of Jesus's birth, death, and resurrection something special and unique to Christianity. They appeared to be common themes used throughout the Greco-Roman world. Slowly I came to the belief that, like the book on Greek and Roman myths I had read in high school, the Bible stories were just not true.

The last belief that I held on to, the resurrection of Jesus Christ, finally fell away when I read Bishop John Shelby Spong's *Resurrection: Myth or Reality?* He portrays the weeks leading up to the crucifixion of Jesus as a very troubling time for the disciples. He believes that they probably fled Jerusalem to avoid being arrested themselves, traveled back to the Sea of Galilee, and took up their fishing nets. At a later time, they realized that even though Jesus was dead and the end times had not come, the message he had been preaching was still good news. Spong proposed that these same disciples returned to Jerusalem to preach this gospel. This made sense to me. There was not a supernatural resurrection, but there was something that moved the disciples to continue the teachings they had learned. I could accept this type of explanation. After letting go of the resurrection, I started to classify myself as an atheist. I didn't feel a huge loss because this had been a gradual process for me over twenty years.

After coming to the conclusion that I was an atheist, I just went on with my life. My husband and I raised our son in a secular home. I tried to teach him the Bible stories so that he would understand all the references used throughout literature. But I couldn't just read him the story of Adam and Eve without pointing out how this story, like many others, was used to reinforce a man's view of the world. The creation story required a current astronomy lesson, and the list continued. Fortunately, he received a degree in engineering, not in English literature. In 2008, I retired to enjoy our gardens, explore my genealogy, and read mystery novels.

Rituals, religious and otherwise, are an essential part of who humans are as sentient beings. Whether it is folding the flag in a special way over the casket of a fallen warrior, attending a funeral when a loved one dies, or something quite mundane like wearing the team colors to a basketball game, rituals help us deal with events in our lives. But today my rituals have nothing to do with religion. I joined the local chapter of the Daughters of the American Revolution after finding an American Patriot in my lineage and became the chapter's regent. Along with my husband, I am active in supporting environmental protections for our local watershed. I belong to two book clubs that meet monthly where we read current nonfiction. I spend hours listening to audiobooks while I remove every weed from our lawns and flowerbeds. At night, I always take up a needlework project as my husband and I watch television. These rituals provide meaning and a rhythm to my life.

Many Christian apologists insist that a personal god is necessary for a moral system. I disagree. I do quite well without god. For me, a moral system starts with family kinship. I do not believe that a list of ten commandments will work. I know that if I had to hurt someone to protect my son, I would. I would also sacrifice myself for him. From there, the circle expands. Humans have lived together with others in communities for over twenty-five thousand years. I don't need the promise of an afterlife to live fully in this one. I wake up each morning excited about what the day will bring. I enjoy my life. I support women's rights. I participate in saving our environment. I contribute to charities. My husband and I travel frequently, forming new experiences and meeting people who are different from us. I don't need a god to tell me to love my husband and my family. I don't need a god to tell me to be kind to others. I don't need a god to be joyful.

I hope that my story and those of others in this book who have let go of a belief in a supernatural deity will show the path for others who are courageous enough to say: "I'm done. I am better than this. I can live a fully useful, moral, and productive life without religion." I invite you to join us.

UNSPOKEN BETRAYAL

Michelle DeBord

There is yet another consideration which is fatal to the Christian religion,
and that is the persecuting spirit. It calls in the aid of Ecclesiastical
and civil laws, and the iron hand of custom to condemn, and if possible to
punish those who may express different opinions to its own . . .
Perish the cause which has no more rational argument in its favour than
that which the stake or prison can supply.

—Emma Martin, *A Few Reasons for Renouncing Christianity*
and Professing and Disseminating Infidel Opinions

I could hear the tightly packed snow crunching under the wheels of the
new Chrysler as we rode down the freeway. It was as if my soul was being
crunched under those wheels. The day was dark gray and dreary outside. I
thought it was fitting for how I felt. As I peered out the window, it looked
like an endless sea of dirty-white snow stretching over the horizon, the
dark-gray skies colliding with it in the far distance. I knew the sun had to
be up there somewhere, but it was obscured from my eyes. I imagined it
was up there hiding behind the suffocating darkness all around it. It was
appropriate weather to say goodbye to my sister, Shannon.

There were only a few other cars on the freeway. Maybe it was because
everyone was part of the betrayal we were somehow lost in, an unspoken
sin that was about to rip our family apart. I am sure it was because of the
weather conditions, but somehow it fit the new feeling of loneliness I was

smothered in. I felt that even if I had screamed at the top of my lungs for help, no one would have heard me. The worst part was that the two human beings I trusted the most sat in the front seat just an arm's length away.

I watched my grandmother as she drove, her hair graying and short. I couldn't remember her hairstyle ever changing since my first memory of her as a small child. That said a lot, considering I was now eleven years old. Her earrings appeared to be homemade beadwork, and I thought I remembered them as a gift she'd received from my sister the year before. She had on her famous red poinsettia sweatshirt that she wore far too long past the Christmas season. Everything about her appearance today would normally have triggered my feelings of love and admiration for her. Not today. Today she was gripping her fingers tightly on the steering wheel. Today she was my enemy.

My mother sat next to her in the passenger seat, her black, curly locks bouncing in sync with the car. I could only see a small part of the right side of her tear-stained face. She appeared to be staring out her window into an abyss. For the first time in my life, I saw her as a coward—no longer my heroine. She was no longer the sweet, safe, loving respite I depended on. She was just a shell of a human being. A puppet.

Next to me sat my thirteen-year-old idol and best friend, the only human on the face of the earth who understood and loved every part of who I was: my sister. I knew every detail of her appearance without having to look at her. She was wearing her favorite jeans, the stonewashed ones with the zippers and bows on the bottom of each leg. Her bright white socks were carefully scrunched up over the seams of her pants. She had on her shiny brown penny loafers, the ones I always borrowed to wear with my slacks. Her sweater, a gift from a leader in the church, was fuzzy gray with flowers bright in color. The turtleneck hugging her long, thin neck reached up past her light-brown bobbed hairstyle. She had ratted her bangs, like she did every morning, about three inches high off her head. Somehow she lucked out with an angelic face and our dad's perfect nose. We shared the same brown eyes. Simply put, there sat an adoring package of love. A "handle with care" package. Something delicate and fragile.

I couldn't look over at her that day. Not this dreadful day. I knew if I did, everything that was exploding just under the surface would come bursting out. I would be a screaming, sobbing mess. I feared one of those sobs that won't stop, the kind that takes your breath away and leaves you whimpering like a baby. Instead I was sitting there, staring at my two new enemies. I was silently begging them to say something. Anything! I hoped for heaven's sakes they would come to their senses and turn the car around!

The tension in the car that horrible day was as thick as the gray fog outside. It felt as dark as a night with no moon. No one would speak of the purpose of this drive, but, oh, I wanted to. I wanted to shout that she wasn't a bad child. That she was just acting like the teenager she was. Thirteen, she was only thirteen. I wanted to tell them that they needed to love her unconditionally. I wanted to scream horrible names at them, tell them that they were traitors and liars. Who cared if she'd had sex? Who cared if it was with our bishop's son? Why couldn't his parents send *him* away? Why was Grandma's "good standing" more important than her love for my sister? Why wasn't our mom fighting for her daughter? (Due to insurance issues, my mom had signed custody to my grandmother for what was supposed to be a year. But Grandma wouldn't sign it back. My grandma then used it to hurt and control my mom.) I kept thinking, *Yell, Mama, yell! Fight, please fight! Custody is just a piece of paper. Grandma has no right. God made you her Mama.*

As we arrived at the airport, I wasn't able to force them to hear my silent pleas for help. Everyone was already exiting the car, and it was too late. The trunk opened, and I could hear my grandma's stern voice scolding my sister, telling her that she needed to stop crying and hurry up. I thought maybe if I didn't get out of the car, then they wouldn't go inside. Maybe that would be the only way I could save my sister from being forced onto the plane. That way she wouldn't be abandoning her little sister. I wouldn't have to lose her for life.

I was ordered out of the car. We waited silently inside the airport for Shannon's turn to board the plane. I was tear soaked, the neck of my shirt wet and clinging to my skin. Still I could not make eye contact with my sister. I was too busy soaking in her smell, mannerisms, and love. The loud voice on the intercom interrupted my thoughts. It was now time for her to board the plane. At that moment, my heart took a picture. There she stood, crying out her last plea to not have to go. There stood the other half of my soul. She looked so helpless, and I knew I was defeated as well.

Our hug goodbye ended my ability to hold in my sorrow. We both were crying and pronouncing our love for each other through sobs. She boarded the plane. I could not watch her leave. When I heard the roaring engines of the plane as it prepared to go down the runway, I imagined my heart being anchored to the wheels. As it sped down the concrete to lift off, it ripped my heart right out of my chest and changed my life forever.

I could not decipher if the chill I felt in the car on the way home was from the cold weather outside or the dark, cold energies between the three of us. There were two things I knew for sure: not one word was spoken the entire ride home, and I now knew the feeling of the word *hate*. It was not my grandma I hated, although I was sure my love clouded my discernment on that—it was the Church I hated. I knew I never wanted to go back, to watch the bishop stand up in front of the ward and tell us that he believed in Jesus Christ. I never wanted to watch his fake reverence or hear his testimony of forgiveness, and I never wanted to stand by and keep his secrets.

I sat back and imagined myself walking up to the podium, on Sacrament Sunday, acting as innocent and reverent as the bishop acts every Sunday. But when I got up there to bear my testimony, I would start screaming out the betrayal and secrets that destroyed my family and not the bishop's. I would scream as fast and as loud as I could before the elders would come and drag me off the podium. Everyone would hate me, but I did not care. I would do it for my sister! Only I knew I would never really do this—I could not hurt my family as they had hurt me.

The car was slowing, and I looked out the fogged-up windows. We were back in our hometown. Had it always been so dreary? Old, broken-down buildings and desolate sidewalks and streets. We slid into our driveway, and I bolted from the car. There was no need to thank my grandma for the ride home, and I wasn't going to hug her goodbye. I could not run for the front door. I couldn't bear to walk past Shannon's room to get to mine. There would be no music coming from her boombox and no magical sound of her laughter caused by the teenage conversation she would be having on her phone. I couldn't face the aftermath of today.

I ran past the houses lining our street. I ran past the school and past the little mini-mart we used to go to get our soda on Friday nights. I ran past the gully where all the neighborhood kids were sledding, where Shannon and I would be sledding if she weren't miles and miles away from me already. I started to feel panic. I wondered where I could go to get out of my head, to make the pain stop. Is there anywhere I could go that wouldn't remind me of her? I fell to the snow and tried to bury myself in it; maybe it would be cold enough that it would numb my heart.

My mind kept racing to questions of fear—Is she scared? Is she there yet? Will they be a nice family? Who will she talk to at night? Who will walk to school with her? Who will clip her favorite red earrings for her? Will she forget about me?

Life turned out to be lonely without her. Shannon was allowed to call home once a week, and I was surprised and devastated to hear her happy tone and good reports on school and home life at my aunt and uncle's house. Were these guys not strangers and enemies in all of this? After all, we had never met them before Shannon was put on the plane to go live with them, yet they were all she talked about now. She bragged about her shopping trips and about the upper-class school she was attending in Southern California. She talked with a bit of a Valley accent already and told me about trying out for and making the cheerleading squad! There was no despair in her voice to match the despair I was feeling in my heart. She had become another soul who betrayed me. She was happy without me, and I was left all alone in my heartache, hatred, and grief.

The one thing she always wanted to talk about that bothered me the most was the Young Women's activities she was involved in with the church there. How dare she! Did they brainwash her or use some scientific invention to erase what the Church had done to us? I certainly hadn't forgotten that the Church was the reason I didn't have her anymore. I certainly remembered that it was because of the Church that I cried myself to sleep on the couch at night and hadn't slept in my own bed in months. I knew it was the reason I couldn't bear to walk by her bedroom. I certainly remembered it was because of the Church that my parents weren't laughing or talking much anymore. I didn't even get out of the car when my parents forced me to leave for church with them every Sunday. I hated Young Women's activities without her, so I didn't go—but here she was telling me how much she loved it!

Our phone calls became shorter and less frequent. I became more withdrawn in life while Shannon excelled. I didn't know her anymore, and I realized I was grieving her. The sister I knew and adored no longer existed. What my sister had become was a mirror image of all I despised in the women and girls in our ward.

Every summer I would board the plane begrudgingly with a small glimmer of hope to go spend a month with Shannon at my aunt and uncle's house. Sure enough, when I got there I would run to hug her, hopeful to find that she was still my precious best friend, only to find that she was a stranger now.

Four years passed before we got the phone call that substantiated my rebellion against the Gospel of Jesus Christ of Latter Day Saints. My sister was being put on the plane that night and being sent home. She had done the unspeakable, had sex with her boyfriend of two years. Again, she was the whore of the family in the eyes of my aunt, uncle, and grandparents. According to them, there was no hope for her. She was damaged goods. Her punishment was that she would be yet again ripped away from all that she loved. She was a seventeen-year-old girl who had only known superficial love her whole life from everyone except for me. A handle-with-care package would soon arrive back home with the belief that she was beyond repair. With the self-esteem of a whore. With the belief that she would never have eternal salvation in the Celestial Kingdom with the rest of the family and that no one would want to marry her because she was defective. With the belief that it was too late to be loved and treated well with money and praise because she had not conformed as their puppet.

I have never stepped foot in the door of the Mormon church again. I will not be part of something so evil and superficial. I will never forget the heartache the doctrine caused in my family or the huge rift it created between all the people I loved. I am haunted by the holidays my family celebrated separately because of my new views on life and religion. I will forever be angry about the years it took from my sister and the damage it imprinted in her soul. After all, Shannon didn't know who she was or how to act—all she knew was she was supposed to be the marionette, but she could only do that for so long. Freedom from the Church meant a lost soul for her. She spiraled into all they had proclaimed she would be, and I followed her.

This went on for several years until we both gained wisdom from life and rid ourselves of all that created dark, heavy energies in us. We did not come to this freedom together or at the same time, but what is real today is that Shannon and I are two amazing women who have found love, desire, passion, and a spirituality that has given us true purpose. Our lives are governed by what we put in them. The beauty of the elements and energies around us create our sanctuary. Life isn't about an unforgiving gospel of man-made rules and fantasies of power in a make-believe kingdom. Life is about love . . .

CRITICAL BELIEVER

Jackie Burgett

We live in a fantasy world, a world of illusion.
The great task in life is to find reality.

—Iris Murdoch

Mysteries of the Unknown

I stood in front of my bookshelf, confused about where to look next. "There's got to be some answers here somewhere," I mumbled to myself. I grabbed a slim, faux-leather book from a series called Mysteries of the Unknown, hoping to land upon some wisdom from the Time-Life series.

The book that preoccupied my thoughts and held my hopes for truth was called *Hauntings*. Since the age of twelve or so, my raison d'être was to have a paranormal experience. I mostly focused on ghosts and spirits and the great poltergeist that I read about in the Time-Life series. It didn't end there, though. Magic of all kinds was part of this territory. I was going to find out what was real if it was the last thing I did.

But where to start? What should I read when so many books said so many contradictory things? It became easier to believe in it all: hauntings, past lives, near-death experiences, and God (but not one particular religion).

I lived in a world awash with information, and in 2002 I had no idea how much that would grow. Although I used the Internet, Google hadn't penetrated our pockets yet and was not the answer machine it has become today. Google would give you millions of answers to your one question.

And I thought the contradictions on my bookshelf were bad: they were nothing compared to Google. The constitution of true knowledge became something I was interested in long before I set foot in a university where ideas where discussed and refined. But for now, as I looked at the cover with a translucent figure pressing a hand to a window in a melancholy fashion, I didn't know how to eliminate any notions from my ever-growing list of beliefs. At this moment in my room, alone with books of the paranormal, I recalled one of the many times I had wrangled my friends into attempting to contact the dead.

Before my thirteenth birthday, I got all my friends together for an overnight sleepover. My parents had a big green-and-white barn out back that had been built in the mid-thirties. The paint was chipped badly enough that you could see the wood beneath. My friends and I walked up the stairs to the second story—the old hayloft. One of them turned to me and said, "So what are we going to do tonight?" I smiled and replied, "See if my barn is haunted."

She was a Christian with a rosy face, a big smile, and expressive eyes. She looked as if I had just said we were going to sacrifice a goat. I had gone with her to church sometimes. Her parents where very religious but seemed to move around denominations, so getting invited to her church events held interesting and vastly different experiences. I wish I remembered what all of them were, but I remember watching people talk in tongues, their mouths moving in what seemed like babbling, and falling on the floor writhing with the "spirit." Seeing full-grown adults in such unfettered flaying was very humorous to my mind. Where else can you go where adults sound like drunken toddlers? Once at a bible camp, I caught dust from the angels. I like to think of it now as a pre-glittered floor so that when you sat on it and inevitably put your hands down, your hands became sparkly—a sure sign that the angels were watching over us.

In preparation for the séance, I had gathered every candle I could find in the house and the cool new multicolored light-up disco ball I had bought at Spencer Gifts. I centered the lights in the middle of the plywood floor, and we all gathered in a circle. We were not ones to hold hands, especially not at the willful and defiant age of thirteen, so we just sat in a circle around the points of light and multicolored dots that flew past our heads. I spoke first. I loved this part. The apprehension of what the night might bring, the slight fear of speaking, and the ease in which the rest of the words came in hearing my own voice amidst the quiet. Later in life I loved the theater and wanted to be an actress. Maybe it all started here.

"My name is Jackie. These are my friends. If you are here, please give us a sign," I said, or some form of that, in the best commanding yet nonthreatening voice I could muster. Silence echoed back, and a giggle arose from within our circle.

"Shhh," I said as I shut my eyes, hoping this would lead to better concentration and more vibes that would pique the interest of the departed.

Weeks before her death, my grandmother had told us that she saw two figures standing beside the barn on her last visit to the farm. She was not scared of them; she thought of them as welcoming her to the other side. Some of her relatives had seen them, too, close to their time of passing. They described them as figures dressed in one color: white or black. They didn't speak; they were just there, waiting.

I pictured what I thought they looked like from her description. I was not sure if I believed my grandmother, but I believed that she believed. I wanted to see some sort of proof and not just anecdotes from others. I wanted it so badly that I thought my only hope was that some ghosts would take pity on me and finally show themselves. If I thought about it enough, maybe they would sense it.

Silence. No ghost, no knock, nothing. After a while we all broke out into talking about the 'N Sync concert that was coming up or the boys we thought were cute. When I blew out the candles, I felt defeated and rejected even though I knew ghosts might not exist. But I was not ready to give up. I'd seen weird things happen: Ouija pointers that moved, creepy sounds in graveyards where I'd led another séance. But of course someone else could have moved the Ouija pointer, and graveyards are by themselves a little creepy. These experiences that so many people hold up as a reason to believe are not definitive. Not proof. Not undeniably otherworldly. However, I still had hope.

Pascal's Wager

I packed up the last of my belongings, and we headed for my parents' house in the country from the small coastal town where we had been living for the past year. My six-month-old son and I. I was twenty. My husband and I had split up after less than a year. There were more than irreconcilable differences; there was a cavern of mistaken personalities.

I wondered how I'd gotten there: How I could have let this happen? Why did I still try even though I knew it would never work? Because I'd felt that a good home needed two parents, even if one parent wasn't ideal. I looked in the rearview at my innocent son's face. I was going to give him a good home, alone.

I had tried my hand at college right out of high school. But I wasn't ready for college then. I was tired of books and papers and the endless amount of memorization, only to forget the memorized details a week later. I just wanted to stop for one minute and be happy. So I dropped out. Leaving school was not the fairy tale of freedom I had been looking for. Now, as I looked at Dean's smile in the mirror, I knew it was time to go home and back to school.

I got to my parents' house late that night. The next day there was a shiny new catalog of class choices I could take from the local community college. Flipping through, I saw health professions, paralegal classes, and a host of other degrees and programs. I wanted something different. I was a new person now, and I wanted my education to reflect that fact.

Closing my eyes, I flipped through the pages blindly. I landed on the page with a welding technology degree. It had everything I wanted. It was different, bold, quick, and lucrative—especially for women. I signed up and thought, *Here we go*.

I loved welding. I hated welding. I wanted to quit and never stop simultaneously. The heat was grueling. The requirements of the welding technology degree dictated that I take a few classes outside my major. So after my morning welding class, covered in slag dust (pieces of metal like flakes of stone), I had to rejoin the academics. Because the one class I had received a good grade in during my one year in college was ethics, I decided to try philosophy of religion.

I sat in the class nodding my head as the professor quoted Pascal: "Belief is a wise wager. Granted that faith cannot be proved, what harm will come to you if you gamble on its truth and it proves false? If you gain, you gain all; if you lose, you lose nothing. Wager, then, without hesitation, that He exists."

A few days earlier, I had raised my hand and said something similar in a moment of passion-driven debate, somewhat less coherently, of course. I did not know the details of God or the universe, but to believe seemed better than to not believe. It seemed like a simple cost-benefit analysis.

Just as I had been fascinated but a little skeptical about the paranormal in my youth, I still couldn't completely believe in any specific religious doctrine. I had a feeling that someone knew what was going on in every point in the vast cosmos, and it certainly wasn't me. Why not believe in a God-like being? It certainly seems like the outcome is better with one, as Pascal thought.

"Although this argument makes intuitive sense, it is not actually evidence for God," my professor said, scribbling names and dates on the blackboard.

What? Of course it is. I felt deflated, like I had been starting to get it and then lost it. Of course the professor talked in a neutral educational manner, explaining the arguments against Pascal's Wager. But to me it felt oddly attacking. I had to shed the idea that belief is a matter of convenience, to embrace that it could be based on a better foundation than my preferable outcome. Along with this, I tackled my irrational conclusion that if I didn't discount any possibilities, I could never be wrong.

I was taking the class with a friend from the welding class. A few weeks in, we walked down the breezeway to the welding shop carrying flashcards about Descartes, Aristotle, and Saint Thomas Aquinas. "So how do you like the class?" I ventured. She was a lovely woman: the most motherly of our small band of welders in the early seven o'clock in the morning class. I was interested to see what she was going to say.

"It's okay. I just wish he would tell us the answers. I feel like I know less coming out of the class than when I went in," she said.

"Yeah, I know what you mean. But I think that's the exciting part."

"I like science and math better. Questions have answers—you don't just win by saying something with more flowery words."

Days later I recalled that exchange as I became more and more disillusioned with welding, mostly because I had been getting more and more invested in philosophy. I liked welding, but when I thought about pursuing it as a career, something was missing. Philosophy felt like hugging an old friend that you hadn't seen for a long time. You have both changed but you still have some history in common. I felt like all the searching for answers I'd done when I was younger and the thoughts I'd explored bumped up against philosophical lines. I just hadn't been aware of it. Now I could build on the thoughts of others that had come before me and change many of my preconceptions.

When my professor told us that Pascal's Wager was not evidence for God, I had to change my conception of the word *evidence*. Previously, I thought that evidence meant connecting dots, like in a detective novel. One continuous straight line. Now I saw evidence as just part of a vast picture holding up a proposition. This deeper knowledge felt exciting. I wondered: Why did I enjoy what my friend had not? Was this because of personal preference, or did it speak to a bigger piece of myself?

The Paranormal Profile

One more philosophy class. I felt I was getting good at it now. Why stop? I still needed more credit for my welding major, so it wasn't like the classes were going to waste. I was excited for the next one. Critical Thinking: Science and the Occult. Perfect!

Given all the time I had spent as an adolescent thinking about the paranormal, I would finally get some answers, some insight into the world of the strange and weird.

As I was walking to the classroom, a woman nearly cut me off with her backpack jangling with key chains. She must've had fifteen weirdly shaped pieces of metal and plastic dangling and clanging to announce her every move. I made a right and another left until I realized we were going to the same place. We both got to the classroom and sat a row away from each other. She introduced herself as Becky.

"Isn't this an interesting topic for a class?" she asked.

"Yeah. I used to be really into ghosts and the supernatural when I was younger. Haven't thought as much about it the last few years, but I'm really curious about what the class is going to be like," I said, trying to gauge her reaction.

"Oh no, I'm still into it!" she said, her enthusiasm nearly bouncing out of her chair along with her. "I have my own personal psychic. Well, she's not just mine, but I have one I go to. And she is fantastic! She is always right on the money. It's amazing how some people can tap into the universe like that, isn't it?" She looked at me with such honesty; I couldn't help but agree.

"Yep," I said as I turned around in my seat and fiddled with my bag.

Although I wasn't wholly opposed to the idea of a very select few people being clairvoyant, psychics were not something I could put any faith in. It wasn't because I thought it was impossible—I just thought that people will do anything to make a quick buck, and the odds that the specific psychic you picked was one of the honest ones that actually had abilities seemed a bit farfetched. But you never know, right? *Gotta keep an open mind*, I thought.

More students started to trickle in. I recognized one or two from other classes even though I couldn't remember their names. We mumbled hi to each other with looks of vague recognition.

The teacher walked in. She was a blonde woman wearing a floral-print dress—quite different from the bow tie–wearing, bearded man who'd taught my last two classes. I sat up in my seat, ready to hear all the secrets she would reveal that I had never been able to understand in my parents' barn or nearby cemeteries.

I wish I could say that I am exaggerating my eagerness for this class. But I can't. The last two philosophy classes had changed my thinking so much that I really thought this class would reveal some momentous truth or ideas that would change my life forever. And it did, just not in the way I anticipated as I sat in the fluorescent-lit classroom on that first sunny afternoon.

The teacher's name was Jenny. She stood up at the head of the classroom and wrote it and her contact information on the dry-erase board.

"The first thing I want to say is a bit of a disclaimer," she said, walking as she talked, passing the dry-erase marker back and forth between her hands.

"If you think this class is going to be a history of the occult or in any way confirm your positive beliefs about the supernatural, you are wrong." Half the class laughed. The woman with the key chains did not. Nervously I let out one "ha."

"This is a critical-thinking class about the occult. It might help shape the way you think about it by the end of the term, or it may not. Whatever your beliefs are about these subjects, that's okay, but this class is not going to be just a story about occult phenomena." She went on lecturing, but I was just thinking, *Dammit!* She described exactly what my first thoughts about the subject of this class had been and smashed them. Becky shot me a glance, and I could tell she was disappointed too.

The first day was filled with what all classes focus on their first day: the syllabus, homework assignments, and questions—housekeeping, basically. We also had one test. Well, not a test, per se, but a profile—a paranormal profile. Our book, *How to Think about Weird Things* by Theodore Schick, Jr.

and Lewis Vaughn, listed fifteen beliefs in the first chapter. You had to rate the beliefs on a scale of one to five, one being that you were sure it was false and five being that you were sure it was true. Three was "neither probable nor improbable." Every single one of my answers was a three. I lived in the in-between. I could not rule any of them out, not even "People have been possessed by demons." Some of the other statements were: "People can read other people's minds," "People can move external objects solely with the power of their minds," and my favorite, "People can talk to the spirits of the dead." Three more threes.

The chapters in this book introduced me to topics I was interested in but had no vocabulary from science, critical thinking, or skepticism with which to evaluate. I began to learn a new way of thinking: the zeitgeist of belief for the sake of believing transformed, for me, into the quote popularized by Carl Sagan, "Extraordinary claims require extraordinary evidence."

It happened slowly at first, but I finally realized that there were templates for thinking; I didn't have to reinvent the wheel each time a new question came along. And I learned that answers could be cumulative.

The chapter on logical fallacies became a road map to gauge whether or not a claim was convincing for its own sake. By evaluating arguments, I could land upon a way to judge a statement without just appealing to what sounds good. The number one reason I held on to the possibility of so many supernatural beliefs was this: if so many people believed something was true or had an experience with the supernatural, there had to be some merit to that, right?

In *How to Think about Weird Things*, I read an analogy that put this argument into particularly poignant language. The fallacy was called "appeal to the masses," and the explanation in the book said: "Mothers understand that this premise is a fallacy. 'But Mom, everyone has a cell phone.' They often counter it by asking, 'If everyone else jumped off a cliff would you do it too?' Popularity is not a reliable indication of either reality or value."

Even though my son was three at this time, I felt close to that logic. It was just a matter of time before he would be in school instead of day care and would ask that same question while telling me how unfair I was. The fact that a lot of people believe isn't evidence. It seemed so simple. *Why didn't I see it before?* Of course that does not mean that a proposition is necessarily wrong either. It just means that you haven't learned any more about something than you knew before.

The more I learned about critical thinking, the better I became about using it in my everyday life. It was especially apparent when I discussed religion and critical thinking with family. I became more interested in the origins of the universe and God. I started applying critical thinking to questions, like how Noah could have fit every single beetle species (at least 350,000) inside the ark. The answer I always received was that God could do anything. Miracles, always miracles.

I wasn't an atheist quite yet, but as I started thinking about the logistics of religion, it was hard to ignore some of the inconsistencies in the stories.

With each new philosophical tactic I learned, my thirst for it all grew. Becky, the woman with the key chains, became exhausted. While the class marched on, her confidence waned, and even the jingling from her key chains sounded less cheerful. She didn't give up on the supernatural, though, and was one of the first to defend psychic readings. But having many of her beliefs dashed wore on her, and she wasn't as cheerful as she had been that first day.

Before philosophy, I'd felt like I was always trying to measure a house without a tape measure. Could be seventy-two feet or ninety feet—I wasn't sure. This new set of ideas about how I could evaluate claims was wonderful, and the fact that many people even thought about the supernatural in a methodical way felt inviting. My enthusiasm for a welding career had waned, and now I knew what I was going to do. I was going to teach philosophy.

Atheist Experience

I transferred to a four-year private university in a college town with a small population of twenty-three thousand. It was perfect. Because I'd grown up in an even smaller town whose population rounded to one thousand, I was not a fan of large colleges: too many people. This one was also just twenty-five minutes away from my parents' house, which is where I was still living. Going there was a big decision. I knew it wouldn't be economical to move out on my own until I earned my bachelor's degree. It was hard enough juggling homework and parenting, and I knew that if I moved out, I would have to get a full-time job and that wouldn't leave enough time for class or my son. In order to be a philosophy professor, I would also need a PhD, which might take another five years. After my parents got over the shock of me going from welder to philosopher (a mere ten serious conversations later), they were very supportive.

It was nice having family around: I didn't feel like I was trying to raise my son alone. We often clashed, but that's what families do. The hardest part was keeping the feeling that I was just living off them at bay, especially when I had to explain it to other people. I always felt like my friends or acquaintances thought I was just lazy, but they didn't think that. That feeling was just my own insecurities with living at home for so long. Balancing homework and parenting was difficult, but my parents helped me and I made as much time to spend with my son as I could. Seeing him happy was always more than worth it.

My first class at Pacific University was an English class. In high school, English had been my favorite subject (after choir, anyway), and I was excited to have it on my schedule. I drove down to the school bookstore and found the section with the book list for the English 112 class. I hadn't looked online for what I needed because I assumed it would be a textbook or literature like *Moby Dick*. Instead of seeing these, though, a yellow cover caught my eye as I read the title *God Is Not Great: How Religion Poisons Everything* by Christopher Hitchens. I couldn't believe it. He was a pretty famous atheist and, as made clear by the book's title, was not a fan of religion. This was not a philosophy class—this was freshman English. Every student had to take it, and we were reading Christopher Hitchens!

I am not sure when, but as my time at Pacific went on, I started to listen to podcasts. I would listen while doing all sorts of chores, and I felt more content. It was like a new attitude: I almost looked forward to doing the dishes. One of the podcasts I listened to religiously, if you pardon the pun, was called *The Skeptics' Guide to the Universe*. The podcast discussed science in a way I was able to understand and gave reasons why many pseudoscientific theories were wrong.

The Atheist Experience was another great listen. The hosts covered topics like the bible and said the word *atheist* with conviction. For a long time, I had been reluctant to call myself an atheist. It felt like I was shutting a door on ideas that I may not have agreed with but didn't want to rule out entirely. *The Atheist Experience* podcast really helped me embrace the term, though. The hosts explained that there is a difference between saying that you do not believe that God exists and saying that you have not found the belief in God to be convincing. And I was the latter. This was how they defined atheism. It was as if a religion was selling tickets, and I just refused to buy one.

A lot of people believe that atheists have a certain arrogance to them. I didn't want people to think I thought I knew better than anyone else: I just didn't believe. Some people think that is agnosticism. Agnosticism means we *cannot* know whether there is a God, and I don't believe that either. Maybe there will be a day when the human race will know so much about the universe that we will all agree on whether I am right or wrong.

What skepticism taught me is that it is okay to be wrong as long as you update your stance with the knowledge you gain. This means that my opinions could evolve with time. Like a scientist, I would explore and analyze to grow a greater understanding of the physical world and, along with it, a better understanding of myself.

After

When I graduated from Pacific University, I asked my Critical Thinking professor about getting a master's degree in philosophy so I could be a professor. She gently informed me about the ratio of jobs to graduates. There were way too many graduates, not enough jobs. I wanted to pursue philosophy, but not if it meant years of competitive stress in a PhD program and many more nights of "No, son, I can't play with you because I have homework" just to have very low odds of finding a job.

Ironically, I did pursue a master's degree, just in library science with a concentration on archives. I had worked at the archives at Pacific and was really glad to get into the program. Most of the classes were online, so I could work and be with my son, which fit my lifestyle as a single parent.

In between this, though, I craved the intellectual discussion I'd had during my time at Pacific. I missed discussions about science, ethics, philosophy, and literature, so I searched for places to have these discussions outside the college classroom. I found Meetup.com. This is a website that allows you to choose areas of interest and see groups of people with similar interests in your area. I signed up for the Philosophical Naturalist Meetup group. The description box read, "We are atheists and agnostics that think the natural world is all there is." And although I'd heard many conversations about atheism, I had yet to really be involved with the concept. I was very nervous at my first gathering. I knew by then I was an atheist, but I had never called myself one.

We talked a lot about what it meant for our lives and philosophies to not believe in the supernatural. I became very involved in the group and several other discussion groups around the area. I got the community that a lot of people get from church, just in a different way.

There are some things about having a secular lifestyle I wish were easier. My son is now eight years old. He has friends, and he loves science and reading. I am very proud of him. I wish he had some of the community that church provides. We do not live in a big city that can provide secular options to the group activities that church can provide. This is of course changing. Groups like the Sunday Assembly have moved toward being a church without the God-bits and have kids' classes.

Overall, it can still be an issue for many people who do not have groups like this in their area. Without belonging to a church, they lack community unless these groups exist for them. It is possible, however, that our society could be realizing that with fewer and fewer people attending churches, we need alternatives. By the time my son is my age, his kids may be going to an alternative place that supplies community in new and fantastic ways.

Until then, I hope to provide him the tools to think critically. I feel a freedom having made a decision to call myself an atheist instead of staying on the fence. I can always incorporate new ideas. Being able to learn new ideas tells us that we are still alive. And maybe that is all we can truly know.

THE LONG ROAD HOME TO MYSELF

Gayle Myrna

*I don't believe in an afterlife. I believe this is it,
and I believe it's the best way to live.*

—Natalie Portman

I first started to question religion as a child. What started me on that road? Well, incidents such as the following may have ignited the long, slow-burning fuse that exploded into a beautiful display of disbelief many decades later. I remember one time when my parents were arguing, again. The cause? Religion. We were on our way to High Holiday services at the Jewish temple we belonged to, and my father had the radio in the car turned on. My mother felt having the radio on was a violation of some religious rule during the High Holy Days. Even as a child, I suspected there was something odd about religion leading to conflict among adults. My parents argued about many things, and the application of Judaism was one of them. But whatever the topic of my parents' disagreements, it was all scary and stomach churning to me as a child.

For those unfamiliar with Judaism, the High Holidays, or High Holy Days, are Rosh Hashanah and Yom Kippur. These observances take place in the fall. Rosh Hashanah, observed for two days, is the Jewish New Year. According to the Torah, the first five books of the Bible, Rosh Hashanah is the anniversary of the world's creation. What's more, the holiday is when God supposedly writes in the Book of Life or the Book of the Dead about whether an individual will live or die, or have a good or bad year. It starts off the ten days of repentance, or Days of Awe. This period of time ends with the Yom Kippur holiday, when Jews try to forgive other people for any problems they have caused them during the last year. Yom Kippur is traditionally spent in fasting and repentant prayer, hoping for atonement before God slams the Book of Life and Book of the Dead shut. After enough praying, Jews hopefully start off the New Year with a slate wiped clean of sin. This, of course, is the short version, and various streams of Judaism have their own versions of these traditions, as do families. As a youngster, I didn't have to fast. Just endure the endless praying.

There are a lot of rules in Judaism, and my family wasn't the assimilated kind of Jewish family. Nope. They kept kosher. There were no Christmas trees in December. We had our Hanukkah menorah and potato pancakes. But Hanukkah to a small child was just not as cool as Christmas with all its societal promotions, dazzling lights, colors, and music. And in modern America, it would take some serious retreating from society to escape Christmas and its entanglements. I later learned that Hanukkah was formerly a relatively minor holiday in the Jewish tradition, but in a kind of religious arms race, it became inflated into the mega-holiday it is for American Jews today.

Beyond maybe a rendition of "I Have a Little Dreidel," Hanukkah was pretty much a footnote at my public school. But there were plenty of Christmas carols, seasonal decorations, and other Christmas holiday–related details. In my elementary school one year, we made Christmas trees out of what—if I recall correctly—was colored construction paper. These were about the size of a greeting card. Figuring my parents would be upset about such an obvious Christian symbol being brought into their home, I hid it in my closet and would take it out to look at it secretly. Today I am aware that Christmas trees are a relic of the pagan past. According to the *Encyclopaedia Britannica*, ancient Egyptians, Hebrews, and Chinese used evergreen trees, garlands, and wreaths as a symbol of eternal life. Pagan Europeans worshipped trees, and this aspect of their culture was incorporated into Christianity. In my understanding, a number of cultures have used decorated trees or other flora as part of their wintertime customs. Nowadays, I enjoy the trees as a seasonal celebration of solstice with no Christian connection.

My mother, who worked on her feet all day as a low-wage sales clerk at a department store, would keep two sets of dishes to accommodate kosher rules. On Passover, she would change out both sets of dishes to keep in compliance with the separate sets of dishes Passover tradition requires. Changing out dishes is related to the thorough housecleaning many observant Jews do prior to Passover in order to eliminate any *chametz*— food items with leavening. In biblical history, Jewish slaves fled Egypt before their bread could rise. Today Jews consume *matzoh*, unleavened bread, instead of conventional bread during the Passover holiday. But, to my mind, all this changing dishes out (and pots and pans, etc.) was another task for my already-burdened mother who took care of my brother, my father, and me. Though both very intelligent, neither of my parents attended college. My mother had a high school diploma and my father had to stop school at eighth grade. My brother was the first in our family to attend college.

As an adult, I have heard that some Jewish people eat Chinese food on Christmas. Not my family. Chinese food is not kosher and has lots of pork in it. Pork, along with shellfish such as shrimp, is forbidden by kosher rules. I did not taste Chinese food until I was fifteen and on an outing without my family. I did not taste pork until I was an adult. Nowadays, while I try to eat a mostly healthy diet with reduced amounts of meat, especially red meat, I will not go all out vegetarian—I had too many religious food restrictions growing up and do not want to be constrained. Ironically, I now try to avoid pork. Not for religious reasons but because I have learned too much about pigs being quite intelligent animals. Shrimp, on the other hand, is now one of my favorite foods.

Meanwhile, as a child I was a believer in God. The monotheistic Jewish God, that is. Now this is where it gets a bit complex. Though I consider myself an atheist, I also would still classify myself as a Jew . . . but not in the religious sense. That is my ethnic ancestry. And I do fondly enjoy some of the traditions of my background, like lighting a candle in remembrance of dead loved ones each year. And I certainly still enjoy foods I grew up eating, like potato pancakes at Hanukkah and lox, bagels, and cream cheese at any time. But no, I don't need the religious trappings to savor a tasty treat or reflect on the life of a long-gone relative.

I grew up in West Los Angeles in a neighborhood that was mostly Christian. I was one of just a handful of Jews in my elementary school. I already knew Jews were a minority in the world, and I did find the larger Christian society somewhat alienating with its—to my mind—bizarre worship of a human being. My best friend was a Lutheran, and we regularly got in arguments over evolution. Naturally, I was on the pro-evolution side and my friend on the take-the-Bible-literally side. Once I learned about evolution in grade school, a lot of stuff now made sense to me. Even as a child, I noted that humans and animals shared a lot of the same traits, such as the need to eat. But my Lutheran friend couldn't accept any of this evidence. She believed in the literal Genesis story. I did not. And as I have gotten older, I notice more and more how we are like our relatives in the animal world. When I watch a documentary on chimpanzees, for instance, I can see how our human behavior is just a more complex variation on what the chimps are doing and how their emotions are similar to the feelings of humans. Sadly, the battle between young-Earth fundamentalist Christians and those who accept the scientific facts of evolution still rages.

But my Lutheran friend could not compare in Christian fanaticism to the two sisters I knew across the street. If my memory serves me well, their father, a snazzily dressed fellow with oiled wavy dark hair, was a convert from Judaism to some kind of evangelical version of Christianity. He was now a preacher and had a congregation in Santa Monica, maybe five or so miles from our home. The sisters had been trying to get me to come to their church for a long time. While I had issues with Judaism, I had absolutely no belief in Christianity and never remotely considered Jesus any kind of deity. While I can't recall exactly how old I was by this point, perhaps ten or so, I had learned enough about Christian beliefs from the media and my friends to find the Christian story about as real as a fairy tale. Plus, years of learning about Christian persecution of Jews did not favorably dispose me to Jesus and his ilk. It's a daunting task to sum up two thousand–plus years of Jewish suffering at the hands of Christians, and I won't attempt it here, but let's say it included stuff like the Crusades, the Inquisition, Jews being forced out of some trades and into others, Jews being kicked out of some countries, laws that constrained Jews but not Christians, Jews made to live apart from their Christian neighbors in ghettos, and vast anti-Semitic outbursts of killing and violence called pogroms that were prevalent not only in Eastern Europe but also in other areas. Eventually the centuries of anti-Jewish hatred fueled the furnaces of the Nazi concentration camps that annihilated six million Jews and others during World War II.

At this point, my family attended just High Holiday services at the temple. My mother usually worked Saturdays when weekly services took place, and my father just didn't attend. I did take confirmation classes on Sundays and Hebrew school during the week. And I always felt my mother would've liked to go to Saturday service on a regular basis, but my father's work as a self-employed inventor of an electronic gadget for cameras did not provide consistent income, so my mother worked.

While my mother may have enjoyed temple, I dreaded it. We did have translations of the Hebrew text into English, but still, being in temple from morning to evening for several days in a row was, frankly, an ordeal. Lots of praying, standing, sitting, praying, standing, sitting, praying. Repeat. Repeat.

While I was conflicted about Judaism, that did not mean I was interested in learning more about Christianity, so I avoided my neighbors' evangelical pressures, but they were relentless. Finally, to appease the sisters, I asked my parents' permission to attend a Sunday service. They agreed to the plan. It was to be my first time inside a Christian church. I can't recall if my father or my friends took me, but I got there and sat down with them for the service. It was different from any Jewish service I had been to. And it was worse. The preacher was of the hell-and-brimstone, come-to-Jesus variety. I knew already I wasn't going to "come to Jesus," so I sat and squirmed as this person ranted and raved and called upon people to come up and give themselves to Jesus. A number of them did. There was a lot of hyper-emotionalism there that I wasn't used to and found upsetting. This went on and on, and to my child's mind, there was no freaking end in sight.

Finally, I figured I could just leave and walk home. Alone. I told my companions I was going to the restroom. I probably went to the restroom and afterward found an exit. I began the walk home. Being a child, I did not think about the implications of a missing youngster. After walking quite a distance toward home, my father came looking for me in his car. I can't recall if he was angry, but apparently my friends had informed my parents that I had disappeared. Maybe my parents were relieved I wasn't going to abandon Judaism for Christianity anytime soon.

Many young Jews are bar mitzvahed (men) or bat mitzvahed (women), which is kind of a welcoming into the adult life and traditions of the Jewish religious community via a special service involving reading of sacred texts in Hebrew. I suspect my failed attempts at mastering Hebrew reading and writing in after-school Hebrew classes kept me from being bat mitzvahed, so instead I got the light version, a confirmation. I did take confirmation classes on Sundays in addition to Hebrew school during the week.

My confirmation class consisted of myself and another young girl who lived across the street from me, taught by a rabbi—a Reconstructionist rabbi. Our temple was Conservative, not as rigid as the Orthodox, but nowhere as liberal as the Reform. Reconstructionism is a modernizing Jewish movement aimed at evolving Judaism to fit with the times. So this rabbi had an approach to teaching Judaism that I wasn't accustomed to. I remember one thing he told us: "Man created God." I was only fourteen or fifteen, so that did not yet sink in, but apparently this rabbi's new approach gave me the confidence to explore and question, because my confirmation speech to the congregation ticked people off. I don't recall the exact bent, but I think I questioned beloved rituals, a big no-no, especially for a congregation of quite elderly people clinging to tradition. It caused so much flack, the speech was reprinted in the temple's newsletter and later published in one of the Los Angeles area's Jewish newspapers. So I got my first writing credit at fifteen. And though I had issues at fifteen with Judaism, I continued to believe in God and the more positive tenets of Judaism.

At seventeen, I briefly became involved with a twenty-five-year-old Vietnam War veteran. Turns out he was a member of Nichiren Shoshu, a branch of Buddhism. Apparently, if I chanted enough, all my life would get better! As a rebellious pseudo-hippie adolescent, I figured I would give it a try. I chanted daily for the required amount of time. I also attended one giant event at the Santa Monica Civic Auditorium. The ushers wore American cowboy garb. They showed a movie about the movement's leader, and the attendees exhibited lots of pep rally–type overenthusiasm. There was also one unfortunate arm salute configuration. It was *not* a Nazi salute, but to me, the similarity of an auditorium full of people repeatedly saluting their leader every time he appeared on screen was unsettling and reminded me of the Nazi rally newsreels I had seen. It felt menacing and just plain wrong. The chanting, meanwhile, had *not* shown any positive outcomes for me. I discarded the practice and immediately felt better. After the event, I also disassociated myself from the boyfriend and the Nichiren Shoshu.

While I still retained a belief in God and considered myself a follower of Judaism, I did question a lot of the stuff we had to deal with, mainly rituals and kosher rules. When I left home at eighteen, I no longer had to attend High Holiday services. During my adult years, however, when I lived near enough, I did continue visiting my family for Passover and Hanukkah. And after my father passed away, I would take my non-driving mother, and sometimes some of her non-driving friends, to one of the shorter evening High Holiday services. But, as a solo adult, I do not keep kosher.

After enough years of building life experiences, reading, observing human behavior, learning details of biology and natural selection, and discussing with others, I have evolved in how I view the universe. And religion. I think I had always questioned religion, and with so much conflict between my parents about what is supposed to be a good thing, I questioned the whole point of religion.

In discussing and observing other belief systems, I found myself questioning most, if not all, of them. I also encountered plenty of people who were positive they had the "One True Answer/Religion/Spiritual New Age Practice," etc., etc. I could easily see that Christians were as convinced as Islamists as Jews as Mormons as New Agers as Buddhists as (fill in the blank) were that their particular version of religion/philosophy/whatever was the only one that was true. And I started to think, *Bullshit.* I reserved a special loathing for the New Agey idea that we are totally responsible for everything that happens to us and that our thoughts can manifest reality. To me, that translated into a view that victims are responsible for the evil acts of their victimizers. In other words, those killed in the Holocaust brought it upon themselves. I mince no words in being disgusted by this repugnant idea.

At one point I lived in East Texas for two long years. I was working as a reporter for a small daily newspaper in Texarkana, Texas, and later for a small radio station in Atlanta, Texas. I had never lived in such a relentlessly Christian area before. Often the first thing someone would ask me was, "What church do you go to?" No one had asked me that in the other places I had lived. I was so overwhelmed by the intrusiveness of the Christians that I found the one Jewish temple in the area, a Reform congregation, and sporadically attended events. It was nice for me just to escape the overpowering Christian influence in the area.

While working on the Texarkana newspaper, I did a set of articles on a Pentecostal tent revival that had set up shop in town. I attended a service in which the mega-emotional-showman-preacher ran up and down and around the giant tent in a whirlwind of maniacal passion. I was not impressed, but it sure seduced the local folks attending. I recall one father had brought his small son to be cured of cancer by the evangelist. I was horrified, as I did not consider prayer a match for cancer, or any disease, for that matter, and I felt the boy should be treated with conventional medicine. I also remember that plates for donations were passed around and around, despite the fact that most of the folks attending were lower income. I'm sure the money they poured onto those plates could've been better spent on everyday stuff like rent, bills, medicine, food. Instead, I suspected the preacher's pockets got nice and fat with green bills.

Accompanied by a photographer from the newspaper, I returned the next day to the revival tent to speak to the preacher and find out more about what was going on. We were turned back by some large, menacing security guards. I'm not sure what the guards' orders were, but at five feet tall and about a hundred pounds, I guess I must've really scared those running the tent revival.

Eventually I returned to Southern California. Except for taking my mother to High Holiday services each year, and my family Passover and Hanukkah celebrations, I wasn't particularly involved in religion. I considered myself a Jew and believed in God, but by now, God had evolved, in my thinking, into some kind of vague cosmic force.

Around '89 or '90, I attended a dance in an Orange County beach town. I was living in Long Beach, California, at the time and was recently divorced from a short, intense marriage. I had a good time and began dating a fellow I met there. At some point, I found out the dances were promoted by the local Church of Religious Science. Religious Science is a spiritual movement that comprises bits from New Age, Christian, and other sources. One of its tools is Spiritual Mind Treatment, which is a prayer technique to tap into God, or something to that effect. I attended services with the new boyfriend. I liked that the services had a lot of music and were nonjudgmental. At that time, Religious Science was considered quite a tolerant group. For instance, it was one place where those from the LGBTQ community could go without rejection, something I found positive about the organization.

The relationship eventually ended, and I began dating a musician I met at the services, one who performed there regularly. He was also a member of yet another religious group, a small New Agey church in Long Beach. This small church was run by its founding minister, who at one time had studied to be a Catholic priest and now managed to combine streams of thought from various sources, ranging from Christianity to New Age to other philosophies. I realized the minister was using a preaching tactic that took a kernel of truth and surrounded it with lies, making it difficult to sift the reality from the fantasy. The church also had a choir, and my musician boyfriend provided piano, voice, and other accompaniment. I wasn't particularly interested in what the minister had to say, but as a singer I wanted the opportunity to sing on a regular basis. Most of the songs we did were inspirational-type pop songs, so I was able to avoid most of the Jesus-type music. The services also involved a "healing" portion, in which someone would sit in a chair and get lots of prayers and attention. The minister had a charismatic style, and during social times, he was often surrounded by fawning followers, something I had no inclination for.

Eventually, it came out that the minister had, some years before, allegedly molested the (now adult) son of my musician boyfriend. The alleged molestation took place at a rural property used for church retreats. This led to my boyfriend rejecting the minister and his church. I also stopped going. While I had never bought into the philosophy, I did miss the community, especially the weekly opportunity to sing.

Several years later, I left the musician boyfriend and moved into my own apartment in Long Beach. In 2003, my health took a downward turn and, to find cheaper housing, I moved to Riverside, California.

While living in Riverside, I came across a flyer on a coffee house bulletin board. I forget all the details, but it asked if you were looking to find people who did *not* believe in superstition, demons, religion, woo, etc. *Wow*, I thought, *I'm not alone in being doubtful about everything from New Age woo to religion.* The group was then called the Inland Empire Freethinkers. We gathered around a table at the local Unitarian Church, which we were not part of but they allowed us to use the space. There were only about ten or so of us, and we'd meet once a month for lively discussion on philosophy and religion. Here I was first introduced to atheism as a positive position. But I still clung onto a vague belief in some kind of cosmic energy that could be charitably called God. So I considered myself an agnostic.

Eventually, the group got larger. When we started a listing on Meetup. com, the name was changed to Inland Empire Atheists and Agnostics, and then the group rapidly grew to several hundred members. Our meetings now had guest speakers, plus there were other activities and events. By this time, I had been involved for several years, and the rational discussions had finally tipped my thinking all the way into full-blown atheism. I could no longer buy into the idea of some entity you prayed hopefully to but that never answered those entreaties. I could no longer buy into some deity that resembled an angry, insecure, misogynistic Middle Eastern patriarch with jealousy and possessiveness issues, as God is portrayed in the Old Testament. I could no longer buy into a God that had the power to create the universe but couldn't figure out how to keep us disease-free. Or one that designed humans so poorly that they are prone to wars, violence, prejudice, hatred, and other negative and destructive traits. The more I thought about it, the more it appeared as if God not only did not exist in the modern world but had never existed. Or, as my Reconstructionist rabbi had put it years ago, "Man created God."

I now think of religion as a weight holding humanity down. As something that causes more harm than good. As something that leads to divisions among people. As a delusion to keep people from bettering their lives now. As something that holds the promise of a life after death . . . but only if you follow so many rules that you screw up the one life you actually have.

In writing this memoir, I can reflect that a lot of my spiritual misadventures were based on my trust of others. As a child, I didn't have much say in what to believe; I just followed my family's lead. Once I reached my teens, I was often persuaded by the men I associated with, as many women were during that time in history. If I were born today, I wonder if I would have the courage to say screw you to religion much earlier than I did. Alas, I have no time machine to go back and undo my religious upbringing or adult choices.

Today I enjoy the one short life I have minus the mental shackles of superstition, religion, and gods. And I do believe that people waste a lot of time fretting over the meaning of life. Hey, we're alive—we have just this one precious chance at consciousness, so let's enjoy it and not spend our lives worrying about mystical fairy tales that were created by human beings with the same weaknesses and prejudices we all have inherited.

In late August 2011, I moved to the Portland, Oregon, metro area. Once I settled in, I joined several secular groups. So nowadays, most of my companions are secular. And no one in the Northwest asks me what church I go to.

THE LONG AND WINDING ROAD

Robin Stafford

I'm an atheist, and that's it. I believe there's nothing we can know except that we should be kind to each other and do what we can for people.

—Katherine Hepburn

Like many ex-Christian atheists, I had a typical childhood. Every Sunday morning, my mother would send me to my brothers' room to drag them out of bed so that we'd be at church in time for Sunday school. Much to my brothers' chagrin, I was very much an early bird and all too happy to sing them a bright and cheery song to wake them up.

I'm surprised they didn't improve their aim.

Most folks know that in the South, there's a church on nearly every corner, and Texas was no different. Around the age of seven, I heard the crucifixion story, focusing on the part that Jesus had died for my sins. I took it to heart. I heard in my innocent little brain that I had put Jesus on the cross. I had killed him with my sins. I felt I had to make things right and the way to do that was to honor his offer to make my soul clean so he could live in my heart, like he did the other members of my family.

Children shouldn't be guilt-tripped like that, but they are. Every day.

I envy those who were able to see behind the curtain at a young age. However, I bought it lock, stock, and barrel. It was easy for me to do so. My family was a great example of Christians walking the walk: very loving, giving people. To this day, my mother humbles me in how much she loves people and does her best to help them. I saw our religion through rose-colored glasses during all of my childhood.

I had quite the testimony during high school, thanks to some physical challenges that came my way. In my freshman year, I suffered through complications from reflex sympathetic dystrophy syndrome. First, I had terrible pain in my back that wouldn't go away. Then a few months later, pain would shoot through my left leg. We'd call them "attacks," and I would have to clamp my jaw down onto a rag to stifle the pain. Between the hospital visits, weeks of physical therapy, and having to do my schoolwork from home, I relied both on my mother's diligence in tracking my condition in a journal and on our deep-seated faith. It was the discovery of multiple follicular cysts pressing against a nerve in my back and the then-prescribed birth-control pills to treat the condition that led to my remission. For my teen years, facing and overcoming such a challenge was the bedrock of my testimony. I was often told how inspiring my faith was to see me through such times.

Things began to change once I was in college. Some of my friends in a tabletop gaming group were spiritualists. Although I had been raised in a Southern Baptist home, I took to heart the more compassionate parts of the bible. I saw no reason I couldn't have nonbelievers as friends, since Jesus reached out to those who were considered untouchable.

But then I had what I would later find out to be called sleep paralysis. I was first out from my family's home, living in a dorm at Stephen F. Austin State University. One night, I had a rather embarrassing but erotic dream that my roommate had let in her boyfriend and they were making out while I was trying not to overhear. It was quite vivid, and no, my roommate wasn't even there at the time. I woke up, and to my senses I was fully awake—just unable to move. I had this overwhelming sense of dread that there was an evil presence in the room. I heard low growls and breathing that sounded like the wind shearing over sheet metal. Even though I couldn't move, I could see, somehow, the silvery black hindquarters of an animalistic demon. I tried to speak. I couldn't. Later, I would describe that I spoke in my heart, intending to say, "Jesus, cast this demon out!" When I got to the word *demon*, the figment screeched, "Demon demon demon!" All of a sudden, it was gone. I could move. With a shaking hand, I picked up the phone and called Mom right away. It was just before Thanksgiving, so she said that Dad would come pick me up in the morning.

What came to follow was something that I am not proud of in the least. It does, however, give me hope that even the most religious people out there can set aside their delusions for reason.

In the weeks to come, my parents were very supportive. However, the church was not. In my Sunday school, I tried to bring up what happened. Everyone was very quiet. Things got awkward. Someone changed the subject. Meanwhile, I was scared and desperate for answers. I prayed. I talked to my gaming community about what happened. One of the players was a spiritualist and recommended I learn how to protect myself spiritually. Others recommended I seek out white witches or Wiccans.

This was before the days of easy Internet access, so to follow my friends' recommendations, I needed to find a metaphysical shop. Over the next couple years, I read up on Wicca and spiritualism in general.

By the fall of 1996, I had learned enough about how rituals had been cross-pollinated from the old religions of Europe with Christianity that I felt I should try being a Christian pagan. On New Year's Day of '97, I began my year as a solitary Wiccan. By the time my father died in October of that same year, I could no longer resolve my upbringing with my newfound beliefs. I laid a small crucifix in my father's casket, saying goodbye to Christianity at the same time I said goodbye to my dad.

I came clean about my conversion to paganism to my mother and immediate family by Christmas Eve. Since then, there have been a few times when Mom or another relative has tried to bring me back into the fold. Over time, my mother has become more accepting and once even said, "Well, at least you believe in something . . ." She's not thrilled that I'm an atheist now, but she's a superstar. Even her deeply held beliefs have not kept us from being close. There are times we just have to disagree, and we've come to an understanding that some subjects are off the table for discussion between us.

I remained a pagan through the years, though I determined that even Wicca was too organized for my tastes. I read tarot for a short while. I performed rituals. There was even a stretch of time when I referred to myself as a "technopagan" because I felt that magic and electricity were aligned. I was deep in the woo. Very deep.

My mother remarried a few years after my father passed away. I returned to college and made friends who were also pagan. While I was staying in an apartment on my own, I continued to play the part of solitary kitchen witch. Finances being strained, I returned to stay with Mom and my stepdad for the last year or so of college.

Under their roof, I was not allowed to keep any of my pagan books or accoutrements. I was not allowed to practice my beliefs. I did, for a time, have to go to church with them on occasion. I played nice. They had sweet friends. Sweet, deluded friends. It tugged at my heart, but I played nice.

To their credit, had they not been so insistent, I may have continued to be pagan to this day. Irony is incredible sometimes.

In time, I thought of myself more as a philosophical pagan. I was in the process of applying to the JET Program, so that I might work abroad and share cultural experiences while in Japan. One wintry night, I drove down to my university town to see the senior art show for some of my peers who were graduating that semester. On the way back, I was driving in the left lane when an eighteen-wheeler semi began to merge into my lane. I had no space to move ahead. I had no time to check for a car behind me. In the space of a breath, the only decision that would spare others was to brake and head into the median of the highway. My car launched from an incline in the median and spun, midair.

I remember saying, "Please," while the world turned upside down in my windshield. I knew that my life was likely to end in the next moment. I felt at peace. I didn't feel any presence but my own. My *please* was not said to any deity, but as a last-minute cry to the universe, that I would have more ahead in my life to live.

I was lucky. I was damned lucky. It had rained the day before, so the median was muddy. When my car's roof and hood hit, they slid some and made a softer impact due to the mud. The door frames held, and that saved my life. I was able to crawl out from the passenger's side window, where already a small group of people had pulled over to assist me.

After the next few days, I had an epiphany. I had been attempting to see the other side of the veil. I was interpreting my dreams. I was trying to see a supernatural world, all those years, in hopes of being strong in case I was being targeted by evil spirits. The wreck showed me that I was allowing distractions into my life, looking for all things supernatural. While others were claiming angels had been working overtime in order to save my life, I was seeing the world with new eyes. People were the ones who came to help me. People were the ones who engineered the car so it wouldn't crumple and take my life. People were the ones who trained for years in order to treat me once I was at the hospital, even though all I ended up needing was a tetanus shot.

It was now more important to me to live a reality-based life than to chase the shadows in my mind.

I had researched various forums when I was first online as a pagan. I revisited these pages again, years later, when I recalled the term *pantheism*, which in its simplest form relates the universe and deity as one and the same. There had been a forum called Keep It Real, which was home to freethinkers as well as some loose pagans and pantheists. By the time I revisited the website, it was no longer functioning as a hub for discussion. I came across other forums for pantheism, then skepticism, and finally atheism. Eventually, I found information regarding sleep paralysis and the medical explanation for it. There had never been a demon or evil spirit that had plagued me. It was my mind reacting to waking up before the rest of my body had.

While I still consider my relation to nature as pantheistic, I am an atheist first and foremost. I spent July 2009 through July 2014 teaching in Japan. There, I learned a lot from Japanese people and their culture. While religion does exist in Japan, it has a special place in the culture, as heritage. Many of the younger people there relate religion to a kind of accessory, like they would blood type or astrological sign. (In Japan, blood types carry a similar personality trait as zodiac signs do in the West.) Religion is secondary in their lives as Japanese citizens. It is a private matter. As a whole, they live an atheistic life.

In the first week of May 2011, I joined other foreign English teachers to volunteer in Northeastern Japan (Tohoku). We traveled to Ofunato, Iwate Prefecture, where a neighboring village, Rikuzentakata, had been obliterated by the effects of the earthquake and subsequent tsunami. *Apocalyptic* is the closest term to describe what I saw. We drove down blocks where buildings lay asunder, fixtures jutting out from the foundations, with belongings piled up high like barricades. It reminded me of pictures I'd seen of warzones.

The people of Ofunato were generous and humble. The firemen and police had been working nonstop to keep the cleanup and rebuilding organized. We were only there for three days, but there was so much to take in to comprehend the living conditions for people who had lost everything. Most of the volunteer work involved cleaning up the riverbanks where the tsunami had spilled over and left debris in its wake. There were boxes of fish mixed in with metal walls, fishing nets that were tangled with all sorts of items, such as shoes, rope, and even handlebars from a bicycle. A friend and I used our muster to unearth a very heavy generator in order for it to be hauled off. One of the days we were there, we helped clean out a very old traditional Japanese home for a lady who had lost her husband. So many of her belongings had been ruined, and we used a bucket brigade to haul away the debris then haul in bags of lye to kill all of the bacteria. At night, we stayed at an English cram, or tutoring, school that was near the coast. Aftershocks were still prevalent and would be heralded in the distance by a rumbling that sounded like a train barreling toward us.

Later that summer, my mother came to visit me. She had been worried for me the day of the earthquake, even though the prefecture I lived in was the safest area in Japan for natural phenomena such as earthquakes and typhoons. I suppose being so frightened, she had to, once again, bring up beliefs. "What do you believe in, Robin?" I recall her asking me.

"I believe in connections. With people, with nature, and with the cosmos." I told her how seeing the effects of the 3/11 earthquake and tsunami showed how powerful nature is, even when Japan has the premier technology to deal with such devastation. That the technology still helped save many people, even though the cost of things was so dire.

Her response was that I was "just being stubborn."

Before I returned to the United States this past year, I understood that there would be reverse culture shock, that I would have moments when my acclimation to Japan would butt up with American life. Staying in the South had always shown a strange dual reality, before, where otherwise genteel people would scoff at me for not being a mainstream Christian, even when they didn't know my atheist stance on religion. I had to go from a daily life in which religion simply wasn't mentioned one iota to one that saturated every aspect of everyday living.

That isn't to say that there aren't good people who are religious. My mother proves that statement false. There are, however, very vocal religionists in the South who are unaware of their privilege. Is it any wonder that shows such as *The Thinking Atheist*, *The Atheist Experience*, and others have been developed deep in the South?

I honestly wish I had the patience that the stars of those shows exhibit. However, many reasons have compelled me to find a new life on the West Coast, where my progressive, feminist, atheist views are held jointly by others and not branded demon-worship. Demons are, after all, internal figments or shortcomings that one must face in order to make oneself a better person. Last I looked, rational freethinkers work every day to do just that.

RUNNING WITH THE DEVIL

Anna Rankin

Two hands working can do more than a thousand clasped in prayer.
—Madalyn Murray O'Hair

As a kid, I didn't learn much about religion, and I don't remember ever praying together as a family. There must have been some praying, at least for a little while anyway. My parents had given up on going to church shortly after my oldest brother was born. My mom wanted to join the Church of Jesus Christ of Latter-day Saints, but my dad, at that time, wouldn't hear of it. He was the man: he had the ultimate authority. From what my mother told me, he was an oppressive, controlling, proud Irish Catholic who was overly ambitious and demoralizing. Keep in mind—I only have my mother's side of the story to go on because my father was murdered when I was eight.

My interpretation of her story goes something along these lines. Their conflict over religion drove a significant wedge between them. After their marriage had a number of "bad years" (they must have been *really* bad), my dad experienced that mighty change of heart described by the prophet Alma in the Book of Mormon. He was compelled through adversity to be humble and hence repented, quit drinking and smoking, got baptized along with my mom, and became a family man . . . at least for the last six months of his life.

The disappearance of my father heavily impacted my ability to connect with the god of any religion. The date of his death and the location of his body remain a mystery. He was in the wrong place at the wrong time. Several months after his disappearance, some of his belongings were recovered when two men were arrested on auto theft charges. One of them accepted a plea bargain and confessed. He implicated another man who was charged, found guilty, spent twenty years in San Quentin State Prison in California for murdering my father, and was then executed. It was hard to believe in a god that was up in heaven somewhere when I needed him down here. Because somehow I knew I should forgive these men, I did. It was around that time in my life that I can remember lying in bed and asking god to help me believe in him. I wanted to believe in him, but I couldn't connect. Believing in god felt contrived.

My mother didn't stay involved in the church long, but I don't know exactly why. I'd ask, but she's dead too. The only memories I have of church during the rest of my childhood were youth activities, which I snuck out of to either smoke cigarettes or get to know some of the young men. I felt alienated; it was almost like these big Mormon families were speaking a foreign language. I could not relate to people who were too good to be true. I was a misfit and didn't feel good about myself when I was around them.

I was alienated at home too. Since I was the only girl out of four children, I was outnumbered all the time. I must have been Daddy's little girl. But without a father, there was no safety net. My mom remarried when I was eleven, and it didn't take long for her and her husband to ship me off to a group home for at-risk teens. By the age of twelve, I was already skipping school and sneaking out at night. These were the days when music began to influence my ideas about god. It is easy to look back and see how heavy metal music affected my thinking and behavior. From the somewhat insane Pink Floyd to the utterly hell-bent Black Sabbath, I found my identity.

One key message about god in heavy metal resonated with my soul: god has somehow abandoned his people on Earth. I definitely related. God had not been there when my father died. My mom had abandoned me also. Van Halen's song "Runnin' with the Devil" contains another message of outright rebellion against god and hence the rebellion against authority too. I embraced this as doctrine as well. Led Zeppelin's music introduced me to the occult. Being naturally curious, I became very intrigued by magic and witchcraft. I must have listened to "Stairway to Heaven" on my Walkman hundreds of times. With my headphones on, I was able to block out everything going on around me. As music became my escape, it also became a source of connection to other people.

The group home for at-risk teens failed to conform me. Now my mother sent me to a boarding school for eighth and ninth grades. The Selwyn School was an Episcopalian college preparatory boarding school. Episcopalian by association, maybe, but I don't remember going to mass or any church services. I had classmates from all over the world: Saudi Arabia, Japan, London, and Highland Park, Texas. I was introduced to a broad array of ideologies, musical styles, and religious beliefs. Taking into consideration that there were other students at the school for reasons similar to mine, I gained partners in crime coupled with an extreme lack of supervision. During the years I spent at boarding school, I learned a few unforgettable lessons.

Even though I was a poor student, often distracted and disengaged, I excelled at biology. I learned that you couldn't just make something come alive. Thus biology added to my confusion about god. I was perplexed by the difference between animate, sentient beings compared to inanimate elements and matter. What spark created the living? The cycles in nature seemed too predictable and repetitive to be completely random. I sensed that there was something magical about the universe, but I was unable to describe what it was.

In English class, I learned critical thinking. I learned that knowing is different from believing, and what we know is far less than what we believe. Even today, I find it hard to go beyond what I can know and confirm.

Another takeaway lesson from my years in boarding school came during an international school trip. I went on an expedition deep into the mountains of Oaxaca, Mexico. The main purpose of the trip was to investigate a canyon for unidentified species of cacti, and incidentally we toured colonial churches along our journey. I had never seen such macabre images before in my life. The horrific depictions of Jesus's crucifixion only further distanced me from believing in god. Alongside the massive, ornate colonial cathedrals, there are *curanderas* in Oaxaca. They are women healers who use potions and folk magic for healing. I saw potions, charms, powders, and healing teas sold at local *tiendas*. I thought this was so bizarre, but great. Consider the dilemma: I saw effigies of gruesome human sacrifice on one hand and superstitious folk medicine on the other. I liked the latter best. The woman was the benevolent healer: her powers were divine and she was imbued with wisdom. Of course I liked her better.

At about this time, I had a small pentagram tattooed on my rib cage, close to my heart. It isn't pretty or inspiring; it is simply a circle with a star inside drawn in black ink. This symbolized to me that I was part of a society of women who rejected the male deity. I liked the idea that through herbalism and natural remedies, I might have the ability to heal myself. It has served as a reminder that at this intersection in my life I had already branded myself a nonbeliever.

It was during those school years that I began experimenting with psychedelic drugs. I am glad I did—those experiences completely changed the way I perceived the world around me. As an example, the perspective of universal interconnectedness now felt natural to me. I started having strange dreams occur occasionally at night. I would be either alert and paralyzed or alert and stuck on the ceiling. When I described my dreams to one of my teachers, she told me they were out-of-body experiences. Sure enough, the profile matched. Regardless of the dreams' origins, they furthered my curiosity about the supernatural.

My next introduction to god was by way of Alcoholics Anonymous. I was bound to get crosswise with the law at some point. At seventeen, I was tried as an adult on felony robbery charges in Dallas, Texas. After repeatedly violating my probation rules, I was given the choice between jail time or six months at a voluntary judicial treatment center. I chose the latter.

I learned the twelve steps to recovery according to Dr. Bob S. and Bill W. In the third step, I was supposed to make the decision to turn my will and life over to the care of god as I understood him. I didn't understand. Ironically, later I learned that the twelve-step program of recovery was simply a modification of Christian repentance. I memorized the step about prayer and meditation to improve conscious contact with god, but I was clueless as to what that meant. There were close to thirty women in the unit. I was the second-to-youngest person. I heard the women's stories and saw their tears. Comments about god occupied a significant amount of the group therapy sessions. Some of the women had been beaten and broken down sufficiently to cause their surrender to a higher power or conversion to Christianity. For them, it was real. When I was praying, I felt like I was talking on the telephone but the line had gone silent: no one was on the other end. I am grateful for this experience because I learned a great deal about life. Hearing other women's stories, I learned that whoring for drugs and having crack babies doesn't work out well.

There is an ironic twist to the story: I started attending community college classes simply out of spite. I discovered that I could get out of paying monthly probation fines if I were enrolled in school. I eventually earned a BS in biology (notice the recurring theme) from Texas Woman's University. Miracles do exist. There was a large feminist population at the university. Feminism was rebellion, and I liked it. I studied molecular genetics and worked in a laboratory on campus. Marie Curie had been one of my childhood idols. Recombinant DNA technology appealed to me because it was the cutting edge of biology. I was fascinated by the human genome project and Dolly, the first cloned sheep. Naturally, there was little talk about god. Except for that one guest speaker. He somehow got onto the subject of science and god. He described how his study of science further confirmed his belief in a god. I could relate to this, but only vaguely.

While I was a student at Texas Woman's University, members of the LDS church in my mom's neighborhood made an exhaustive effort to influence my younger brother. They were successful: he went to seminary, received his endowments, served a mission, got married in the temple, and then procreated. While he was serving his mission in Portugal, during my last two years of college, my mother decided to become active in the LDS Church again. She decided to tidy up her life and go to the temple. The Church became an overpowering force in my mother's life. Everything revolved around church commitments. When my brother returned from his mission, the two of them ganged up on me. They both wanted me to read the Book of Mormon, be heterosexual, and shave my legs.

During this time, I was diagnosed with right temporal lobe epilepsy. I remember feeling random, strange sensations for very brief periods of time. I had never had a seizure, so I had no reason to suspect that those weird déjà vu feelings were, in fact, simple partial seizures. Here is the background information on the diagnosis: after falling asleep at a friend's house, I had a seizure. My friend looked alarmed when I woke up. She told me that I'd been convulsing. Even though I knew that there was no reason to doubt her story, it was difficult to believe her because I didn't remember anything. When I had my head checked out, the doctors saw no physical cause, such as a tumor or blood clot, for the seizures, so surgery wasn't an option. It is impossible to determine the exact reason that the seizures started happening, but they coincided with a time when I was taking Wellbutrin for depression. This was the beginning of a burgeoning pharmaceutical roller-coaster ride.

The epilepsy diagnosis was a turning point. I was terrified and exhausted; there was just too much wrong with me. I felt empty and broken. I was hungry for love and attention and a sense of community. I had a huge psychic void. This was the prime opportunity for my mother, brother, and the missionaries to close in on me. By the time I was twenty-eight, I had experienced enough tragedy and disappointment to be contrite and brokenhearted. All I wanted was relief. I wanted to have the 180-degree turnaround in my life just like my dad had. I figured that if even my onerous dad had eventually joined the Church, I should too.

I read the Book of Mormon, bought a dress, let my hair grow, shaved my legs, and started going to church. Immediately, there was pressure to find a husband. I conceded and got involved with the singles group. Take into consideration, my last romantic relationship had lasted two years and was with a woman, so I was completely unprepared to be a good girl by the Church's definition. These people were from another planet. How was I supposed to find a mate? My previous interactions with the opposite sex had been entirely negative. Because the Mormons believe that attaining the celestial kingdom is impossible without getting married, there is a lot of pressure to wed. The idea behind this is that as a person grows spiritually, he or she becomes more like god. And something about making babies in heaven and then populating your own planet is in there too.

I wanted relief from the adversity that had plagued me for the last twenty years. I thought I could make a deal with god: I would surrender my will in exchange for a more peaceful life. I was tired of running. I met my future husband at an activity he attended while he was in Dallas for business. Several months later, he traveled to Texas again and stayed for a couple of weeks. We were compatible in two ways: we both liked hiking outdoors and attended the same church. He was ten years older than me, had a stable income, and knew how to be a good Mormon. I remember making myself kiss him with the hope that I would feel something. It would have been helpful to have someone tell me that I should *want* to kiss the person I marry, not just be willing to tolerate it. He was thirty-nine when we got married. By the measure of his Church upbringing, he was about twenty years overdue for finding a wife. Along with the advice I needed about kissing, I needed someone to tell me that if a man is still a virgin at forty, then there's a problem somewhere.

At this point in my life, I was employed by the University of Texas Southwestern Medical Center in a biomedical laboratory. My primary responsibility was maintaining embryonic stem cells for experiments. The laboratory made mutant mice for studying cardiac tissue development. Altering genes and observing the results were fascinating, but the hands-on, day-to-day bench work was dreadfully boring. I had an inner-city, third-floor apartment in a gritty industrial area in Dallas. I was disillusioned by the anti-climactic transition from college into the working world. Laboratory work at the technician level doesn't pay well.

There happened to be an epilepsy clinic on campus where I found a neurologist to help manage my seizure disorder. I decided to participate in a clinical drug trial he suggested for Topamax, the latest greatest pharmaceutical. It was a double-blind study where neither the doctor nor I knew the dose I was taking. I remember getting on elevators and forgetting to push the buttons to go up or down. My cognitive functions declined to the degree that I could not do basic arithmetic. Not being able to think clearly made molecular biology impossible, and it made me miserable. How was I to know that this was the wrong time to make major life-altering decisions? I was afraid and looking for an escape. I agreed to marry my new boyfriend.

When he suggested that I move to Oregon to be with him, I was ready to be someone and someplace else. I headed west with every square inch of my little truck packed to maximum capacity. So far my bargain with god seemed to be working. After three months in Oregon, I was engaged to be married. As the wedding approached, I sensed something uncertain in my heart. My gut instinct was to go back to Texas, but I lacked the courage to pick up and leave. When I told him how much I wanted to go home, he begged me not to go. I was tired of running, so I stayed. I didn't know how to stand up for myself; I was totally intimidated by him. Wounded by life in the fast lane, I was vulnerable to manipulation. I knew marrying him wasn't the right choice, but I lacked faith in my intuition and myself.

I still have a photograph of me standing outside of the Portland LDS temple following my initiation and endowment. In order to be married in the temple, a person has to go through both of these ceremonies. The photo shows a classic gray Oregon sky appearing behind defoliated trees. I am wearing my grandmother's black cashmere cardigan over a long red dress as I stand with a look on my face similar to someone who has been seriously shell-shocked. I am not even smiling.

The pressure to conform was suffocating; I felt violated. My mother and brother flew in from Texas to go to my endowment. All of my soon-to-be extended family was there as well. I clearly remember the point during the ceremony when the initiate is instructed to stand up and leave if there is any doubt or reluctance about receiving their endowment ordinance. There would be no turning back. There was a covenant that carried everlasting destruction as a consequence of even casually talking about the temple ceremonies outside of the perimeter of the building. I was cornered—surrounded on both sides by people expecting me to proceed through the temple ceremony. I resented them and wanted to run, but I stayed. I associate my experiences that day with the story of Lot's wife turning back for one last look at her homeland, Sodom. What was it that we were leaving behind?

After being married for two months, we moved to Albuquerque, New Mexico. Early on I felt resentment emerging from the balance of power being in his favor. Since I was trying very hard to keep up my end of the bargain I'd made with god, I got pregnant right away. Unfortunately, this made me more trapped than ever. I tried to morph into a baby-making, bread-baking housewife, but I couldn't quite fit myself into that box. I tried following the prophets, like one of the primary songs suggests, but I got lost anyway. Over the course of the two years we lived in Albuquerque, I had two sons. I really was someone else, someplace else.

We moved back to Oregon in 2004. This time I had a two-year-old, an infant, and a very sick husband. We bought a house near his sister and parents. I was in for serious culture shock. He had been born into the Church from pioneer progeny. They were like the Mormons I remember as a kid—the ones I thought were from another planet. Shortly after we moved back, there was a cascade of unfortunate events. First, my father-in-law died, leaving a wake of chaos with his passing. It meant that I had a chance to really get to know my in-laws. Clearly I was either the black sheep or the ugly duckling.

There wasn't much time for the dust to settle before my mom died too. I won't write much about her death now other than it was unexpected and tragic. God was really letting me down. The trauma I experienced from watching modern medicine try to save her was amplified by her funeral preparation. I dressed her cold corpse in ceremonial temple clothing in preparation for burial. For months following her death, every night I would close my eyes only to begin seeing images of her in my mind. One night I dreamed that I was a greeter at a local Walmart. It was my job to say hello to the public as they walked into the store. In my dream, a young woman began talking to me as if I knew her. She told me that she was my mother resurrected, and she wanted to let me know that she was fine. Weird dream or personal prophecy? You decide. The advent of my mother's death started a downward spiral in my health. I should have seen a psychiatrist, but my husband didn't want it on my medical record, so I didn't get the help I needed. My neurologist simply prescribed more pharmaceuticals.

Seven very difficult years passed before my husband asked, "Why will you not just submit?" Those were the words that struck an undeniable, instinctual nerve that shattered my delusion that I could make a marriage manageable based on principle. Looking back, I had tried to be part of the clan by holding callings, going to the temple, wearing their underwear, and being a good girl, but it just felt so phony. I often think of the children's story by Hans Christian Andersen titled "The Emperor's New Clothes."

Earlier this evening, when I sat down to finish this essay, I heard a knock at my front door. Two young Mormon elders stood at my door with eager faces, wearing white shirts, dark ties, black pants, and dress shoes. Their hair was cut above the ears off the collar. Instantaneously I knew who they were. The conversation was awkward from the beginning. For a moment I felt pensive, and then I reacted instinctively. Rather than just telling the young men, "No, thank you," I paused while I formulated my thoughts. Then I shared with them some of my experiences with the Church that had ultimately led me away.

In that moment, I experienced a strange blend of emotions. I felt compassion because they were so young and inexperienced with the world and they were just doing what they were told. I felt sorry for them, but then I realized I started to feel a twinge of silent rage. I was angry because they were pawns sharing a scripted message without a complete understanding of the religion that they were preaching. I verified that they were from the ward I had attended last. I told them a story about their bishop that I thought they should know.

A couple of years ago, I was homeless, unemployed, and unable to drive due to a seizure, and three-quarters of my body was covered with an allergic reaction to poison oak. I described to the elders the day that I finally asked for the bishop's help. I will never forget the conversation the bishop and I had. We were talking in the library of his mansion when he said to me that he really just didn't know how to help, that he didn't know what he could do. In other words, he was clueless. He offered me assistance with food and a referral to the church employment office.

I told them about this essay and described how I'd felt when Karen asked me, "Do you believe that Jesus Christ is the son of god?" I also told them that women really get the shaft. They are expected to accept that their husbands have ultimate authority over them. Women who work full time outside of the home by choice instead of financial desperation are frowned upon. Women are expected to be meek and subservient. Clearly, that didn't work for me. I told the elders what my brother had said after he left the Church. He said that it is too bad that people at church talk about the great calamity that ensues when someone leaves the Church, but they never tell the stories of when peoples' lives actually got better. Mine did.

After all is said and done, I'd like to die happy. I realize that's a worn-out sentiment, but I wonder how many people have failed. I'd like to end this memoir with a few words about resilience and serenity. For many years of my life, I failed to let go of the past. At the same time that I was despondent, I was also afraid . . . afraid of almost everything. Desperate emotions gave rise to my delusion: the idea that if I could be someone else someplace else, then all of my pain would go away. I tried so many times and in so many ways to pacify the vacuous void in my soul: relationships, drugs, music, sex, travel, and religion. All of these diversions had their joys and pleasures, but they were ephemeral.

What I lacked was love. And, most importantly, love of myself. As I age and continue to grow in wisdom, I am better able to understand that in order to have self-esteem, I have to do estimable things. I learned that the Buddha wrote, "Suffering leads to compassion." I am grateful to have learned compassion. As I get older, not much frightens or intimidates me anymore. I consider my many trials a strange gift because through them I learned resilience.

Today the delusion that god will magically bless me if I obey his rules has ultimately been shattered. I quit searching for answers from the divine, and today I find peace in solitude—in particular, solitude in the wilderness. Also, instead of seeking my reward in heaven, I simply seek to be useful here on Earth.

NOT QUITE AN ATHEIST (AND WHERE DOES THAT LEAVE ME?)

Nancy J. Wolf

All the atoms of our bodies will be blown into space in the disintegration of the solar system, to live on forever as mass or energy. That's what we should be teaching our children, not fairy tales about angels and seeing grandma in Heaven.

—Carolyn Porco

"You think too much," my mother gently scolded me periodically as I was growing up. It was true. Even as a kid, I had a passion for the big questions: Where do we go when we die? What is the purpose of my life? Who am I really—and what do I stand for? I watched the puffy, sun-clad clouds in the summer sky and wondered what my purpose in life was—or if I even had one. I wondered what lay beyond the stars and tried to imagine infinity or God or Jesus risen from the dead. "You think too much," my mother would say gently. *But how can you not think?* I asked myself. These are matters that will affect how you live your life. What you believe, what the meaning of your life is, why you are here, whether there is a God—all of these issues are the foundations of everyday life, the decisions we make on big and small matters. How can I not think about these things?

Being raised in the Lutheran Church, my thinking self, of course, believed in God and in Jesus. I prayed sincerely and fervently, but never for frivolous things like going swimming on Saturday or getting a dime for the Dairy Queen. I prayed for important things like for God to feed the poor and clothe the poor children whose homes had been hit by an earthquake in Turkey. (Well, okay, I admit I also prayed for Diana Nash—the most popular girl in sixth grade—to like me; but mostly, I believed that if God was going to answer my prayers, he was more likely to answer a prayer I made on behalf of someone else than a prayer I made for myself.) In my Christian heart, I harbored the religious spirit of Christmas. I was filled with wonder and an inner peace at the thought of the shepherds and the angels rejoicing in the birth of the Prince of Peace. I loved listening to Handel's *Messiah* and Bach's cantatas, the melodies and surging choruses and the words so moving that I thought that if a human being could write music that seared my soul, surely God must have inspired him. I even thought that, when I grew up, I might want to be a Christian missionary to the country that was then called Tanganyika, in East Africa.

But as I grew, I continued to think and by thirteen or fourteen, I had a lot of questions about Christianity that I was afraid to pose to anyone, as I knew in my heart that no one would be able to answer them. How could Jesus possibly raise Lazarus from the dead and heal a blind man? (Didn't these supposed occurrences completely contravene common sense?) Did God really part the Red Sea for the Hebrews to escape slavery in Egypt? If these miracles really occurred, why did such miracles happen only in biblical times and not in my lifetime? And after all, it was the miracles recounted in the Bible that made me (and other Christians, I assume) believe that God existed. For if these things really never took place as the Bible said, what evidence would we have of God?

If God wanted to save us from our sins, I wondered, why didn't he (as the omnipotent God) just simply forgive us and send a prophet to tell us we were forgiven? Why did he instead send himself in human form to suffer and die on the cross, when the act of forgiveness could have been so much neater and cleaner if he just announced it himself? And it always seemed to me that Jesus's "gift" of extreme suffering to save us from our sins seemed so overblown. Hadn't "regular" human beings suffered just as much for other reasons that were just as worthy—and, more tellingly, for reasons that were unworthy? Why were we singling out Jesus's suffering? And weren't Jesus's miracles—the loaves and the fishes to feed the multitude, raising Lazarus from the dead, turning water to wine—what Christians relied upon to believe that Jesus was divine? And if Jesus hadn't really performed these miracles, wouldn't he just be an ordinary guy with a great philosophy and a message of compassion?

How did I know that no Christian had answers to these questions that were in my mind? To me, the questions themselves were obvious, but no one ever addressed them. The minister never preached on why there were no biblical miracles of epic proportions in modern times. The Sunday school teacher never offered to explain why Jesus had to die to save us from our sins. If there were answers to my questions, I knew that Christians would have been discussing these answers—and the fact that no one even posed the questions in church (where we were supposed to be learning about God and Jesus) meant to me that Christians either (1) were so indoctrinated in their religion that they had no questions, or (2) had no answers and so didn't bother to ask the obvious questions about the problems with Christian faith.

At fourteen, I read the 1965 *New York Times* best seller called *The Passover Plot* by New Testament scholar Hugh J. Schonfield which posited that Jesus, during his ministry, came to believe that he was the Messiah prophesied in the Old Testament and that he deliberately faked his own death and resurrection specifically to fulfill the Old Testament prophecies about a Messiah, the Son of God, and thus, to himself *become* the Messiah. In 1965, this was a well-known and, of course, very controversial book. The premise of the book was far-fetched but nonetheless seemed to me less far-fetched than believing that Jesus died and literally rose from the dead to save me from my sins.

While the premise of *The Passover Plot* was suspicious, Lutheran beliefs about the Trinity, the resurrection, and heaven were also suspicious. Why should I believe something that feels so counterintuitive to me just because my mother believed it or because the minister and my Sunday school teachers believed it? Wasn't it possible that, as fallible and limited human beings, my mother and the minister and the Sunday school teachers were just wrong? Anyway, how would they know that Jesus died and rose from the dead and that I was saved from my sins? Didn't they just get indoctrinated from *their* parents and minister and Sunday school teachers? And didn't all of this belief come from the Bible? And how did anyone know that the Bible was accurate?

Also at fourteen, I was confirmed in the Methodist Church. I almost didn't go through with it. Although I understood God the Father and God the Son, I didn't understand the Holy Spirit—and thus, without a firm belief in the Trinity, I felt I couldn't honestly affirm that I was a Christian. Nonetheless, to avoid embarrassing my family and raising questions about how I—as a mere fourteen-year-old—could possibly question the tenets of that long-standing institution, the Christian Church, I got confirmed and just went on believing what I believed (i.e., that Christianity was suspicious). I had no guilt about this choice, as I felt no deep connection to God anyway, and I thus exonerated myself of blasphemy. I felt, without being able to articulate the feeling at the time, that at my confirmation I had professed a belief in an empty shell, an external system (religion) without any real substance inside of it that I could relate to.

At seventeen I was in a high school sociology class and also a high school humanities class that introduced me to new views of the world— views based on research, critical thinking, analysis, and introspection. Those classes shaped my life, even to this day. These teachers introduced us to existentialism (from Sartre to Kierkegaard), critical and analytic views of the functioning of American society, questions about history that encouraged critical thinking (Was it right to drop the bomb on Hiroshima without giving the Japanese notice of the destruction our new technology could wreak?), and issues of morality, of the role of government in people's lives, of the essence of being, and of the essence of truth. I was encouraged to ask questions, read critically, and examine my own life and beliefs. At this time, the sociology teacher encouraged each student to choose a book of interest, to read it critically, and to share our thoughts and analysis with him privately as a mentor and guide. I chose to read *I and Thou* by the Jewish mystic Martin Buber. This book introduced me to a highly abstract philosophy that encouraged thinking of other beings in their own light, as essential beings unto themselves rather than always resorting to the default—viewing other beings as implements of utility in our own lives. The concepts in *I and Thou* resonated with me: I found I was more interested in the mysterious, hidden, ineffable characteristics of being and the universe than I was in religious doctrine or in orthodox religious systems. The broad scope of my spiritual inquiries opened me to many possibilities beyond Christianity—and, although I knew atheism was one such possibility—I was not ready to commit to a firm belief in anything.

All of my learning and reading opened me to multiple possibilities. I began to believe that there is not one right way of thinking. The Christian beliefs that I had been taught were not the only way to interpret the world. (And, indeed, even Christians disagreed among themselves about what constituted the correct Christian belief.) I finally had the courage to doubt the Christian faith I had been raised in. I would say that, at this time, I believed in God, but I had no way to ascribe any characteristics to "him." I believed in God the Father and in the possibility of heaven but without being able to articulate what role God played in my life.

At eighteen I went away to a private Christian college—not to practice or deepen my feeble faith—but because it was the best place to get the best, most individualized education and as a place to continue my musings about the Christian faith I had been raised in. I took the two required semesters of Christian Bible history—and I was delightfully surprised that my professor, a Lutheran minister and scholar, welcomed my doubts and questions and musings. He encouraged my thoughtful approach to Christianity. In the end, the class confirmed my beliefs that I was probably not a Christian. But what was I? Had I a faith in anything? However these were not questions that troubled me. In truth, I was enjoying the search, the thought process and the many possibilities of what there was to believe in. I didn't have to choose. I felt fulfilled by wondering, questioning, reading, and discussing.

As an adult, I had to let go of my philosophical and religious questions. I had a career and a family and little time to contemplate the beautiful abstractions of religion and philosophy. I attended a Presbyterian church occasionally but mainly because the music was so beautiful and because the minister, educated at Princeton, preached thought-provoking sermons replete with references to literature and social issues and philosophy. It was an intellectually inspiring church environment, and I enjoyed the service for itself, not because the Church fed my faith. Eventually, I stopped attending church all together. Much later, after I was married and when my daughter was old enough, my husband and I joined a Methodist church (which welcomed a variety of members who were anywhere along the path of their faith journey), and we enrolled our daughter in Sunday school. I even taught her Sunday school class for five years, every Sunday, without fail. Why did I do that? I sometimes ask myself. I think I believed that Sunday school would give her a foundation to believe in *something*. I wanted her to have the opportunity to decide for herself what she believed.

Some religious upbringing, some religious information, was necessary for her to understand what religion had to offer and was essential to give her a basis to examine her own beliefs.

She, like me, didn't want to be confirmed in the church. She said she had too many doubts. In tenth grade, she was taking an intense world history class. She came home one day and, in awe, told me that her class had been discussing how religion had been used to repress people throughout history. She was quite disgusted and, after a few weeks of thought, said that religion was just a superstition and that she thought she was an atheist. I did not react to her declaration of unbelief but rather was happy that she was thinking for herself.

I had never confided in my daughter that I also had doubts about Christianity. I had never declared myself an atheist—and in fact, at that time, I wouldn't have said I was an atheist. As for my church attendance with my daughter, I had always just let my church attendance speak for itself, hoping that going to church was just a way to tell her that Christianity was available to her as a way of life. I was not shocked by her firm and heart-felt expression of atheism. I knew she was a thinker, just as I had been, and I knew she had a genuine compassion for others, she had a social conscience, and she had the high level of integrity that her father and I had tried to instill in her. Apart from expecting her to live a life of honesty and compassion, I did not care to insert myself into her faith life. In fact, her expression of atheism gave me a sort of permission to re-examine my own religious beliefs and gave me the courage to re-acknowledge my own doubts—subjects that I had abandoned or avoided for many years in favor of a demanding career and a family.

In the end, however, despite my daughter's protests, I convinced her to be confirmed, only because I knew that people's beliefs change throughout a lifetime and I believed that if she were confirmed, she would be better positioned to take up her faith again if she later decided she wanted to partake in a Christian life.

So what does this say about me? What does it mean that I basically eschew the Christian faith but cannot declare myself an atheist? Am I an agnostic, one who admits that she does not know enough to confirm or deny the existence of God? What *do* I believe? I cannot say that I am an atheist or an agnostic: I like to say that I am a hoper. I want God to exist. I want a god who breathed life into me and who has my best interests at heart. I want there to be satisfying answers to the mysteries of life, and I want these answers to be personal—not just explanations that refer back to the random meanderings of atomic particles and light waves and random mutations in cells that eventually evolved into human beings. I want the answers to show that I am special, made in the image of a loving God, and endowed with a unique purpose on Earth. But I doubt that my hopes will be realized. I hope, but I don't think it's likely.

In the end, though, what is it that makes me doubt the Christian religion that I was raised in? What is it about Christianity that I find unfulfilling and improbable?

Why Bad Things Happen to Good People:
Maybe because There Is No God

A distant relative of mine once came to a family gathering, arriving in a flurry, announcing that she had almost not been able to bring the photos of her newborn to the celebration because she had misplaced them. She obviously really wanted us to see what the new baby had looked like in the moments after birth, but as she was packing her suitcase, she just could not find those pictures. She explained that she had prayed to God that she would find the photos before her flight to Minnesota and, in fact, she found them. She thanked God for answering her prayer.

Compare this story to the iconic photo of a starving, emaciated African boy, about three years old, tiny, sitting alone in the dirt of the African plain, just minutes or hours from death, with a vulture, the same size as him, sitting not ten feet away, staring at the boy—waiting for the boy to die so that it could have a meal.

If there is a Christian God and if, as Christians believe, God is good, why would he help my relative find her family photos but allow this African child to starve in the dust?

Let's consider more about the state of the world as we know it. Women in Sudan are gang-raped when they go to gather firewood to cook a meal. Men and women on Wall Street have raped and pillaged the American economic system for their individual benefit, causing other American families to lose their homes, their dignity, and their hope for the future. Women in India are murdered for having sex before marriage, and others are burned to death on the funeral pyre of the deceased husband simply because that is a long-held custom in certain regions of the country.

Catastrophic events and deeds have befallen people in every country, among every ethnic and racial group, from time immemorial. We have all witnessed that there are billions of individual people who, throughout history, have suffered mentally, emotionally, and physically; have lived and died alone, with a whimper or a scream; and who are faceless to us. And although we do not see these people in this essay, we know in our minds and our experience that this kind of extreme suffering has existed since human beings first appeared on Earth—sick, repressed, abused, neglected, hungry, powerless, poverty-stricken, empty-hearted, hopeless, in pain, uneducated, serving in war-torn lands, unfulfilled for reasons beyond their ability to change, and grief-stricken for any one of innumerable reasons. My relative believes that God was gracious enough to help her find her photos in time to bring to the Christmas festivities, but where is God, where are his miracles of biblical proportions in cases of real need?

Many look at seas, little children, and sunsets and, moved, they say, "Surely, such a sunset could not exist if God did not create it." Many survive a terrible illness or live through a horrendous accident or see the starving being fed and say, "Surely God is good because, even in the worst situations, good things happen."

I, however, cannot compartmentalize what I see. I cannot see the beauty of a sunrise and forget that children and old people are dying and alone. I see trees blossoming in spring and I rejoice, but I do not forget the hundreds of thousands of dead bodies littering the road of Rwanda in 1994. So which do we choose to say? Do we choose to say that the world is so full of beauty and goodness that there must be a God who created this? Why couldn't we also say the world is so full of evil and ugliness that maybe there is *no* God? Or we why can't we say that the world is so full of evil and ugliness that maybe, if God exists, he is evil? Based on the beauty and goodness in the world, we can say that God is good. Based upon the horrors we see in the world, why can we not likewise say God is evil—or that there is no God? Do people choose to see only the beautiful part because it reinforces the religious view they already choose to hold? Do they believe so strongly that they cannot admit how horrible the horrors are—and they cannot question why such horrors exist?

The religious often say that evil exists for a reason, and they also say that we cannot understand the mind of God. The religious say that God has a grand plan that we cannot fathom, implying that God may have a reason for the existence of evil that will ultimately be revealed as a means to a greater good. They say that God moves in "mysterious ways."

If this is so, I still cannot compartmentalize evil. Catastrophic, tragic life events occur. People suffer and live in inescapable misery. That God may be acting "mysteriously" or that God may have a "grand plan" does not negate that, in the meantime, God allows horrendous things to happen to human beings. There is no way to minimize or discount these miseries. To me, human misery is evidence of an arbitrary and random universe, a universe where bad things happen to righteous people, where good things happen to depraved people, where the innocent suffer, where the unexpected and inexplicable govern. A plan, on the other hand, if it existed, would be orderly and logical. A grand plan would be masterful, organized, systematic, and coherent. I do not believe that a loving God would have a grand plan that causes human suffering on such a vast scale. Human misery is evidence of randomness, not of a loving God.

Let's Play Telephone—What Can We Believe?

Leap of Faith

I have heard Christians say that you will never believe in God if you use only your brain—your reasoning powers—that belief requires the proverbial leap of faith between what we know and what cannot know. But for me, that leap of faith is unjustified.

If I were to have a belief in God through a leap of faith, I must leap *from* somewhere to reach the faith of a Christian believer. If I leap into the river, I must leap *from* somewhere—from the boat, from the riverbank. If I leap to the ground, I must leap *from* somewhere—from the balcony or from the tabletop. Likewise, to leap to a Christian faith, I must leap from somewhere. I must be grounded in something before I leap. Most Christians look to the Bible as the source of their religious belief, the platform from which they leap. Many Christians trust the Bible because they say it was divinely inspired and, consequently, it reflects the mind and nature of God (the Christian God) to the extent that we can know and understand God.

First, before I discuss my lack of faith in the Bible, I must ask: what is it about the Bible that induces in people a belief in God and in Jesus? Certainly, many of the "characters" in the Bible—from Moses, to King David, to the Apostle Peter, to the Apostle Paul—had a belief in Yahweh, the

Hebrew God. The books of the Bible reveal that faith. However, I personally choose not to base my belief in the Christian religion based on what some individuals I do not know believed thousands of years ago. Furthermore, the Bible recounts Jesus's message of love, compassion, and forgiveness. Yes, this is a message I can believe in, but this message alone does not make Jesus divine. Jesus did not, in my mind, become the Son of God just because he preached a message of love and humanitarianism that resonates with me. After all, mere mortals (Mother Teresa, Albert Schweitzer, Eleanor Roosevelt, humanitarian Dr. Tom Dooley, Pope Francis, and many other philosophers and humanitarians) have propounded the same message over time, but preaching the message itself did not make the messenger divine.

No, there must be *something else* about the Bible that, for believers, establishes the existence of God and that establishes Jesus was the divine Son of God. I think that the feature of the Bible that establishes the existence of Yahweh (God the Father) and Jesus as the Messiah is the recounting of miracles, supernatural events effectuated by God or Jesus that mere mortals could not bring about: the plagues visited upon Egypt to convince Pharaoh of the power of the God of the Israelites, the Great Flood, the rendering of Lot's wife into a pillar of salt at Sodom and Gomorrah, the bounty of manna to feed the Israelites in the desert—these are the miracles of the Old Testament that instill a sense of a divine intervention in the lives of men, intervention by God. In the New Testament, Jesus rises bodily from the dead. He miraculously heals the lame and the blind and the lepers. He survives in the desert for forty days and forty nights. (Indeed, Yahweh himself tells Aaron and Moses to perform supernatural acts—turning a shepherd's staff into a serpent—to convince Pharaoh that Yahweh is in fact a mighty god. Yahweh himself thus relies on miracles to prove that he is the real God.) An ordinary human being could not do these things and thus, a man who *can* do these things, such as Jesus, *must* be extra-worldly. It is the miracles wrought in the Bible that persuade us of the divinity of Yahweh and Jesus. So if the miracles of the Bible are not true, then how can I believe in Yahweh and in Jesus Christ?

You Can't Trust Hearsay

I cannot leap to faith based upon the Bible. Consider that the Bible was written by many different authors, authors that we do not know. In the Old Testament, biblical scholars have distinguished as many as four different writers of the Pentateuch, the first five books of the Old Testament. We do not know who these authors were; they are lost to history. Because no one knows the identities of these four writers, we cannot talk with them or determine how they learned what they revealed in their writings, nor can we reveal any biases they may have had when they wrote or determine the source of their supposed divine inspiration.

Similarly, the New Testament was written by almost eight different authors, each with a different story to tell. We do not actually know exactly who all of these authors are, but we do know that Jesus's disciples did not themselves write the books of the Gospels. The actual witnesses to the life of Jesus never recorded what they saw or experienced. Biblical scholars assert that the writers of the books of the New Testament did not personally witness any of the acts of Jesus, but rather they *heard* about them from the apostles and others. The Gospel of Mark was probably written first, and the books of Matthew and Luke appear to borrow heavily from Mark. The Apostle Paul, who wrote Ephesians, Romans, and other letters to nascent Christian communities around the Mediterranean, never met Jesus and was probably a boy living in what is now Turkey while Jesus was preaching. Thus, Paul wrote his epistles based upon what he personally chose to believe based on what he experienced and what others told him.

In short, the written biblical record about God and Jesus is hearsay—and hearsay is a risky basis for belief. In fact, in American courts hearsay is generally not allowed into evidence at a trial because it is inherently unreliable. Hearsay is suspect because we often cannot establish the veracity of what is reported. Hearsay does not allow us to obtain information directly from the original source of the information: in this case, for example, we cannot talk directly to Moses or to the Israelites personally or to Jesus or to his disciples or to those with whom Jesus came into contact. We have no way to verify the accuracy of what biblical writers reported based on a story that passed from mouth to mouth over a period of years. Without the direct ability to confirm the correctness of what is reported in the Bible, I am unwilling make a leap of faith based on hearsay.

Time Erodes Memory

Furthermore, time erodes memories. The first of the four Gospels was first written in approximately 50 or 60 CE, at least one generation after Jesus's ministry, considering this was a historical period when lives were short.

How many times were the stories of Jesus passed down until they were finally written down? And what level of accuracy did they lose over time?

We have all experienced this phenomenon: As time passes, we do not remember details of events, even of those events that we personally witnessed. Some memories are hazy, or we do not remember some parts of an incident at all. We frequently fill in the gaps in our memory, not with what actually happened but with what makes sense with the rest of the story we are telling or with what makes sense from our individual and distinctive point of view. We are not lying, but we are subject to the fallibility of human memory. How many times have we argued with a family member about what exactly happened when we were children or what happened at an event that is part of the family's collective memory? Who said Dad was the best salesman in the United States—was it Uncle Jim or Uncle Bob? Who got drunk and fell flat on her face at Aunt Sue's wedding thirty years ago—was it Aunt Louise or Cousin Linda? Even in a family, where people witnessed the same event firsthand, we do not always agree on what happened.

This failure of memory with the passage of time casts doubts upon the accuracy of biblical accounts of events in the Old Testament and events involving Jesus. I have asserted that Christian faith is based upon stories about the miracles that Jesus wrought. But these stories are the product of hearsay and are thus very likely inaccurate or, at least, only partly accurate. If these miracles had not occurred—or were misreported or exaggerated—wouldn't that undermine the likelihood that the miracles happened at all? And if Jesus did not create miracles, wouldn't that fact undermine (or obviate) Christian beliefs? If Jesus did not bring about the miracles reported in the Gospels, wouldn't he be just a regular human being who lived long ago and who had a particularly compelling philosophy of life? Similarly, if God did not in fact create a miracle to save the Israelites from Pharaoh or if Jesus did not in fact raise Lazarus from the dead and if the other miracles told in the Bible didn't happen, then is there a god at all? Is Jesus really a divine being? In short, the accuracy of biblical hearsay has been adversely affected—not just by being filtered through multiple storytellers and reporters but also by the passage of time, by the fact that what we remember over time is unreliable, that much of memory is lost or exaggerated or added to over time.

Galvanizing Christian Beliefs

Jesus never personally declared himself the Son of God. Belief that Jesus was the long-awaited Messiah prophesied in the Old Testament only arose after Jesus's death. Early Christian sects held a variety of disparate beliefs about Jesus. Some sects believed that Jesus was coexistent with God. Other sects believed that Jesus was divine but was not in the same category as the all-powerful, omnipotent God. The Roman Emperor Constantine, who converted from paganism to Christianity, convened a council of Christian sect leaders to decide the issue of the divinity of Jesus. This was the Council of Nicaea, held in 325 CE. The council, consisting of more than three hundred Christian bishops from various parts of Europe, decided that Jesus and God were of the same "substance," that Jesus coexisted with God, and that Jesus— like God—had no beginning and no end. In other words, Jesus was in fact God in a physical form, rather than the two being separate entities.

I find this council and its decision troubling. A group of Christians, holding a variety of beliefs about Jesus, came together and formulated the doctrine that Christians still hold today (as expressed in the Nicene Creed). Weren't these council members mere human beings? How can they decide that Jesus is one with God the Father? What made their beliefs right? Again, fallible human beings were entering the province of the divine—and I do not trust that these council members necessarily made a true or accurate determination about whether Jesus was divine or coexistent with God the Father.

In addition, we must consider how the books of the New Testament were effectively selected and organized into the Bible we accept today. Many writings about Jesus were extant in the years after his death, beginning about 50 to 60 CE, but not all of those writings were eventually accepted as the divinely inspired New Testament. The canon of the New Testament was chosen by a succession of religious and scholarly councils, which determined whether various texts written about Jesus were worthy to be designated as the inspired word of God. Most of these later councils re-endorsed the books that had been selected by earlier historic councils, but some changes were made by each council until about 400 CE, when the Bible as we currently know it was adopted.

I have questions though about those who selected and designated these ancient writings as divinely inspired or God-given. Were the selections driven by political or personal motives that we cannot discern today, many hundreds of years later? Did those on the councils who designated the books as divinely inspired unanimously concur—or did they make trade-offs with one another, swapping votes? Were there dissenters? After all, those who chose the books of the Bible were human and undoubtedly approached the task of selecting the "genuine" New Testament texts with fallible human motives. Although Christians will say that they believe what is in the Bible because the Bible was divinely inspired, how do they arrive at that conclusion? How did they know what was divinely inspired? How did the council members know that certain writing, most notably the Gnostic Gospels, were supposedly not worthy to be included in the final version of the Christian Bible? How did they know which writings were the accurate words and acts of Jesus? How did they, as fallible human beings, presume *themselves* to be worthy to select what should be included in a Bible that would guide millions of people over thousands of years?

My own answer is that these early Christians were not infallible in their determination that Jesus was coexistent with God and they were not infallible in their choices of the canon. They were influenced by other fallible humans, and they were influenced by their own cultural, political, family, and educational biases. All were human beings; they were prone to err and thus are not a credible, solid foundation for my own choice to believe or not to believe. Their opinions are no better than my own in deciding what is the truth about God.

The Biblical Writers' Indoctrination Agenda

A further problem arises from the fact that the authors of the books of the Bible wrote with the purpose of convincing us to believe in their cause. The biblical authors (whether unwittingly or purposefully) already believed in the divinity of Jesus. They were writing about Jesus's ministry to perpetuate their own faith. In doing so they embellished their memories to serve their own purposes and to communicate their inspiration and their faith. They were not communicating bare facts, but rather they were communicating with a gloss, with their own biases in favor of the divinity of Jesus or the omnipotence of Yahweh, the God of Israel. The biblical writers did not write to help us make up our own minds; they wrote to persuade us to believe as they believed. They wrote to convince us of the rightness of their own viewpoint. I, however, cannot choose a faith just because others, long ago and far away, chose that faith for themselves.

Thus, here again, we are confronted with the vagaries of human memory. Because the biblical writers were human, it stands to reason they sometimes remembered things as they wish they had happened. Or they inserted into their stories an interpretation of what happened or what they understood the story to mean. The books of the New Testament were written by people who believed in the divinity of Jesus, and they wrote with the specific intention of persuading people to believe their point of view.

This is a trait that exists in modern, twenty-first-century humans. When we recount a story, we often tell not only the facts of the story (as we best recall them) but also what the story *means* to us: that my uncle was jerk, that I was a smart baby, that my grandmother loved us, or that my neighbor was a failure as a parent. Surely, the biblical writers did likewise.

Cultural Interpretations

Finally, I find it difficult to accept the Bible as a source of faith because historically biblical culture was so different than our own. Consider when the Bible was written: in the first century CE, people had a greater belief in unknown, inexplicable cosmic forces. They believed that plagues arose as punishments for bad behavior. They believed that animal sacrifices would bring a good crop. They believed in enchantments and superstition. They could not interpret the events of Jesus's life and death without recourse to their own irrationality, as they existed in a time before science, filling in the blanks of what they saw and heard using their own cultural and religious biases.

From my perspective, the books of the Bible are suspect as a source of faith because they were written in a time when supernatural interpretations were the only explanations for inexplicable occurrences such as disease, repression, weather events, military victories, and crop failures. Biblical culture supported a belief system made up of demons, superstition, and miracles only because biblical peoples had no alternative scientific explanations for what they saw and experienced. Then, when the biblical authors later wrote about those events, they attributed them to divine, supernatural forces because, based on the limited knowledge of the period in which they lived, they had no other choice.

In modern times, when scientific explanations can be offered for so many phenomena, science and religion do not necessarily have to conflict. There exist many phenomena that have a scientific explanation but where the scientifically explained occurrence could have a divine source. We know, scientifically, that the universe is made up of atoms and molecules. Our knowledge of atoms and molecules does not obviate the possibility that the atoms and molecules were put in place by God. This idea is often referred to as intelligent design.

On the other hand, science does conflict with religion where religion describes a supernatural event that cannot be explained by science or that defies what we know through science. I am doubtful that Jesus's miracles occurred because raising Lazarus from the dead or turning water into wine contravenes what science says is possible. The culture of the biblical writers gives rise to fallacies that defy the scientific culture's laws of possibility.

Playing Telephone

Reading the Bible is like playing the game of telephone: One person whispers a sentence to another person. The second person whispers it to a third, and then the third person to the fourth, and so on. By the end the original message has been garbled and often bears little resemblance to the sentence announced by the last person. "I haven't got a gun," for example, can end up as "I have bought a bun." But in the biblical game of telephone, the original message is further garbled by the time that has passed between the life of Jesus and the time the New Testament was written, the foreign culture that filtered the message of the biblical writers, and the human fallibility of those who chose the books of the Bible and designated them as the inspired word of God.

The writings included in the Bible are thus marred by the biases of superstition, by the cultural viewpoint of each writer, by the passage of time from the date an incident occurred and the date it was recorded, by the inescapable loss and distortion of information as it is passed orally from one source to another before it was written down, and by the fallibility of human memory. I cannot make a leap of faith from such a tenuous platform.

Where Does This Leave Me?

So where *does* this leave me? Not willing to deny the existence of God. Not willing to affirm the existence of God. Trying to understand the Gospels. Hoping that there is a God, but thinking there probably is not.

What I Know (Or, At Least, What I Think I Know)

My analysis of the deficiencies of religion are not necessarily dispositive, however, as my analysis deals only with facts or supposed facts and does not take intuition, sensations, or the experiences of the inner life into account. Many Christians have had flashes of insight or experiences that they "know" comes from a cosmic force, from a higher power, from God. These experiences cannot be proved or disproved. Such experience transcends facts. If such an experience becomes the basis for a religious belief, I cannot dispute the legitimacy of others' experiences, nor can I dispute the religious belief that comes to them based on these experiences. I, in contrast, have had no such experience—and I probably would distrust such an experience even if it struck me, as the human brain is so prone to teasing itself, fooling itself, and carrying prejudgments. (Think, for example, of people who hallucinate, have delusions, or have other mental processes that present untrue "realities.") In such instances, the brain is not reliable. The brain is subject to fancifulness and self-deception. Although I respect those with religious beliefs, I cannot make their acceptance of religion into my own acceptance. So one thing I know is that I am probably not open to a transcendent religious experience.

In the midst of doubts about the existence of God, I subscribe to a philosophy of compassion that reflects the life of Jesus. If Jesus is not divine (and I don't know whether Jesus is divine or not), I nonetheless believe in his message. If there is no God, no heaven, no afterlife, then all we have is the here and now. All we have is how we treat one another on this earth, as there is no place that each human being will get a second chance, a better option. I do believe that how we live our lives is more important than whether we believe in a divine being. If God exists and loves me, he knows that the acts of my life reflect all he would have wanted me to be—and he forgives my unbelief because he knows I have been seeking him and that I try to live his message of peace and compassion.

In fact, I liken myself to a newborn, just out of the womb. As such, I am born into a world that I can never conceive of—a world of quantum particles, credit default swaps, calculus, neurological research, milk vs. dark chocolate. I have no concept of the simplest things: sleeping, food, parents, love. Nonetheless, these realities do exist, even though I, as a newborn, cannot conceive of them. In the face of an infinite and complex universe, the newborn me knows next to nothing. Maybe my minuscule, fallible self, facing the unfathomable universe, is the same as a newborn. Maybe, like a newborn who cannot conceive of mother, father, or food, I similarly am of such limited capacity that I cannot, with my puny brain and my limited ken, understand God. In my human condition, I realize that maybe God does not exist. But I also see that maybe God does exist but that I just cannot reach him.

Hoper as Seeker

I have sought an answer to the question of God for much of my life. I have read numerous scholarly Christian works: *Jesus Christ and Mythology* by Rudolf Bultmann, *Zealot: The Life and Time of Jesus of Nazareth* by Reza Aslan, *Mere Christianity* by C. S. Lewis, and other books by Christian apologists and books about the historical Jesus. I have never read a book about atheism, as I want to avoid so-called confirmation bias that can come up when reading only those ideas that reflect what I already believe. I want my doubtfulness to be challenged. I do not want to read about what I already believe, but to read in a way that opens *new* ways of thinking. Thus, I have read only about Christianity to determine if any Christian or historical writer can give me an insight that can become the basis for a leap of faith.

I have also read books about cosmology, about the scientific study of the origins of the universe, and about quantum physics (books for a lay audience, I must add). These books explain such concepts as the origin of the Big Bang, how there may be an infinite number of universes (not just the single universe we are familiar with but the multiverse), how physicists theorize that there may be an infinite number of each of us (multiple copies of each individual human being that live in different universes of the multiverse), and how reality is not immutable but takes different forms and may actually move among the various universes of the multiverse. I have read about the time-space fabric of the cosmos. (My favorite is *The Fabric of the Cosmos* by Brian Greene.) Much of this science is just theory, but the theories are posited by physicists and astrophysicists who concur that there is more to the cosmos than just this one universe. To the extent that I grasp these concepts, they inform my spirituality. The universe (the multiverse) is so vast, so mysterious, so unexpected, majestic, unfathomable. What must there be in the cosmos that I cannot imagine? What unbelievable, unimaginable things—even perhaps God?

I subscribe to a thought expressed by William Shakespeare:

There are more things in heaven and earth, Horatio,
Than are dreamt of in your philosophy.
—*Hamlet*, Act 1, Scene 5, lines 167–8 (Hamlet to Horatio)

I also see the universe as so complex that I cannot fathom what it holds. I see the universe as full of possibilities presented by myriad forces I know and do not know; forces seen and unseen, of quantum physics, God, multiple universes, universal love, spirituality, the flow of time and space, dark matter, energy, forces known and unknown. The Bible verse in 1 Corinthians 13:12 speaks deeply to me: "For now we see through a glass, darkly; but then face to face: now I know in part; but then shall I know even as also I am known."

To me, this passage means (if I may offer my personal interpretation): Now, our understanding is fuzzy, faulty, occluded, but someday we will know the truth fully. If there is a God, we will see him. But if there is no God and no afterlife, I hope I will nonetheless no longer see through a glass darkly: I hope I will receive the answers to all universal, philosophical, and religious questions upon my death. I can only hope that in my death, I will understand—that all will be revealed to me.

Something Is Happening

The multiverse is so vast and dense and incomprehensible that I feel *something* is happening here. Something transcendent. Something that affects all of humankind. I do not know what it is. It could be God, a higher power with a consciousness. It could be a higher power without a consciousness. It could be that there is no higher power and that I am an essential part of the stream of humankind that flows through time eternal. Whatever it is, I am a witness to something I cannot describe. Such a sweet mystery! I do not despair to have no answer, for I love the mystery.

APPENDIX:
THE SUBORDINATION OF WOMEN
IN THE JUDEO-CHRISTIAN TRADITION

Karen L. Garst

Culture in the United States, while not homogeneous, has been strongly influenced by the tenets of Western civilization. While Western civilization's roots date back to early societies in the Middle East, many of its characteristics can be traced to the Judeo-Christian tradition. Because the first immigrants who came to this country did so to escape religious persecution in Europe, the Bible was probably the most common book found in their belongings. Even today it might be difficult to find someone in the United States who has not heard of this book or who could not name a story or person portrayed in it. It would be less likely, however, outside church leaders, academics, and the very devout, to find those who have studied it in depth or read it cover to cover. Many people might be surprised to learn that one of the justifications used to deny women equal rights over the centuries comes from this core religious document. Some authors in this book point out stories from the Bible and how their church or synagogue leaders interpreted them, how these interpretations affected them, and why they came to reject them. For those readers who want to learn more about the treatment of women in the Bible, the following synopsis is provided.

* * *

Up until the second millennium BCE, most people worshipped a pantheon of gods and goddesses. This is the mythology most of us learned in high school: a dizzying array of names, cultures, religious practices, stories, songs, poems, and customs. Conquering nations brought their deities with them and often were satisfied with incorporating them into the existing practices of the people they subjugated. Trying to tease out the origins of these gods and goddesses has occupied historians for over 2,500 years. With few exceptions, the presence of a female deity in the pantheon did not translate into equal treatment for men and women living in that culture. Most societies have been patriarchal since at least the establishment of cities and the accumulation of property. But a group of people was poised to exacerbate this by eliminating any female deity or concept of the feminine divine from worship.

The first reference to this group of people, the Israelites, is found on a stone stela dated to the year 1207 BCE. On this stela, the Egyptian ruler Merneptah recorded his victories, including one over a people referred to as Israel who lived in Canaan (present-day Israel and Palestine). Over hundreds of years, the stories of the Israelites were written down, edited, and expanded, resulting in the text that Jews refer to as the Tanach and Christians refer to as the Old Testament. Today, three monotheist religions are based on these Israelite origins: Judaism, Christianity, and Islam. In contrast to the many religions that preceded them, the books of the Old Testament are unique in promoting the worship of one single god, a god that is referred to as male. There is a possibility that this god, Yahweh, initially had a female consort. However, when the Israelites returned from captivity in Babylon in the sixth century BCE, the religion was almost exclusively monotheistic.

While the Israelites were captives in Babylon, they were exposed to a somewhat similar transformation in the worship of the Babylonian deities. The male Marduk had asserted himself over the other gods and violently killed Tiamat, the strong female deity, in the Babylonian epic *Enuma Elish*. This ascendency of a male deity is also seen in other cultures' worldviews and creation stories. In the Bible, however, women are not only eliminated as part of the divine and subordinated to males as in other patriarchal societies, but they are also blamed for introducing sin into the world.

This raises the subordination of women to a whole new level. It is hard to underestimate the role that the story of Eve has played in the treatment of women in Western civilization.

Eve, the first woman, is the transgressor in the Garden of Eden, a paradise created by god. By eating the fruit of the forbidden tree of knowledge and tempting the first man, Adam, to do so as well, Eve later becomes responsible in Church doctrine for original sin. Once discovered by Yahweh, they are both banished from paradise. It is not by accident that what becomes the devil in later interpretation is portrayed in this story as a serpent. Asherah was a goddess worshipped in Canaan, the land the Israelites eventually came to rule. The Israelite leaders often railed against her worship by some members of their tribes. Female deities, such as Asherah, were associated with fertility, regeneration, and cycles. Serpents or snakes were used as symbols of the important power of renewal because they shed their skin and grew it anew. In Egyptian, the written word for goddess *is* the symbol of the cobra. What better way to put down this goddess worship than by portraying the devil using a classic symbol associated with her? Other common symbols of goddess worship were present in this story as well, including a tree of knowledge, a setting in nature, and female sexuality. As stated above, when male deities were introduced to many cultures, the goddess figure was usually incorporated in some fashion in the worship, often as a consort to the male god. It is clear from the opening chapter of Genesis, however, that this is not going to be the way of the Israelites: there will only be one deity, and he will be male.

Banishment from paradise isn't the only punishment for Eve. In addition to putting her under the rule of man from this time forward, god tells Eve that she will also endure great pain in childbirth. Having children was so important to our early ancestors that there is evidence of pregnant full-breasted women in the form of clay figurines from at least twenty-five thousand years ago. In contrast, the Bible equates female fertility with sin. As Annie Laurie Gaylor writes in *Woe to the Women*, this passage about punishment of pain for women was used by clerics in the 1800s to attempt to deny women any anesthesia during childbirth! What omniscient, omnipotent god would make the wonderful and amazing event of giving birth a painful punishment? How much have women suffered needlessly because of this one passage?

Early Christian leaders expanded upon the biblical account of Eve to further denigrate women. Tertullian, a prolific Christian writer (155–240 CE) in the Roman province of Carthage, summed up the Church's attitude toward women in the following in *On the Apparel of Women*:

> And do you not know that you are Eve? God's sentence hangs still over all your sex and His punishment weighs down upon you. You are the devil's gateway; you are she who first violated the forbidden tree and broke the law of God. It was you who coaxed your way around him whom the devil had not the force to attack. With what ease you shattered that image of God: Man! Because of the death you merited, even the Son of God had to die. . . . Woman, you are the gate to hell.

While there are some positive portraits of women in the Old Testament, they are few and far between. This is a society that was patriarchal in virtually all aspects: men were the only priests at the temple, men owned the property, men decided whom they married, and men made the laws. Numerous passages in the Old Testament reflect a view that women are indeed the mere property of man. Laban, who doesn't think he should house his sister's son Jacob for nothing, asks him, "Tell me, what should your wages be?" (Gen. 29:15). Jacob answers, "I will serve you seven years for your younger daughter Rachel" (Gen. 29:18). Laban ends up making him work seven years for his older daughter first. Thus, Jacob uses his "wages" to buy two wives for himself. In the book of Joshua, Caleb, a Hebrew soldier, offers his daughter to the man who takes down a city. "Whoever smites Kir'iath-sep'her, and takes it, to him will I give Achsah my daughter as wife" (Josh. 15:16). The most expensive price paid for a woman is undoubtedly Michal, the love of King David. He paid "the price of a hundred foreskins of the Philistines" (2 Sam. 3:14). Most women living in the United States today might find it hard to imagine what it would be like to be sold to a man, to become his wife, to have his children, and to have no say in the matter.

In a patriarchy, men continue their lineage and pass on their property through their sons. As a result, a man wants to be sure that the children his wife bears are his children and not someone else's. This is likely one reason the Israelites were obsessed about the virginity of women. This obsession still continues in our culture today in many religious communities. In the Old Testament, if a man married a woman and the "tokens of her virginity" could not be proven, she would be killed—"then they shall bring out the young woman to the door of her father's house, and the men of her city shall stone her to death with stones" (Deut. 22:21). As a highly prized commodity, virgins are used for barter as seen in Lot's willingness to give his two virgin daughters to the mob threatening him rather than let them take the two angels he is harboring. "Behold, I have two daughters who have not known man; let me bring them out to you, and do to them as you please; only do nothing to these men, for they have come under the shelter of my roof" (Gen. 19:8). Restitution must be made if a man sleeps with but isn't able to marry a virgin, as seen in the following passage: "If a man seduces a virgin who is not betrothed, and lies with her, he shall give the marriage present for her, and make her his wife. If her father utterly refuses to give her to him, he shall pay money equivalent to the marriage present for virgins" (Exod. 22:16–17). In one of only two books in the Old Testament named for a woman, the story of Esther is told. The king of Persia, Ahasu-e'rus, seeks out a queen among the beautiful virgins. Esther, a Jew, wins out after spending twelve months being beautified with the other contestants (Esther 2). No need to wonder why women and not men wear makeup, high heels, and elaborate wardrobes today.

Another aspect of the male lineage through sons is women's duty to produce more of them. According to the Bible, a brother has an obligation to marry his brother's widow if she has no sons so that the property can be conserved through a male heir (Deut. 25:5). Lot is an old man and does not have any sons. In order to preserve offspring through their father, his two daughters get him drunk and have sex with him (Gen. 19:31–32). They both bear sons who become tribal leaders. No negative comment is recorded about this incest. In another story, Leah, the previously less preferred wife of Jacob, proclaims, "Now this time my husband will be joined to me, because I have borne him three sons" (Gen. 29:34). The value of the sons is also seen in the length of time a woman needs to be purified after their birth (thirty-three days) as opposed to a daughter's birth (sixty-six days) (Lev. 12:1–5). God even outlines to Moses a price difference for male slaves twenty to sixty years old (fifty shekels of silver) versus that for a female slave of the same age (thirty shekels of silver) (Lev. 27:3–4). As historians have noted, when slavery was legal in the United States, a similar price differential based upon sex applied for this age group. Young females able to bear children were undoubtedly prized in both eras.

The importance of virginity and the woman as male property are key reasons why adultery was severely punished. When men were punished for adultery, it was because they had stolen the property of another man. "If a man commits adultery with the wife of his neighbor, both the adulterer and the adulteress shall be put to death" (Lev. 20:10). But in reality, most men didn't need adultery to satisfy their desires because they had multiple wives and concubines . . . plus their maids. Abraham has a child with Hagar, his wife's maid, because his wife, Sarah, is at first barren (Gen. 16:3). Rachel gives Jacob her maid Bilhah for the same reason (Gen. 30:3).

In warfare, women, particularly virgins, are seen as the fruits of the victorious in many biblical passages. After destroying the Midianites, Moses is angry that his soldiers have let the women live, as they had allegedly caused a plague. He instructs them to kill every woman "who has known a man," but "all the young girls who have not known man by lying with him, keep alive for yourselves" (Num. 31:17–18). Women are valued so little, they are seen as easily expendable. A beautiful woman may be taken in battle and kept as a wife, but "if you have no delight in her, you shall let her go where she will" (Deut. 21:14). In a tragic story, Jephthah makes a vow to god to give him the first person that comes out of his house if he returns victorious from fighting the Ammonites. Unfortunately, it's his daughter. After lamenting for two months that she will die as a virgin, she is put to death (Judg. 11:29–40). Notice that this vow was to god. God could have rescinded it, as he did when Abraham lifted the knife to kill Isaac, his son, but he didn't, thus condoning the sacrifice of Jephthah's daughter.

While conquerors throughout history have committed atrocities, what is different about the stories in the Bible is the fact that they are not just part of our past. We can be horrified by the genocide at the hands of Nazis during World War II and fight to assure that this never happens again. We can fight the lingering problems of slavery by promoting equal rights for all races and by punishing abuses and violence when they occur. But when this violence is contained in scripture, something different occurs. For many, these events are not just history. They are sacred events, which Yahweh commanded the leaders of his chosen people to commit. Furthermore, they are in a book that is in every pew in every Christian church and in the scrolls of every Jewish synagogue. They are seen as divinely inspired. These stories are read from the pulpit; they are taught to children. What impact does this have on the prevalence of violence today? What impact does it have on the justification for war? What impact does it make on the status of women and their rights?

Another group of women is also the subject of violence—harlots, or prostitutes. Indeed, they are constantly maligned and even threatened with death. When Judah finds out his daughter-in-law is pregnant (not by her husband), he says, "bring her out, and let her be burned" (Gen. 38:24). In this instance, he finds out the child is actually his and rescinds the punishment. One of the reasons the prostitute is maligned is likely the presence of cult prostitutes in the other local religions. "There shall be no cult prostitute of the daughters of Israel, neither shall there be a cult prostitute of the sons of Israel" (Deut. 23:17). If a daughter of a priest plays the harlot, the punishment is the most severe—"she shall be burned with fire" (Lev. 21:9). The temple priests are high up in the hierarchy, and more is demanded of them.

The story of Rahab is one of the very few instances in the Old Testament where a prostitute is seen in a positive light. She harbors Joshua's men and saves them from the king of Jericho's men. She does this to protect her family from the devastation that Israel intends to bring down on her town. In this instance, the men of Israel swear to save Rahab and her family.

There is, however, no punishment for the man who frequents a prostitute. Three thousand years later, our police forces jail prostitutes but rarely arrest the men who purchase their services. Some things never change.

Rape is one of the oldest forms of violence against women. In the context of a patriarchy where women are submissive to men, where they are the booty of war, and where they are considered merely property, there is no question that rape will be prevalent. In the book of Judges, a man is sojourning with his concubine. After he's searched for a place to stay, an old man invites him to his house. When the men of the town want to attack the interloper sexually, the old man offers his daughter or the sojourner's concubine. They do not want to take the old man's daughter, so the sojourner himself offers them his concubine and the men "knew her, and abused her all night until the morning" (Judg. 19:25). The sojourner sleeps through the night and finds his concubine lying on the porch the next morning, dead. The ten commandments state, "You shall not commit adultery," but there is no similar prohibition against rape (Exod. 20:14). We rarely go a week when we do not hear of a woman who has been raped. Where does this violence in men come from? Is a religion that is replete with violence against women part of the problem? Can men ignore at a basic fundamental level the impact of hearing about this violence toward women in what is deemed a holy book? While some of these stories are rarely discussed from the pulpit, they are clearly part of the legacy that this religion has to bear.

A culture that charges women with the cause of all evil, treats them as mere chattel, threatens them with rape, and obsesses about their virginity impacts the image women have of themselves. Imagine being a woman and hearing these stories repeated over and over again and living with the consequences. Today when reciting these very same stories in synagogue, church, or Sunday school, do pastors have any inkling of the impact they have on women's views of themselves? Do Christian fathers as they read bedtime stories from the Bible? Can men see what they are doing to the next generation of women? Or is the renunciation of patriarchy and violence solely on the shoulders of women?

Many Christians want to focus on the New Testament instead of focusing on the subjugation and violence toward women in the Old Testament stories. This approach is not much better because Jesus affirms his support of the Old Testament. "Think not that I have come to abolish the law and the prophets; I have come not to abolish them but to fulfill them. For truly, I say to you, till heaven and earth pass away, not an iota, not a dot, will pass from the law until all is accomplished" (Matt. 5:17–18). Any notion of a peaceful transition is smashed when Jesus says, "Do not think that I have come to bring peace on earth; I have not come to bring peace, but a sword" (Matt. 10:34). Jesus tells a crowd getting ready to stone a woman to death for adultery, "Let him who is without sin among you be the first to throw a stone at her " (John 8:7). While the stoning may have been stopped in that one instance, the Old Testament commandment against adultery still stood in full force and effect. In addition, many scholars believe that this text was added much later.

Unfortunately, throughout the New Testament, a similar denigration of women occurs as was seen in the Old Testament. Even though it is not mentioned until the gospel of Matthew, written toward the end of the first century CE, the virgin birth of Jesus plays an important role in Christianity and especially in Catholicism. Most scholars today agree that this focus on the virginity of Mary was an attempt to fulfill a prophecy in the Old Testament book of Isaiah (7:14). It was discovered later that the word *virgin* did not appear in the original Hebrew of this verse. Matthew was using a Greek translation. Today, the Revised Standard Version of the Bible corrects this mistake and uses the phrase *young woman* in Matthew.

Some will say that Mary, who came to be venerated through Christian art and Church doctrine, serves as a positive image of women. But in examining this further, this is only a truncated view of women. A virgin who is impregnated by the holy spirit only serves as a vessel for god's work. She is not a full woman. She may intercede between people and god, but as Gerda Lerner writes in *The Creation of Patriarchy*, "She has no power for herself, and the very sources of her power to intercede separate her irrevocably from women. The goddess Ishtar and other goddesses like her had power in their own right."

Many of the passages that belittle women in the New Testament are found in the letters of Paul. Scholars believe these letters were written about twenty years after the death of Jesus, around 50 CE. Written to early congregations of Christians, they gave instructions on how to practice their faith. The subordinate role of women is clear in Paul's view, as shown in the following citations: "But I want you to understand that the head of every man is Christ, the head of a woman is her husband, and the head of Christ is God" (1 Cor. 11:3); "For man was not made from woman, but woman from man. Neither was man created for woman, but woman for man" (1 Cor. 11:8–9); "As in all the churches of the saints; the women should keep silence in the churches. For they are not permitted to speak, but should be subordinate, as even the law says" (1 Cor. 14:34). Paul explains that they can always ask their husbands at home if they have questions. In 1 Timothy, an epistle probably not written by Paul, the admonition against women in the Church is even stronger: "I permit no woman to teach or to have authority over men; she is to keep silent. For Adam was formed first, then Eve; and Adam was not deceived, but the woman was deceived and became a transgressor" (1 Tim. 2:12–14). In yet another letter, it is stated, "Likewise you wives, be submissive to your husbands, so that some, though they do not obey the word, may be won without a word by the behavior of their wives, when they see your reverent and chaste behavior" (1 Pet. 3:1–2).

Again, women are reminded to fulfill their key role by bearing children. "Yet woman will be saved through bearing children, if she continues in faith and love and holiness, with modesty" (1 Tim. 2:15). Christian apologists argue that these passages reflect the society of first-century Palestine. They are, however, the sayings upon which Church doctrine was built. Jesus himself did not leave any writings.

There are instances in the New Testament that portray a more positive treatment of women. Jesus performs a miracle and banishes seven demons from Mary Magdalene, who follows Jesus and his disciples, along with Mary the mother of James and Salome (Mark 15:40). A woman cleanses Jesus's feet with tears and hair. Jesus rebukes the owner of the house who disapproves of this woman (Luke 7:36–50). His disciples marvel when he is found talking to a woman at Jacob's well (John 4:27). Women also served as hostesses to gatherings in their homes of early Christians, and a woman named Phoebe is referred to as a deaconess of the church at Cen'chre-ae (Rom. 16:1). Unfortunately, by the second century CE, men began to take control over Christianity, and the plight of women took a turn for the worse.

Abstinence from sex, which first appeared in the New Testament as a temporary measure because of an apocryphal prediction of the end times, becomes the ascetic ideal in the second century. As Karen Jo Torjeson writes in *When Women Were Priests*, when Thecla, an aristocratic woman, renounced an arranged marriage, "a new ideal of womanhood was created—that of the consecrated virgin." While there is an acknowledgment that refusing to marry someone may indeed have been a liberating act during the time, what a shame the only way for a woman to be free was by renouncing sex and becoming a chaste virgin. John Chrysostom, a church leader writing in the second half of the fourth century, can't even acknowledge the value of what a woman like Thecla has accomplished without using male language. "Don't say 'woman' but 'what a man!' Because this is a man, despite her physical appearance."

Once the end times did not come, another attitude toward sexual relations appeared. Saint Augustine of Hippo, called the Father of the Western Church, spent his life focusing on the cause of original sin. His journey led him to postulate that it was concupiscence, or lust at its core. Since Eve was seen as the temptress of man, she was the origin of the Church's negative portrayal of women. This negative focus on sexual relations eventually led the Catholic Church to condemn birth control because procreation was seen as the only justifiable goal of sex. In 1968 Vatican II removed the sex-for-procreation only doctrine by postulating responsible parenthood. The Catholic Church, however, still bans birth control, even refusing to distribute condoms with its missions to Africa. It assumes that its doctrine of sexual relations only within marriage will control the spread of AIDS. We know, however, that condoms are a much more effective measure.

Certainly these doctrines about procreation impacted women and the society's view of sexual relations. But more sinister acts were to come. Starting in 1095, the Papacy in Rome sponsored at least eight major crusades to recapture the Holy Land. How many men, women, and children were killed? In the fifteenth to eighteenth centuries, it is estimated that, at the very least, hundreds of thousands of people, mostly women, were murdered because they were deemed to be witches. The *Malleus Maleficarum*, published in 1486, outlined the requirements for being considered a witch. It posited that dependence on the movements of the celestial bodies was a greater factor than the devil in creating witches. Building on Saint Augustine's work, the authors stated, "All witchcraft stems from carnal lust, which is in women insatiable." Author Starhawk states, "At times, hundreds of victims were put to death in a day. In the Bishopric of Trier, in Germany, two villages were left with only a single female inhabitant apiece after the trials of 1585." The obsession with sex continued unabated with a discussion of how witches could use magic to remove a man's penis from his body. Marija Gimbutas refers to these witch executions as the "most satanic event in European history in the name of Christ" and sets the number killed at a much higher level.

Today, most people would see the Crusades and the burning of witches as horrific acts. The problem, however, is the fact that the Bible, once used to justify these acts, is still seen as the basis for a code of morality. William Lane Craig, a leading Christian apologist, claims that the only path to morality is through belief in a personal god who informs you of the righteous path. As we have seen through this study of the treatment of women, the morality laid down by Yahweh in the Old Testament, writers in the New Testament, and the official doctrines of the Church from the second century onward, is not a morality that women should support.

So how does someone who rejects this biblical deity form her notions of morality? Betty Brogaard, in *The Homemade Atheist*, sums it up well:

"Morality is a code of conduct. It can be either 'good' or 'bad.' 'Right' morality, from my point of view, is the best path through life, as summed up in the so-called Golden Rule. This axiom is taught in one form or another in every religion and humanistic philosophy of which I am aware." Starhawk, in *The Spiral Dance*, cites the philosophy of modern witches:

> Witches do not see justice as administered by some external authority, based on a written code or set of rules imposed from without. Instead, justice is an inner sense that each act brings about consequences that must be faced responsibly. The Craft does not foster guilt, the stern, admonishing, self-hating inner voice that cripples action. Instead, it demands responsibility. "What you send, returns three times over."

For Julian Baggini, the root of morality is a concern for others—a recognition that their welfare counts too, adding that mental illness can be defined as a total indifference to others. Robert Green Ingersoll summed it up well by saying:

> While I am opposed to all orthodox creeds, I have a creed myself; and my creed is this. Happiness is the only good. The time to be happy is now. The place to be happy is here. The way to be happy is to make others so. This creed is somewhat short, but it is long enough for this life, strong enough for this world. If there is another world, when we get there we can make another creed. But this creed certainly will do for this life.

These codes of morality do far more to benefit humanity than the codes contained in the Bible. Today women in the United States and in many countries of the world are experiencing more and more opportunities: for interesting and rewarding careers, for equal pay as men performing the same job, for the ability to decide when and when not to have children, and for an ever-increasing voice in the political sphere. Hopefully this small insight into the portrayal of women in the Bible will lead some women to take a second look at their religion and decide if now is the time to give it up and embrace a new secular view of the world that values all men and women equally.

ABOUT THE EDITOR

Karen L. Garst has a bachelor's degree and a master's degree in French. She obtained her PhD in Curriculum and Instruction from the University of Wisconsin, Madison. She moved to Oregon in 1980 to serve as field representative of the Oregon Federation of Teachers. In 1988 she was selected to serve as the executive director of the Oregon Community College Association and in 1996 as the executive director of the Oregon State Bar. She retired from that position in 2008. She is married and lives in Oregon.